CICERO ON THE EMOTIONS

CICERO ON THE EMOTIONS

Tusculan Disputations
3 AND 4

Translated and with Commentary by

MARGARET GRAVER

THE UNIVERSITY OF CHICAGO PRESS

CHICAGO AND LONDON

Margaret Graver is assistant professor of classics at Dartmouth College.

The University of Chicago Press, Chicago 60637
The University of Chicago Press, Ltd., London
© 2002 by The University of Chicago
All rights reserved. Published 2002
Printed in the United States of America
11 10 09 08 07 06 05 04 03 02   5 4 3 2 1

ISBN (cloth): 0-226-30577-5
ISBN (paper): 0-226-30578-3

Library of Congress Cataloging-in-Publication Data
Cicero, Marcus Tullius.
    [Tusculanae disputationes. English. Selections]
    Cicero on the emotions : Tusculan disputations 3 and 4 / translated
and with commentary by Margaret Graver.
       p.   cm.
    Includes bibliographical references and index.
    ISBN 0-226-30577-5 (alk. paper) — ISBN 0-226-30578-3 (pbk. : alk. paper)
    1. Emotions—Early works to 1800.   2. Happiness—Early works to 1800.
I. Graver, Margaret.   II. Title.
    PA6308.T7 G7313   2002
    158′.1—dc21

                                           2001003526

CONTENTS

The third and fourth books of Cicero's _Tusculan Disputations_ present the reader with a self-contained treatise on the nature and management of human emotion. Cicero sets himself the task of presenting, first for grief, then for emotions in general, the insights that had been gained in Greece over many years through philosophical debate and also through practical experience in the ancient equivalent of psychotherapy. His own support is given for the most part to the Stoic position, which he admires for its thoroughness and close reasoning; indeed, his work now stands as the oldest complete text documenting Stoic views on this subject. But he also pays considerable attention to the views of other Hellenistic thinkers, notably the Peripatetics and the Epicureans, setting their arguments in dialogue with those of the Stoics. Recommendations from all the schools are combined in the advice he offers to counselors on the means of allaying grief and other strong emotions.

Scholars in the field of ancient philosophy have over the last decade become increasingly interested in the analyses of emotion that were posited by various thinkers during the Hellenistic period, that is, the two and a half centuries following the death of Aristotle in 322 B.C.E. The majority of scholarly attention has rightly been devoted to reconstructing and interpreting the positions of the primary Greek thinkers of the period, figures like Zeno of Citium, Chrysippus of Soli, Epicurus, and later Posidonius of Rhodes. But progress in this area is frequently uncertain and always methodologically difficult because of the nature of our evidence, much of which is fragmentary and heavily mediated by the opinions of later writers. Cicero, by contrast, provides us with a continuous account which, though it comes from a slightly later time period and from a different culture, can still serve as an invaluable point of reference for the Hellenistic thought which preceded it. For Cicero is well informed about his subject through many sources, oral and written, that are now lost to us, and his treatment is both intelligent and relatively impartial. By following his argument on its own terms, working out its motivations, and then comparing it with other available sources, we learn much about Stoicism in particular which could not be gained from any other source.

But for many readers, this work will have an appeal in and of itself. The topic has a perennial interest, and the position Cicero takes, though unlikely to win wide adherence, will nonetheless command respect, challenging its opponents to construct equally thoughtful and rigorous responses. The manner of presentation is lively and accessible, for Cicero's intention is not to enter the debates of professional philosophers but to engage a wider public in disciplined reflection upon a matter of importance. It is my hope that both scholars in ancient philosophy and others new to the subject will find in his work material for many fruitful discussions.

This project has benefited from research funds supplied by the Walter and Constance Burke Research Initiation Awards for Junior Faculty at Dartmouth College, as well as from leave time provided under Dartmouth's Junior Faculty Fellowship program. Among the many individuals who have assisted me in various ways, I would like to thank Martha Nussbaum, Charles Fornara, and Victor Caston, who guided my graduate studies in Hellenistic ethics and epistemology; Christopher Gill, who provided the initial inspiration for this project and waded patiently through my first efforts; and David Konstan, who did much to clarify my understanding of the Epicurean material in book 3. Brad Inwood and two anonymous scholars read complete drafts for the University of Chicago Press; their comments have not only saved me from numerous errors but also materially improved nearly every page of this book. Bruce Graver has been my technical support and for many years my source of strength and model of exacting scholarship. I wish to dedicate this volume to my parents, Harry Robson and Roberta Steffe Robson, without whose love of learning and deep commitment to truth I could not be what I am today.

Abbreviations and Matters of Citation

Acad., Acad. Pr.	Cicero, *Academics* and *Prior Academics*
Ad Brut.	Cicero, *Epistulae ad M. Brutum* (Letters to Brutus)
AM	Sextus Empiricus, *Adversus mathematicos* (Against the Professors)
Att.	Cicero, *Letters to Atticus*
D.L.	Diogenes Laertius, *Lives and Opinions of Eminent Philosophers*
EK	*Posidonius: The Fragments*, ed. Edelstein and Kidd 1989
Ep.	Seneca, *Epistulae morales ad Lucilium* (Moral Epistles to Lucilius)
Ep. Hdt.	Epicurus, *Epistle to Herodotus*
Ep. Men.	Epicurus, *Epistle to Menoikeus*
Fam.	Cicero, *Epistulae ad familiares* (Letters to Friends)
KD	Epicurus, *Kuriai Doxai* (Principal Doctrines)
LSJ	*Greek–English Lexicon*, ed. H. G. Liddell, R. Scott, and H. S. Jones (Oxford, 1968)
ND	Cicero, *De natura deorum* (On the Nature of the Gods)
NE	Aristotle, *Nicomachean Ethics*
Off.	Cicero, *De officiis* (On Appropriate Actions)
OLD	*Oxford Latin Dictionary*, ed. P.G.W. Glare (Oxford, 1982)
PHP	*Galen: On the Doctrines of Hippocrates and Plato*
QFr.	Cicero, *Epistulae ad Quintum fratrem* (Letters to Quintus)
Rhet.	Aristotle, *Rhetoric*
Stob., *Ecl.*	Stobaeus, *Eclogae* (Anthology)

SVF   *Stoicorum veterum fragmenta,* ed. von Arnim 1921
Tusc.   Cicero, *Tusculan Disputations,* books 1, 2, and 5

Cross-references to the translation are to book and chapter.

Translations are my own unless otherwise noted. Where the commentary makes assertions as to the derivation or meaning of specific words and phrases, I have relied on the relevant entries in the standard lexica as noted above, including a citation only if needed to pinpoint a section of a long entry.

Dates for persons and events are given in accordance with the relevant articles in the *Oxford Classical Dictionary* (ed. S. Hornblower and A. Spawforth, Oxford, 1996). All dates in this volume are B.C.E. unless otherwise indicated.

The bibliographical notes provided with each section are meant to direct the reader to important recent treatments of specific topics, with emphasis on works in English, and to indicate which modern treatments have most influenced my reading of the evidence. They are not by any means comprehensive. Fuller bibliographical resources for matters treated in this volume can be found especially in Everson 1998, Barnes and Griffin 1997, Griffin and Barnes 1989, and Long and Sedley 1987.

Introduction

CICERO AND THE PHILOSOPHERS ON EMOTION

To the philosophers of Greece and Rome, it seemed obvious that the emotional experience of humans was a proper topic for philosophy to address. Grief and anger, delight and desire, fear and pity had always belonged to ethical discourse, for formal moral education was first and always foremost the province of poets, and the most respected poetic forms of antiquity were also the most deeply emotional. Emotion, its causes largely mysterious, figures centrally in the narrative strategy of Homeric epic, motivating gods and humans alike to acts of prowess, of cowardice, of caring and deceit. In Athenian tragedy, the unexplained and intensely problematic power of emotion figures large both in the actions on stage and in the critical responses of the viewers. It is not surprising, then, that when the philosophical writers set themselves to provide explanations for the behavior of individuals in social settings, they inquired closely into the emotional dimensions of motivation, asking on the one hand psychological questions about how emotions are generated and how they are related to conscious thought processes, and on the other hand broadly ethical questions about the nature of emotional health, the function of emotional responses in a divinely ordered universe, and the extent to which we can be blamed or praised for the emotions we have. Both Plato and Aristotle developed positions on the subject, and the views of their predecessors and contemporary opponents are often mentioned in their writings. The hedonist philos-

opher Epicurus, a generation later than Aristotle, made questions of fear
and desire central to his ethics; his views, too, were widely influential.

By the time Cicero came to study philosophy, however, the most highly
developed position was that of the Stoics, a series of scholar-philosophers
working primarily at Athens, all of whom were deeply influenced by the
thought of Zeno of Citium (335–263 B.C.E.).[1] In modern English, the word
"stoic" has come to mean "deliberately unemotional," and it is quite true
that for Zeno and his followers, a reasoned approach to ethics makes necessary a radical overthrow of many of our usual assumptions about emotion. For these thinkers, emotional responses are essentially activities of the
mind's judging faculty (rather than, say, unthinking instincts or drives) and
must be counted as voluntary actions: we are accountable for our emotions,
although this need not mean that they remain under our conscious control
at every given instant. Moreover, while there are in theory several different
species of affect, not all of them blameworthy, emotions as we know them
are deeply and essentially flawed, logically dependent on certain kinds of
judgment which humans operating to their fullest and best potential would
not be inclined to make. Real moral and intellectual seriousness requires us
to do away with them.

Cicero is not himself a Stoic: he professes allegiance to what he calls the
"New Academy," a skeptical stance which requires of him only that he
study the views of others and accede to those which appear most plausible.
The Stoic view appears to him extreme, on first view scarcely human. He is
well aware that some of his readers will be more attracted to one of the
competing views, possibly to that of the Peripatetics, who insist that emotions are natural and serve a useful purpose, or even to that of Epicurus,
who frames all questions of value in terms of pleasure and pain. Nonetheless, it is the Stoic position which he recommends to his readers in these
books as the best-reasoned view, the one most suitable for statesmen, and
the only one which is able to confer real happiness on its adherents. This is
in contrast to some of his own earlier writings, for in his earlier work *On the
Orator*, as in some of the letters, he tends to favor the Peripatetic view as one
well suited to a man in public life.[2]

His reasons for taking the Stoic line here are of more than one kind.
His admiration for its intellectual bases cannot be discounted, for it is
clear throughout the work that he respects the Stoic authors for the power
and coherence of their reasoning on this as on many other issues. It is
these same features of Stoicism which have attracted the attention of
some modern philosophers. But Cicero was also faced with considerations of a more personal and political nature which made it expedient

that he should make a public display of Stoic leanings at this time. These we can trace especially through his letters in the spring and summer of 45 to his lifelong friend T. Pomponius Atticus. The letters reveal what the work itself could not make explicit: the extent to which Cicero's own emotional behavior was under scrutiny, at this time of crisis for the Roman Republic, by other members of his own aristocratic circle.[3] Concern for this important audience may well have influenced his choice of positions in the work, although this does not make it any less a serious and considered choice.

In mid-February of 45, with his public position more than ever precarious, Cicero suffered a devastating bereavement at home. His only daughter, Tullia, the member of his small family whom he loved most tenderly and unreservedly, died a month after giving birth to his first grandchild. We do not have any letters from the three weeks following her death, since Cicero was then staying in Atticus's house, but in early March they were apart again, and he writes several times of his experience with grief: of his desire to be alone, of long walks in the woods, of uncontrollable fits of weeping.[4] Over and over he entreats Atticus, who often served as a liaison in business dealings, to assist him in purchasing some suitable piece of land for a memorial, a little shrine which would consecrate her name in the public eye long after he himself was gone.[5] He speaks also of efforts to find consolation in books, at first primarily in books on grief and in the self-directed *Consolation* which he was himself composing, later in reading and writing on other topics in philosophy. "Reading and writing do not comfort me," he tells Atticus, "but they do distract me."[6] Indeed, he was not certain that he wished to be comforted. "I try in every way I can to repair my countenance—though not my heart. I think sometimes that I am wrong to do so, at other times that I will be wrong not to."[7] Not until May 17 could he bear to return to the house at Tusculum, a day's ride from Rome, where Tullia had spent her last hours.[8]

Unable to face the social round at Rome, Cicero had to do what he could from a distance to protect his fragile reputation. Expected to attend a dinner in honor of the quaestor M. Appuleius, who had recently been appointed augur, he instructed Atticus to get him excused on grounds of ill health.[9] This required a sworn deposition and witnesses, for the obligation was legal as well as social. But it was well worth putting Atticus to this trouble, for although Appuleius himself was understanding, others would be sure to notice an unexplained absence and would draw their own conclusions. Significantly, Cicero felt even on March 7 that he could not afford to draw attention to the anguish he really felt.

But the rumors could not be controlled so easily. As the weeks drew on and Cicero failed to reappear, Atticus wrote to him repeatedly, urging him to make a show of fortitude. A letter from M. Iunius Brutus was even less gentle.[10] In response, Cicero points to the philosophical writings on which he spent every hour of the day.

> You urge me to dissemble, to conceal how deeply I am grieving. Others, you say, are becoming aware of my failure to do this. But am I not doing the most that I can in this regard, when I spend entire days writing? Even if I am not doing it for the sake of concealment, but rather to comfort and heal my mind, still it should serve to make the pretense. It does little else for me.[11]

When these writings were circulated, they would silence any charge of unmanliness:

> So you think I should do something to show my strength of mind. According to your letter, certain people are saying things about me even harsher than what you and Brutus have written. But if those who think my spirit is broken or weakened were to find out how much writing I have done, and what it is like, then (if they are human beings at all) I think they would make a different assessment of me: either I have recovered enough to write with full concentration on these difficult subjects—in which case I am not to be criticized—or I have chosen to distract my mind from grief in the manner most fitting for a person of my class and education. And in that case they ought actually to praise me.[12]

His productivity alone, he felt, should be a sufficient demonstration of equanimity, for by mid-May he had completed not only the *Consolation*, but a first draft of the *Academics* and a political pamphlet addressed to Caesar. Five books *On Ends* and a complete recasting of the *Academics* into four books would be completed before the end of June.[13] But what mattered even more was that the works themselves should show their author to be as energetic and eloquent as ever, a man of principle and action, dedicated to the public interest. If readers could not get this message from the erudite *Academics* and the fiery *On Ends*, then perhaps they could find it in a work which confronted the reality of death, pain, and emotional disturbance, and argued the superiority of the human spirit to all of these. But that work would have to take the most rigorously intellectual, most selflessly courageous line available. The Stoic position was the only one which would serve.

Between mid-July and mid-August, the time during which the bulk of the *Tusculans* was composed, the letters are again infrequent, and we no longer have such immediate access to Cicero's thoughts about his work. But the work itself speaks clearly enough. It shows the author at his estate in Tusculum, passing his days in intellectual pursuits—the mornings in oratorical practice, the afternoons in philosophical discussion.[14] It alludes pointedly to his earlier period of grieving, and even more pointedly to his conquest of grief.[15] Tullia herself is never named.

The Format of the Discussion

While the five *Tusculan Disputations* are linked to one another by many internal connections of thought, it is to a large extent the formal manner of presentation, rather than continuity of thought, that holds them together as a single work. Here, alone among his major philosophical works, Cicero employs what he calls the "disputation" format or, Latinizing a Greek term, the *schola*.[16] In place of dialectical exchange between named speakers, the *schola* gives the lion's share of the discussion to an unnamed principal speaker whose voice will usually be recognized as that of the author himself. The exceptionally docile interlocutor speaks only at opening and closing and at points of transition. His chief function is to supply the thesis, a one-sentence statement of opinion which is eventually to be proved wrong.[17] Within these formal constraints, the discussion ranges with some freedom over a number of points more and less closely related to the thesis. In the book on grief, for instance, the formal case against the thesis is quickly expanded to take in the causes of distress, its relation to the other emotions, the techniques that have proven effective in treating it, and practical suggestions for the writers of consolatory discourses. This flexibility gives opportunity for a livelier, more accessible treatment and for the incorporation of a greater variety of philosophical views than would have been possible in a more tightly structured assault upon the thesis.

Both books express the thesis as an assertion concerning the experience of the wise person: in book 3, that "the wise person is subject to grief," and in book 4, that "the wise person cannot be free of every emotion." Readers unfamiliar with Hellenistic ethics will be puzzled by the importance given these particular assertions. Why not begin with ourselves? In Cicero's philosophical context, though, questions about ordinary humans are regularly approached by asking first what humans would be like if they were wise—that is, if they were living the best possible human life. For it is assumed that the purpose of studying philosophy, as of any purposive action, is to improve our condition, and improvement can hardly be understood if we cannot say what it is for one condition to be better than another. In both the formal theses, then, Cicero is posing a problem concerning the norm with which ordinary humans are to be compared.

A more succinct way of putting the same question might be to ask whether grief, or emotion in general, is natural to human beings. For within the discussion Cicero is now entering, it is common to say that those characteristics, actions, and experiences which make up the best and wisest human life are also natural to humans; and, conversely, that everything which is natural to us is also part of our norm. But, then as now, the use of the term "natural" may tend to cloud the issue. For although its connotations are almost universally positive, the word is rarely defined, and ethical views claiming to defend what is natural may turn out to have widely divergent practical implications. As a point of entry into the ancient debates, it is helpful to note that both the Latin word *natura* and its Greek equivalent *phusis* retain the force of their etymological connection with words for conception and birth. It is for this reason that Cicero's discussion of grief begins with a description of what tendencies are present already in newborn babies. Of course, not every philosopher need give the same account of what is contained in the minds of infants. But all parties to the Hellenistic debate agree that any tendency which is truly innate in humans must also be retained in a good account of human wisdom.[18]

Cicero's decision to treat grief first and separately from the other emotions is perhaps sufficiently explained by the personal and political considerations mentioned above. But this approach proves convenient in other ways as well. Inasmuch as grief is mental pain, it follows naturally on the discussion of pain of body in book 2. It matters, also, that within Cicero's literary tradition were many examples of philosophical and semiphilosophical works claiming to provide consolation for distress, the species of composition to which he had himself contributed in writing the *Consolation.* By giving separate treatment to grief, Cicero is able to draw upon the body of shared opinions and experiences recorded in that consolatory tradition, finding in them both practical utility and insight into the causes of emotion.[19]

Finally, there is a strictly philosophical consideration. Distress is treated by the philosophers as a response to present circumstances perceived as bad for oneself. But not all schools of philosophy agree that in our best and most natural state we *can* perceive any present circumstance as evil. Stoics in particular will deny this, for reasons to be considered below. This means that in a work which means to take the Stoic line, arguments concerning grief and distress must develop in a different way from those on the other emotions. In book 3, then, Cicero will concentrate on the experience of ordinary humans, exploring the causes of grief and other emotions in us. He can then proceed in book 4 to the more difficult arguments that contrast the emotions with the "well-reasoned" affective responses of the sage.

ARISTOTLE AND THE PERIPATETICS

Although the position of his principal speaker in each book is in opposition to the thesis, Cicero also lays out, more or less fairly, the views which led some ancient thinkers to support it. These thinkers he generally calls Peripatetics—that is, followers of Aristotle—although he also speaks in this connection of some members of the fourth-century Academy, notably Crantor, and undoubtedly believes that the position he describes was held by Aristotle himself.[20] And indeed that position has clear affinities with elements of Aristotle's thought as known to us from the *Nicomachean Ethics* and *On the Soul.* That it is not quite the same as Aristotle's view should not surprise us, for Cicero had only limited knowledge of the works we now read as Aristotle's.[21] His knowledge of Peripatetic thought on this issue comes largely through later and far less distinguished thinkers, men like Lyco (c. 300–c. 226) and Staseas of Naples, whom he had known as a young man.[22] The position against which he contends thus emerges as a simplified version of what we have from Aristotle. Yet its deepest motivations are still Aristotelian, and if its claims are attractive, it is in part because Aristotle himself sets out to construct a view which will appeal to the moral intuitions of educated persons generally.

When Aristotle writes of emotion, it is within the context of a much broader investigation into the functioning of all living things. At the heart of this investigation is the observation that while humans and non-human animals have certain life-functions in common with plants (growth and reproduction, for instance), they also share certain other functions which plants do not have, especially perception and purposive self-locomotion. And humans have in addition the faculty of reason, through which we are able to make judgments about what things are good (and not merely pleasant) for ourselves and to plan suitable means of obtaining those things.

Where will the emotions fit into this classification of functions? In Aristotle's view, it would not make sense to count them among the functions most characteristic of humans as reasoning beings. For fear, desire, anger, and other emotions often motivate us to act in ways other than what we should choose on a reasoned calculation of what is best for us. They belong rather with the functions which we have in common with animals. In fact, they are essential to our functioning at that level, since it is fear which causes us to avoid some objects, and desire which causes us to pursue them.

Approaching the subject from this direction, we can see why Cicero's Peripatetics lay great emphasis on the claim that emotions are useful, indeed indispensable, to our everyday lives. Emotions, they say, are of a piece with our ability to perceive and respond to our surroundings, so that without them we would be insensate, "numb in body, and in mind scarcely human" (3.12). Moreover, it is emotion that provides the effective energy we need in order to act forcibly for our own self-preservation and the furtherance of our various aims. Anger, for instance, is useful in armed combat and in political oratory; fear enables us to avoid danger; and desire is fundamental to all forms of endeavor, even the endeavors of philosophers (4.38–47). For these reasons, it would hardly be expedient to try to eliminate emotions from ourselves, even if it were possible. And it is by no means clear that it *is* possible, for the level of functioning to which they belong is independent of our choosing, just as it is not a matter of choice for us whether we will digest food we have eaten or see objects that are before our eyes.

But this is not to say that the choices we make as rational beings can have no influence at all over our emotions. Both Aristotle and his followers hold that the involvement of reason is a definitive feature of emotions in humans, making our emotions quite different, both qualitatively and ethically, from anything that might take place in non-human animals.[23] For Aristotle, the fact that humans have all three classes of function suggests a model in which the emotions are intermediate between our characteristically human rationality and our more plantlike functions such as digestion and growth. They may be functions of a different order from reason and yet "heedful" of reason, responsive in various ways to our reasoned determination of what is best for ourselves. For those of Aristotle's followers whose works are known to Cicero and to Seneca in *On Anger,* the responsiveness of emotions to reason appears primarily as a matter of limitations: reason imposes a "limit" *(modus)* or "moderate amount" *(mediocritas)* which emotion should neither exceed nor fall short of. This is not quite what Aristotle says in the *Nicomachean Ethics,* but it is close enough to claim Aristotelian descent.[24]

Other versions of this approach sometimes speak of the control exercised by reason as a matter of one *part* of the soul or mind overcoming another.[25] On this model, those moments when we feel ourselves to be acting against our better judgment are times when the emotional part of the mind takes control of the person as a whole and causes her to pursue its own objectives, rather than the objectives of the reasoning part. This description, too, has some precedent in Aristotle, though it owes most to Plato's arguments from mental conflict in Books 4 and 10 of the *Republic*.[26] Cicero himself, however, has little to say about any such partitioning of the mind. He does speak at one point of a division between rational and irrational parts but does not employ this division to explain mental conflict; in fact, he considers it to be part of the case *against* the thesis.

THE STOIC POSITION

The Stoics share some of the assumptions mentioned above concerning the functioning of living things in general. They, too, hold that humans function at a higher level than either plants or animals; and they, too, attribute that extra level of functioning to our possession of reason, which endows us with the ability to understand what is good for ourselves and to plan and act accordingly.[27] Within this broad framework, however, they proceed to very different conclusions about the nature of emotion and its place in human life. They will not condone even the moderate emotions advocated by the Peripatetics. For them, emotions are indeed rational in one sense of that word, but they are not natural to us and have no place in the best possible life.

To understand how these differences come about, we need to devote some attention to the Stoics' unusually careful analysis of what it means for humans to be rational animals. It is important first of all to note that the English word "rational" may have more than one meaning. We sometimes describe a person's behavior as "rational" when what we mean to convey is that that behavior is not undertaken blindly or randomly but has some kind of thought behind it. In this sense, the word is merely descriptive; there is. no implication that the speaker approves of the chosen course of action. In some other context, however, we might speak of someone's behaving "rationally" in a normative sense, meaning that the action in question is actually the right and appropriate thing to do. A similar duality can be traced in the Greek word *logikos* as it is used in Stoic texts on rationality. Again, both a descriptive and a normative sense are available, and both are clearly delineated: although the surviving fragments sometimes mingle the two with more freedom than we might like, a careful reading invariably makes it clear which is intended.[28] Let us consider each of these in turn.

The descriptive account of rationality begins from certain fundamental assertions about the world and about our own life processes. In Stoic thought, the universe itself, if viewed from a wide enough perspective, would be revealed as a perfectly orderly and coherent structure. This central postulate is expressed in Stoic texts in many different ways: by talk of a material continuum and of an unbroken causal nexus, by descriptions of the universe as an "animal" or as "god," and also by mention of an all-pervasive "active principle" or "designing fire" or "seed."[29] But while the system as a whole is orderly, not every smaller portion of it will exhibit the same degree of orderliness within itself. On this point Stoics will say that the "breath" (pneuma) which permeates all things, imparting to them the designing fire, may exist at varying levels of "tension."

This is strange language, but the underlying thought is comprehensible enough. Zeno and his followers are clearly interested in patterning and complexity, both of structure and of function. To say that pneuma is present in a starfish at a higher level of tension than in a strand of kelp would be to say that the starfish has a more complicated structure and more elaborate life functions. And if humans occupy a special position on this scale of pneumatic tension, it must be because we exhibit some further kind of complexity, either in our physical structure or in our ways of perceiving and responding to the world.

This additional level of complexity consists in a particular mental capacity, a capacity manifested especially in our use of language. Language and rationality are synonymous in Greek (both logos), and the coincidence is important for Stoics. For to use language (as opposed to merely producing the sounds of language, parrot-fashion) is to be aware of the meanings of sentences, what Stoics call lekta ("things said") or propositions.[30] It is characteristic of us as rational beings that when we take in and process information about the world, we do so by means of stated or unstated lekta. Even our actions can be described propositionally. For just as my believing that something is the case involves a mental commitment or "assent" to the truth of some proposition, so also do my conscious actions imply a commitment to propositions of which I myself am the subject. Of course there are some things I only happen to do, like blinking at regular intervals or rolling over in sleep, but these are not properly called actions.[31] These excepted, for me to do a thing means that I believe, at least at the very moment of acting, that this, and not something else, is the thing for me to do.

A being whose mental processes were not propositional could not act on the basis of assent and thus in Stoic usage is not properly said to *act* at all. A rational being, however, cannot act in any other way. One thing this means is that all the actions of adult humans are attributable to their agents, in a way that the behaviors of animals or young children are not. This is true even of what we do in moments of strong emotion. Even when we feel ourselves "carried away" by desire or anger to act against our perceived best interests—for Stoics do not deny that we have this experience—our impulses are still generated in this characteristically rational way, through the workings of assent. Thus emotions, considered as impulses to act, belong to us as (descriptively) rational agents, and we have to accept responsibility for them.[32]

But rationality also opens to humans an exciting possibility. If all our actions imply beliefs, and if all our beliefs take the form of propositions, then there can be patterns of logical coherence among our beliefs and actions, and we as rational beings can become aware of these. In fact, we have a natural liking for such patterns. After all, the statements that seem to us to be correct are normally those which cohere with the beliefs we already have; and if we become aware of some flat contradiction between two beliefs, we do tend to reject one or the other of them. In theory, it should be possible—though perhaps only rarely—for some particularly reflective human to bring *all* of her beliefs into line with each other and with the larger natural order.[33] One who exhibited this perfect coherence in belief would be rational in the further sense of right or sound reasoning—the normative sense mentioned above. Her thoughts and actions would be fully consonant with universal reason and would also resemble universal reason in working together as a perfectly orderly system. This, for Stoics, is what it means to be wise or to have knowledge, and also what it is to be virtuous.

This ambitious notion of human potential now serves to ground a system of value which applies to all circumstances in our lives. For Stoics assert that virtue as defined above is the only good for a human. Goodness is defined not by what appeals to some individual, but with reference to the internal coherence of some system. Just as in the universe it is good that everything fits into a providential order, so in a human life, given that humans are capable of their own comprehensive order, what is good ought to be that which fits into some pattern which is orderly and complete relative to that person. But only my own actions, sayings, and affective responses can be meaningfully compared with that particular pattern which is *my* life. So if something I do, say, or feel is part of a fully coherent pattern extending throughout my life, it should be called good for me; if it does not, it should be called bad.

Other kinds of objects—maintaining one's health, earning money, or winning an election—are not, properly speaking, either good or bad. Stoics refer to them as "indifferents," meaning that such things make no difference in our condition: we need not possess any of them in order to attain the human good. It does not follow, however, that we ourselves should be indifferent to this class of objects; indeed, it is entirely proper that we should spend most of our time trying to obtain or avoid them. From birth, say the Stoics, we have preferences for many things: material resources, good health, the well-being of friends and family, life itself. And these are in fact the kinds of things it is usually appropriate for us to pursue. But we also, and in quite a different way, value certain things about ourselves, certain traits of character and ways of believing and acting. If I am a doctor, for instance, I may regard it as very important that my patients should get well, and I may also regard it as very important that I myself should do everything in my power to make them well. Both kinds of objects matter: if the first were not important to me, the second would hardly be possible. But only the second counts as part of my good.[34]

We can see, then, why Stoics deny that emotions can ever be rational in the normative sense. They reason that emotions as we know them are always dependent on a belief which is inconsistent with the value-system just described. Most of us do think that good health, for instance, is not only something which it is usually appropriate for us to pursue, but is actually good for us; and that death, pain, bereavement, and the like are actually bad. If I did not believe that financial ruin is bad for me, I would not fear it nor be distressed when it occurs, though I might still try to avoid it. But if I do believe this, I believe what is false: such ruin cannot be bad for me, properly speaking, since it is not really up to me to determine whether it occurs. And a similar account could be given for every one of the emotions with which we are familiar, showing its dependence on false attributions of value or disvalue to things outside our own control. Therefore, since what depends on a false belief cannot be part of the wise person's coherent pattern of human functioning, emotions as we know them cannot be part of the human norm, and anyone who wishes to live the best possible human life should seek to eliminate them.

But can humans live without emotion? The Peripatetics have asserted that we cannot: without desire and fear, we could neither pursue nor avoid anything, and the existence that would be left to us could hardly be called a human life. But Stoic psychology does not make emotions the sole motivators of pursuit and avoidance. Rather than distinguishing the reasoning function (or part) of the mind from its motivating and emotional function, they give all our functions simply to the mind itself, that is, to a single "directive faculty" (*hēgemonikon*). And while this mind, with its integrated functioning, may sometimes misevaluate its surroundings, producing in us those sensations we recognize as fear, anger, delight, and so on, it may also move us to action without having made any error of this particularly powerful kind, indeed without necessarily having made any error at all. For the impression to which it assents when it produces an impulse does not necessarily imply an evaluation in terms of good or evil, but only a belief that some possible action is appropriate (*kathēkon*).

Suppose for instance that I have an opportunity to pursue a particular deal in business. I may pursue this on the false assumption that wealth is a genuine good for me, and if I do so, my pursuit is an instance of desire, an "ill-reasoned reaching." But I may also pursue the same deal merely on the assumption that it is appropriate for me to do so at this time; and this assumption, while not necessarily true, at least *might* be true. Reaching after things on this basis is an instance of what Stoics call "selection" and is how those of us who are not sages perform any appropriate actions we do perform.[35]

Moreover, the theory has not by any means asserted that a good human life must be devoid of *all* affective response. Ordinary emotions were excluded not because of the way they feel to us, but because of their dependence on false belief. If a person can have strong feelings on the basis of correct ascriptions of value, there is no reason these feelings must be denied. Thus a wise and good person who is considering some feature of his own conduct or condition might, in theory, respond to that object with a strong feeling which would be analogous, in some ways, to the feelings we identify as emotions. Such a feeling would necessarily be very different from any ordinary emotion: it could not be fear, for instance, as we know fear, but rather a strong inhibition from doing wrong; not desire, but a strong inclination to behave well; not pleasure, but joy in doing good and being good. A different terminology is called for, and Stoics will provide this.[36] For now, though, the point of importance is that the human capacity to feel strongly toward what we see as good or bad for ourselves remains a natural capacity, in Stoicism as in other ancient systems. It is not in having feelings that we go astray, but in our judgments of value.

THE ANTIOCHAN SYNTHESIS

Not everyone who studied these questions was convinced that Stoic and Peripatetic views were irreconcilable. Respect for Plato and Aristotle, and a

sense that the controversy surrounding the Stoic view was somehow mis-
guided, had led more than one philosopher to seek an intermediate position. Thus Panaetius of Rhodes (185–109) had softened Stoic claims about
value and rejected outright their central claim about impassivity (*apatheia*),
and Posidonius, the most influential Stoic of the early first century, had
retained the claim about impassivity while rejecting some of his predecessors' more counterintuitive psychological premises.[37] More important for
Cicero's contemporaries, however, was the Academic philosopher Antiochus of Ascalon (130–68). Like Posidonius and the Stoics, Antiochus insisted that the wise person will not experience emotion. His position was
unusual, however, in that he regarded this Stoic doctrine as fully compatible with early Academic and Peripatetic views. Indeed, he claimed that those
supposedly conflicting positions were in fact the same position, distinguished only by trivial differences in terminology. If Cicero in *Tusculans* 3–
4 appears absorbed in the controversies of the past, mentioning Antiochus
only once (and then only in passing, at 3.59), it is not for lack of knowledge
about this recent development in ethics. For the evidence of his other works
of the same period—the *On Ends,* the *Academics,* and also the fifth of the *Tusculans*—shows that he was deeply interested in Antiochus's ethical views.
One possible reading of his project in the emotion books is that he here
calls into question the synthesis which Antiochus had attempted, reopen-
ing the debate between the major schools as one which makes a substantive
difference in ethics.

The name of Antiochus is now usually mentioned in connection with a
reversion to dogmatism within the Academy. Reacting against the skeptical
stance that had prevailed in that school since Arcesilaus assumed its direction in the early third century, Antiochus had adopted what was essentially
a Stoic epistemology, maintaining the possibility of knowledge through the
"grasp" of impressions (*katalēpsis*), and insisting that such dogmatism was
fully in harmony with the views of Plato and Aristotle. His position in
ethics was similarly synthetic. Like his Academic forebears, he recognized
the traditional "three classes of goods" (goods of the body, of the mind,
and of life), but at the same time he insisted that virtue is preeminent
among these goods to such an extent that it is still possible to say, with the
Stoics, that the possession of virtue suffices to make one happy.[38] Not
supremely happy, for the presence or absence of the other goods must still
make some difference, and yet still happy as philosophers count happiness.
And it must have been for this reason that he also considered emotion incompatible with wisdom. The Antiochan sage must know that while health,

reputation, financial resources, and the like are indeed good things, and the loss of them indeed a misfortune, such things cannot make any real difference in his happiness.

Antiochus's views were influential at Rome. Cicero had studied with him in person (see on 3.59), as had others among his acquaintance. Two of Cicero's most respected contemporaries considered themselves Antiochans: Varro, the dedicatee and principal speaker of the *Academics;* and Brutus, the dedicatee of the present work and of several other Ciceronian works.[39] Brutus's own treatise *On Virtue* will have taken the Antiochan position. Yet Cicero himself has many reservations about Antiochus's ethics. In *On Ends* 5.77–86, and again at greater length in *Tusculans* 5.21–82, he argues that Antiochus's position on value is not viable. If Antiochus wishes to maintain the Stoic claim that virtue suffices for happiness, he cannot consistently maintain that there are other goods which the virtuous person might lack.

In the *Prior Academics,* after summarizing these same points, he had also confronted Antiochus directly on the emotion question:

> But at what point, I would like to know, did it become the doctrine of the old Academy to say, as you do, that the mind of the wise person is not stirred by emotion? Their support was given to "moderate amounts," and they wanted there to be some natural limit in every emotion. We have all read the little work *On Grief* by Crantor of the old Academy, for it is not long (though it is made of gold, and worth learning by heart, as Panaetius told Tubero to do). They indeed used to say that those emotions of which you speak were given to us by nature for a useful purpose—fear to make us cautious, pity and distress to make us merciful; even anger they called "the whetstone of courage." We shall investigate on some other occasion whether or not they were correct. But this brutishness [i.e. impassivity] you speak of—how *that* got into the old Academy I do not know.[40]

Cicero is careful not to give the impression that he himself supports the Crantoran position: as we shall see, the *Tusculans* will present it as a "very human" way of thinking about emotion (3.12), but will on the whole find it considerably less plausible than its Stoic competitor. About Antiochus, however, he can be direct. The modifications Antiochus has proposed in the Peripatetic system of value can never bring that system into consistency with Stoic ethics. And a synthesis which results in inconsistency is a failed synthesis. The differences between philosophers are sometimes more important than their similarities.

Epicurus on Emotion

Cicero could not claim to offer a balanced review of emotion theories if he did not also give some attention to Epicureanism. For Epicurus, too, recommends that we reconsider and reject those false beliefs which underlie most forms of desire, anger, and fear, with a view toward eliminating those emotions from our lives. But these recommendations come from within an ethical system fundamentally different from either of those which Cicero treats as the philosophic mainstream. For Epicurus's ethics is closely integrated with a physical science which flatly denies that the universe exhibits any overall structure or plan. This means that for an Epicurean, the Aristotelian and Stoic claims about virtue and honor will frequently sound hollow. The best and most natural life for a human cannot be defined in terms of nature's purpose for us, or god's. Rather it will be that life which is most satisfying to us when we set aside all cultural influences and make an honest and comprehensive evaluation of our own sensations. And it is by this standard that emotional disturbances turn out to be incompatible with the good life.

Epicurus is therefore a hedonist: like other Greek hedonists (notably the Cyrenaics mentioned in 3.28–31), he holds that the human norm and all human motivation can be understood in terms of pleasure (*hēdonē*) and pain. In humans, as in non-human animals, it is simply a fact of our nature that we are so constituted as to pursue pleasure and avoid pain. Indeed, our sensations of pleasure and pain, both of body and of mind, are one important way we gather information about our surroundings.[41] But humans happen also to have powers of reason sufficient to maximize our pleasure through intelligent management. We can choose slight pains in order to obtain greater pleasures or to avoid other, greater pains; we can experience mental pleasures so great that they overbalance pain of body, and we can direct our attention to some objects rather than others, disregarding pains in favor of present or even remembered pleasures. We can also eliminate many disturbing feelings by examining our beliefs and rejecting those which do not stand up to scrutiny, for some of our most powerful desires and fears are dependent on misconceptions which we have absorbed from literature and from other cultural influences.[42] Erotic love, for instance, is largely a cultural construct.[43]

It is the broad ethical foundations of Epicurus's position that Cicero is most concerned to attack here. He recognizes that many who espouse Epicureanism do so believing that the system promotes decent and upright behavior: he claims, in fact, that it is this belief that is responsible for the popularity of Epicurean views at Rome.[44] For Epicurus insists that a truly intelligent understanding of one's own interests and the means of obtaining them, freed of all false assumptions about the nature of the universe, will actually motivate us to behave in accordance with conventional standards of courage, justice, and self-control. His ethical system thus formally upholds the conduct most Romans would recognize as moral, even while it questions the use that other philosophers make of terms like "virtue" and "honor." Cicero can respect individuals who have adopted Epicureanism for this reason. Atticus, foremost among his friends, was an Epicurean, and the choice of views did not come between the two men. But Cicero also feels that despite the merits of individual Epicureans, the system itself remains open to self-indulgent interpretations which are entirely incompatible with a life of public service. So pressing is his concern that he devotes a sizable portion of book 3 (3.36–51) to a full-scale assault on Epicurean ethics, repeating many of the same points he had made in *On Ends*, book 2.

On Epicurus's actual strategy for consolation he has less to say: he doubts that it can be effective but does not pursue the matter in any detail. Nonetheless, even the bare sketch he does provide (at 3.28–35) is of considerable interest, for it preserves some shreds of information about an otherwise very obscure controversy between Epicurus and other fourth-century hedonists on the nature of mental pain.[45]

THE MANNER OF PRESENTATION

Even when most deeply engaged in evaluating the ethical views put forward by the major schools, Cicero is also much interested in comparing the achievements of philosophers as writers and speakers. By this criterion it is the Peripatetics and early Academics who receive his warmest approval.[46] He writes in *On Ends*:

> What a legacy they have given us in oratory, not only instructions in handbooks but also actual examples of speeches! First, they spoke aptly and with elegance even upon subjects requiring subtle argumentation, sometimes offering definitions, at other times classifications. . . . And then on subjects which called for a grander and more ornate style, how wonderfully they spoke! How splendid are their speeches on justice, temperance, and courage, on friendship and the conduct of life, on philosophy, on politics![47]

He goes on to speak of the superiority of Peripatetic writings on consolation and public policy, and especially of their rhetorical works. For it is the

Peripatetics who provide the practical rhetorical training. Thus the site of declamation-practice at the Tusculan villa is to be designated the "Lyceum," and when young Marcus Cicero is to be sent abroad for training, it is to the Peripatetic Cratippus, "the principal philosopher of our generation," that he will go.[48]

On Stoic achievements in this area, Cicero is more equivocal. Their language is certainly less mellifluous:

> You address these matters as well, but your manner is unkempt, while theirs, as you see, is highly polished. . . . *Theirs* was not the speech of plucking out the thorns, of laying bare the bones. It is Stoics who speak that way.

Yet this is not the contempt with which he elsewhere dismisses the language of Epicurean writings. Stoics are charged not with bad style but with an overly technical style, a style which concerns itself with rigorous argumentation and precision in terminology, caring little for the approbation of non-specialists.

As directed at serious philosophical writing, this might not seem to be much of a criticism, indeed rather the reverse. But Cicero does find grounds for complaint. In his view, the Stoics' lack of interest in rhetorical training misses an important opportunity for moral action. To be sure, some early Stoics did write rhetorical handbooks, but those books are a failure—ideal reading, he exclaims, for prospective orators who wish to be struck dumb! And the failure is symptomatic of a deeper problem. There is in Stoic ethics an implied imperative to encourage ethical reflection in *all* persons, not only in professional philosophers. An unrelieved technical idiom is to this extent a fault.

> What great things they attempt! To convince a resident of Circeii that his true city is this entire world! A subject to kindle the heart! But would a Stoic speaker set fire to anyone? No, he will rather quench any enthusiasm he finds. . . . For they prick at us with narrow little needles of argumentation. Their hearers, even if they are convinced, find their minds unchanged and when they depart are the same people they were when they came. The views are certainly important, and may even be true, but Stoics do not handle them properly. Their treatments are a good deal too minute.

It is the potential appeal of Stoic thought that makes existing works on Stoicism unsatisfactory.

This is the same complaint Cicero had voiced a year earlier, in the *Stoic Paradoxes* of 46. In that work he had himself attempted to remedy the deficiency in a small way, by arguing the truth of a series of ethical dicta in the manner of popular oratory.[49] But the program laid out for the *Paradoxes* did not have room for any very serious exposition of Stoic thought. Nor could *On Ends* itself demonstrate the full power that Stoic ideas might have when handled by a skilled orator. For Cicero had set himself the task of responding in his own person to each of the views presented there and could hardly commit his own officially skeptical voice to the service of Stoic ethics. In the *Tusculans,* however, the use of the *schola* format offered a less restrictive form of dialogue and dispensed with the need for refutation. Cicero could maintain his usual skeptical stance in some sections, but in others could let his authorial voice be subsumed by the more dogmatic voice of his principal speaker. Meanwhile, the earnest but unhurried manner of the work allowed him to explicate Stoic thought with some degree of patience.

The structure of books 3 and 4 is designed to illustrate the point about Stoic style with samples of different types of philosophic discourse. Each of the two books is built around a contrast: an initial section presents the Stoic position "in the Stoic manner" (3.13), while the main portion of the book defends the same views in the more expansive manner which Cicero claims for his own. Before a ship can spread its sails, explains the author, it must first be rowed slowly and laboriously out of harbor (4.9). Thus 3.14–21 consists primarily of a string of syllogisms, and 4.11–32 presents a long stretch of definitions and classifications very similar in style and content to surviving handbook material. In each case, the material is followed by a second exposition whose more combative manner and livelier, more accessible style calls to mind the author's experience in the courtroom. There is some irony in this, in that Cicero's Stoic speaker triumphs only by adopting the methods of his opponent. But the real victor, we are to understand, is Cicero himself, whose rhetorical skill here demonstrates its enduring worth.

It may be doubted whether the finished product achieves everything its author intended. Concern for his readers' patience sometimes leads Cicero to abbreviate his arguments to such an extent as to obscure the point being made, and his interest in contrasting modes of discourse sometimes results in excessive repetition. For the most part, however, he has been more than successful in shaping his material into graceful and coherent treatises. His stated intention is to express the ethical thought of

Greece in a way his contemporaries will find compelling, and it is clear that he has made a strenuous effort to do so. The works are spattered with human-interest stories, bits of verse, and an occasional excursus into etymology, a subject Roman intellectuals seem to have found fascinating. Whatever his private feelings may have been, his public presentation was to show him calmly but earnestly engaged in a study which might well appeal to any intelligent person.

NOTES

1.   Those new to the subject will find in Sedley 1980 a brief review of the fourth-century philosophical scene in Athens, in Long 1986 a useful conceptual overview, and in Inwood and Gerson 1997 a convenient anthology of source materials. More comprehensive resources include especially the texts and commentary in Long and Sedley 1987 and the recent *Cambridge history of Hellenistic philosophy* (Algra et al. 1999).

2.   For Cicero's position in the rhetorical works see comm. 4, IIc (on 4.47–57). Many scattered remarks in the letters bespeak a common-sense commitment to the view that emotions are necessary and/or useful. Two examples especially worth noting in this connection are the consolatory notes to Atticus (*Att.* 12.10 "your grief is human but should be kept very moderate") and to Brutus (*Ad Brut.* 1.9.2 "to grieve, but moderately, is a matter of expediency for others, but for you a necessity"). A remark in the long advisory epistle to Quintus, written some fifteen years earlier, is equivocal: one should avoid the appearance of sluggishness (*lentitudo;* cf. *Tusc.* 4.43), and yet both Quintus's high station and "perfect wisdom" require that anger be eliminated (*QFr.* 1.1.38).

3.   For the political situation see esp. Griffin 1997, 8–14. For the chronology and text of the letters see the standard editions by Bailey, together with the narrative in Bailey 1971, 200–15. The argument that follows works from the assumption that the stand Cicero takes in his circulated philosophical works is often fruitfully interpreted by reference to his political and personal concerns of the moment as understood from the letters. For more sustained recent ventures in this line see Griffin 1995 and 1997, Murphy 1998.

4.   *Att.* 12.13.2, 12.15, 12.21.5.

5.   *Att.* 12.18.1, 12.23.3, 12.37a, 12.38a.2, 12.41.4, 12.43.2. The proposed dedication would likely have struck contemporary Romans as peculiar; see Bailey 1971, 209–10, and in more detail Bailey 1966, 404–13. Cicero tells Atticus he found the idea in books (*Att.* 12.18.1), meaning perhaps in the treatise of Crantor; compare passage [h] in Appendix A.

6.   *Att.* 12.16; cf. 12.38.1. For the *Consolation,* see Appendix A, and compare also *Att.* 12.28.2: "As to my consolatory epistle to myself, I do not regret its success. I lessened my mourning, but grief itself I could not lessen, nor would I have wished to do so."

7.   *Att.* 12.14.3.

8.   *Att.* 12.46.1.

9.   *Att.* 12.13.2, 12.15.

10.   Cicero remarks to Atticus on the severity of its tone; *Att.* 12.14.4, 13.6.3. From what he writes to Brutus the following year (*Ad Brut.* 1.9.1), it appears that Brutus's consolation chided the grieving father for "softness" (i.e., effeminacy) and for being untrue to the advice he himself had often given to others. A surviving letter to Cicero by the jurist Servius Sulpicius Rufus (*Fam.* 4.5) gives a taste of the way one ex-consul could address another on such an occasion. Lofty but by our standards rather chilly in

its formality, it urges Cicero to think less of this small personal loss in comparison with the magnitude of the current political calamities. Cicero's response (*Fam.* 4.6) is heartrending. Others wrote as well: L. Lucceius (*Fam.* 5.13, 5.14, 5.15) and Caesar himself (*Att.* 13.20.1), though nothing of Caesar's letter remains. See Hutchinson 1998, 59–77, together with Bailey 1977, 2.415–19.

11.   *Att.* 12.20.1.

12.   *Att.* 12.38a.1. *Att.* 12.40.2, written two days later, is even more defensive in tone.

13.   *Att.* 12.14.3, 12.20.2 (finishing touches to the *Consolation*); 12.44.4 (*Prior Academics*); 12.40.2, 13.26.2 (letter to Caesar); 13.12.3 *(On Ends)*; 13.13.1 *(Academics)*. Griffin argues convincingly that the *Hortensius*, sometimes assigned to the period after Tullia's death, was in fact composed sometime during the winter of 46–45 and in circulation by March (Griffin 1997, 8). On the revision of the *Academics* see Reid 1885, 28–38, together with Plasberg 1922, i–xv. Evidence dating the composition of the *Tusculans* themselves is less secure. Cicero appears to have had it in the planning stages by May 29, when he requests from Atticus a copy of Dicaearchus's *On the Soul* "for a project I have in mind" (*Att.* 13.32.2), but it is not otherwise mentioned until May of the following year (*Att.* 15.2.4). This might mean that the work was not fully completed until that time; so Ruch 1958, 168–74. But the ordering of Cicero's list in *On Divination* 2.1–4 suggests that at least the bulk of the writing was done in the summer of 45, between the completion of the *Academics* in late June and the beginning of *On the Nature of the Gods* in mid-August (*Att.* 13.38.1, 13.39.2).

14.   *Tusc.* 2.9.

15.   The personal note is most explicit in 3.76 and 4.63, but can also be heard earlier, in 3.58. Erskine 1997 explains Book 3 as an introspective exercise in self-consolation. There is some validity in this, but for this as for all Cicero's circulated works it is important also to become attuned to the rhetoric of public presentation.

16.   The *schola* (Gr. *scholē*) was an oratorical as well as a philosophical format; see *Tusc.* 1.7–8, 2.9, and compare *On Ends* 2.1–3 and 2.17. Douglas 1995 gives a convincing analysis of the evidence, arguing that the term "diatribe" has been improperly applied to the *schola*. For the terminology see further Glucker 1978, 160–62.

17.   The example of the *Stoic Paradoxes* shows that one might argue for the thesis, rather than against it; note *pref.* 5 "in disputations thesis-fashion" *(in scholis thetikōs)*. Cicero sometimes associates the *schola* with argumentation on both sides: according to *On the Orator* 3.80 and *On Ends* 5.10, this is the manner of Aristotle particularly. But he also speaks in these same passages of a more specialized use of the *scholē* by Arcesilaus and Carneades to argue *against* every thesis. See Long 1995, 52–58, and compare Cicero's report about Carneades' pupil Clitomachus in 3.54. *Tusc.* 5.11 names Carneades as a model for Cicero's own disputations.

18.   Brunschwig 1986 discusses the use of the "cradle argument" in Epicureanism and Stoicism, with particular reference to Cicero's *On Ends*. Questions of innatism and experience in Plato and the Hellenistic schools are treated at length in Scott 1995.

19.   Cicero was not alone in this endeavor. I argue in comm. 3, IVA (on 3.52–61) and 3, VA (on 3.75–79), and in the appendixes, that philosophers of several Hellenistic schools made use of the consolatory tradition in much the same way.

20.   Crantor is in fact the principal authority cited here for the "Peripatetic" view; see Appendix A and comm. 3, Ic (on 3.12–13).

21.   The evidence for Cicero's knowledge of various works of Aristotle has recently been reviewed in some detail in Barnes 1997b, 44–59 and Long 1995, 52–58. In what follows, I am primarily concerned with the broad bases of Aristotle's position as suggested by On the Soul 2.2–5 and NE 1.13–2.8, rather than with the more specific observations in Rhet. 1.10–11 and 2.1–11. Cooper 1988 provides a useful point of entry into the secondary literature, and see the essays collected in Rorty 1996, among which the treatment by Striker (1996b) is especially relevant here.

22.   Antiochus of Ascalon was another source; see p. xxiv–xxv below. For Lyco see on 3.78. Staseas was an associate of M. Pupius Piso Calpurnianus; he is mentioned . in On the Orator 1.102–5 for his abilities as a speaker and in On Ends 5.8 and 5.75 for his position on value; see Moraux 1973, 217–21.

23.   The Stoics are notorious for denying emotions to animals, and Cicero will follow his source in this (4.31). But it should not be forgotten that even those ancient philosophers who assert that animals can be angry or in love see crucial differences between the mental experiences of animals and those of humans. Neither Stoics nor Peripatetics were necessarily interested in non-human minds for their own sake; rather, they argued for or against attributing emotions to animals as suited the understanding of human experience they wished to defend. For a broad-based treatment of the issue, see Sorabji 1993.

24.   But Diogenes Laertius attributes the adjective metriopathēs directly to Aristotle (5.31). For differences between the Peripatetic view and Aristotle's own view, see further comm. 4, IIIB (on 4.38–47).

25.   This is the view of Galen and Plutarch in the second century C.E. and also of the handbook Platonist Alcinous, whose dates are uncertain. But Cicero's earlier contemporary Posidonius of Rhodes may also have put forward a part-based account. Some of the relevant texts and bibliography for Posidonius's position may be found in Appendix D.

26.   Aristotle, NE 7.3, 1147a31–b5, Plato, Republic 4.435c–444e, 10.603e–604d. Cicero's division of the mind at 4.10 is labeled by him "Platonic," even though it does not proceed in what would appear to us to be Plato's direction. See further comm. 4, IIA (on 4.10–14), section 1.

27.   Origen, On Principles 3.1.2–3 (SVF 2.988). For this and other texts on Stoic psychology, see Long and Sedley 1987, 1.313–23, to which my own summary account is much indebted.

28.   Galen at PHP 4.2.20 attributes to Chrysippus an explicit statement of the distinction between the two senses of logikos, though for reasons of his own he denies that Chrysippus uses the distinction correctly.

29.   See especially D.L. 7.134–39, with Cleanthes' *Hymn to Zeus* (*SVF* 1.537) and Long and Sedley 1987, 1.286–89. Cicero was soon to give his own account in book 2 of *On the Nature of the Gods*.

30.   Sextus, *AM* 8.275–76 (*SVF* 2.223). See further comm. 3, IIA (on 3.13–21), section 1.

31.   Seneca, *On Anger* 2.4.5. The point is connected by Seneca with the (also morally insignificant) "pre-emotion," on which see comm. 3, VB (on 3.80–84).

32.   See further comm. 3, IIB (on 3.22–27), section 1, on the causal history of emotions; 3, IVC (on 3.64–71) on responsibility; and 4, IIB (on 4.14–22), section 2, on being "carried away."

33.   It is of course perfectly possible for a set of statements to be internally coherent when some or even all statements in the set are false. I take it that the Stoics are ready to insist that within those possible sets which can constitute the belief-set of a human being, the process of sorting and elimination which produces full coherence will always result in a set of true beliefs. The underlying premise is, again, teleological: certain foundational truths will always be present in us, even though in some cases they may be very deeply hidden.

34.   Fuller treatments of the role of (cosmic and human) nature, value, and the indifferents include Irwin 1998a, 227–38 and 1998b, Long 1971 (together with Long 1996, 152–55), Annas 1993, 159–79, and Striker 1991.

35.   For texts on "selection," see comm. 4, IIIc (on 4.47–57).

36.   The class of affect which Cicero calls "consistencies" and Greek authors *eupatheia* ("well-reasoned affect"). See 4.10–14 with comm. 4, IIA (on 4.10–14), section 2.

37.   Reports of Panaetius's views on the subject include Aulus Gellius 12.5 (fr. 111 van Straaten) and Cicero, *On Ends* 4.23. Panaetius was enthusiastic about the Old Academy (*On Ends* 4.79, *Tusc* 1.79), but we have no clear indication what arguments he used to support his attempt at synthesis. See also on 4.4. Evidence for Posidonius's views is presented almost exclusively by Galen, in a polemical work, and analysis of the material has been much disputed. We have some reason to question whether Cicero was familiar with Posidonius's views as reported by Galen; see Appendix D, where the point is argued in detail.

38.   See further Dillon 1996, 52–105, Barnes 1989, and Glucker 1978, 98–120.

39.   Barnes 1989, 60–62, reviews the evidence for Antiochan views among Cicero's contemporaries. For Brutus's treatise *On Virtue* see on 3.1.

40.   *Prior Academics* 2.135.

41.   The "feelings" (*pathē*), i.e. pleasure and pain, are listed by Epicurus as one criterion of truth; see further comm. 3, IIIB (on 3.32–35) and Appendix B.

42.   On the relation between emotions and false belief, Annas 1992, 189–99, Nussbaum 1994, 102–15.

43.   For Epicurean texts on love see on 4.70, together with Lucretius 4.1058–1191, and see Nussbaum 1994, 149–54.

44.   *On Ends* 1.25. See further comm. 3, IIID (on 3.47–51).

45.   For discussion see comm. 3, IIIA (on 3.28–31) and 3, IIIB (on 3.32–35) with Appendix B.

46.   The point is developed in detail in Long 1995, 50–58. The rhetorical preeminence of the Peripatetics, including Aristotle, is established early in the *Tusculans;* see *Tusc.* 1.7, 2.9.

47.   *On Ends* 4.5–6. The two following quotations are from the same passage.

48.   For the Lyceum see on 3.7; for Cratippus, on 3.22.

49.   The format of the *Stoic Paradoxes* is closely allied to that of the *Tusculans;* see note 17 above, with Lee 1953, xxii–xxiv. For further information on the *Paradoxes* see the annotated edition by Ronnick (1991).

About the Translation

My aim in the translation is to provide a readable and contemporary version of the text that will enable the reader to perceive the structure of Cicero's thought. For the sake of clarity I have not hesitated to break the longer sentences into shorter units, or occasionally to recast the structure of a sentence entirely, but I have tried to keep clauses in their original order insofar as possible. If the result is less elegant than the original, it cannot be helped; however, I may point out that many passages in the philosophical writings are intended to be simple and conversational in style, and that Cicero himself is often willing to forgo stateliness in order to represent his sources accurately and comprehensibly.

I have tried to be consistent in terminology, particularly for those terms which have a technical import in Hellenistic philosophy. Thus *visus* in the sense of Gr. *phantasia* is always "impression," *motus* in the sense of *kinēsis* always "movement," and so on. It should be observed, however, that Cicero himself does not attempt a one-for-one correspondence in translating philosophical terms. A comparison with Greek treatments of the same issues often finds him alternating between two different Latin words where the Greek authors employ a single standard term. Sometimes this practice helps to disambiguate a Greek word used in two distinct senses. For instance, *hēdonē* is rendered by *voluptas* in Epicurean contexts, where it refers to bodily and mental pleasure together; but by *laetitia*, sometimes paired with *voluptas*, in Stoic passages, where it refers to the emotion of delight. In other instances, a single Greek term may be given multiple renderings for the sake of emphasis, as in the repeated double or triple renderings of *kathēkei* ("it is appropriate"; see on 3.61) or merely for variety, as when *epithumia* ("desire") is called alternately *cupiditas* and *libido*. In such cases, I have generally preferred to stay with a single standard term, except where both Latin words occur together.

Less commonly, we may find a single Latin word standing in for more than one Greek term. In a few cases, the reasonable assumption is that Cicero has lost hold of a distinction made by his sources. Thus he may use *opinio* of beliefs held by the wise, where the parallel texts in Greek are scrupulous to avoid *doxa*. Elsewhere, the ambiguity seems to be created by the usual difficulty of finding equivalent terms in the target language. Thus *voluntas* in the nominative is pressed into service for *boulēsis* in 4.12, even though the ablative of that same word had been used extensively in book 3 in the sense of *eph' hēmin* (see comm. 3, IVc (on 3.64–71)). *Hormē* ("impulse") at 4.11 is rendered, reasonably enough, by *appetitus*, but having done this, Cicero has no good term available to use for *orexis* ("reaching") in 4.12, and settles for *appetitio*. Here and in similar cases it has seemed best to me to preserve the distinctions made in the Greek, at least in those places where I am satisfied that the language of Cicero's source must have resembled that used in texts known to us.

A few words and phrases present special difficulties. *Animus* is nearer to "mind" than it is to "soul," and I have in general insisted on this. The usage of certain Greek authors, however, sometimes precludes rendering their term *psuchē* as "mind," so that "soul" has occasionally had to be retained in the introduction and commentary. I render *virtus* as "virtue," standardly but with some reluctance: the English word hardly suggests rugged masculinity, as *virtus* does for Cicero; and in any case, few of us would now use English "virtuous" to describe a person we admire. "Excellence" or "merit" or even "goodness" would perhaps capture the connotations of the Latin term more faithfully. The word *aegritudo* is used in book 3 especially for distress at the death of a loved one, what 3.81 calls "that one type of distress which is the most grievous of all"; in book 4, however, *aegritudo* is used only in its broad generic sense (as at 4.14), distress specifically at bereavement being called *luctus*. For the sake of consistency I have rendered *aegritudo* as "distress" throughout both books, even in a few passages (3.27, 3.61) where a more specific translation such as "grief" would have been well suited to the immediate context.

Cicero's phrase *perturbatio animi*, which I regularly render "emotion," is literally "a disturbance of mind," and the force of the metaphor is never entirely absent: Cicero can exploit it, as he does, for instance, in 3.18 and 4.54.

But *perturbatio animi* is also his standard rendering for Gr. *pathos*, naming the class to which fear, desire, grief, and anger belong, and is as close to a standard usage as was in existence in Republican Latin (see further on 3.7). To adopt a stronger rendering in English, such as "passion" or "disturbance," would imply, wrongly I think, that the Hellenistic schools were interested only in especially powerful versions of emotions and not in emotions generally. I have, however, added "disturb" or "disturbance" to "emotion" in a few places where the verbal notion comes into play in the argument. Another difficult phrase is the one here translated "happy life." Cicero uses the words *beata vita* as his equivalent for *eudaimonia*, in philosophical Greek a specialized term for that ideal human life which is completely satisfactory on both a subjective and a long-term objective evaluation. This is not, I think, what most English speakers mean by "happiness." I have tried through the notes, and once through a rather studious translation ("that life which is properly called happy") to remove any possible confusion between "happiness" in this sense and the emotion of delight.

One other point of interest is the way Cicero deploys language of gender. By scrupulously rendering *homo* as "person" or "human" and insofar as possible employing gender-neutral default pronouns, I have sought to bring out the deliberate emphasis with which Cicero employs "man" and "manly" (*vir, virilis*) and, conversely, the opprobrium which attaches to "womanish" (*muliebris*; examples at 3.13, 3.70, 3.72). Another less obvious sexual innuendo can be heard in *fractus*, idiomatic Latin for "effeminate" (cf. Seneca, *Ep.* 115.2, *On the Happy Life* 13.4, Persius 1.18) and so rendered here. All these are standard usages in the public discourse of the period; see L'Hoir 1992, Richlin 1996. It does not follow that Cicero was or could be unconcerned about the viewpoint of potential female readers. We do well to remember that the first reader of *On Ends* was the inquisitive Caerellia (*Att.* 13.21a.2).

A Note on the Text

In preparing the translation, I have for the most part followed the Latin text of Pohlenz's 1918 edition, but have also consulted the editions by Dougan and Henry (1905, 1934) and by Giusta (1984), together with Giusta 1991 and Lundström 1964, 1986. In a few places the translation adopts a different reading from that printed by Pohlenz. These are as follows:

3.8–9 *omit* id est . . . insaniunt
3.52 ergo . . . repentina *transfer from end of 3.55*
3.76 *no supplement or lacuna after* accidisse; *for* nihil mali *read* nihil non alii.
4.1 *for* is *read* his
4.32 *no lacuna after* enim; *for* multa *read* in ulla
4.66 *for* cavere *read* confidere
4.68 *no lacuna before* quem contra
4.73 *for* amnipotens *read* omnipotens
4.78 *omit* defervescere . . . excitatum
4.80 *for* diffidentia *read* opinio; *omit* sunt in malo

Textual decisions which are of significance for the understanding of Cicero's thought are explained at the appropriate points in the commentary.

TUSCULAN DISPUTATIONS

BOOK 3

PREFACE: WHY WE NEED PHILOSOPHY

1 ⋅   What am I to think, Brutus? Are we not made up of a mind as well as a body? But while a method for the care and preservation of the body has been sought after and found, one so useful that it has been called the invention of gods immortal, for the mind no such method was thought necessary, until one was actually discovered. Why is this? And now that such a medical science has been recognized, why has it not been studied with the same devotion as the other? Why are so many people suspicious and hostile toward it? Perhaps it is because we make judgments about pain and afflictions of body by means of the mind, while sicknesses of the mind are not felt by the body. Because of this, the mind has to make judgments about its own case at a time when the judging faculty is itself infirm.

2 ⋅   If nature had made us such beings as would be able to see and comprehend that same nature, and to accomplish our life's journey under its excellent guidance, then we would have no need for any analytical teaching. But what nature has in fact given us are only the tiniest sparks of understanding, which we, corrupted as we are by our wrongful habits and beliefs, quickly put out again. Then nowhere can our natural light be seen. Seeds of the virtues are inborn in our characters, and if they were allowed to mature, nature itself would lead us to perfect happiness. But as it is, no sooner are we born and received into the family than we are surrounded by all kinds of corrupting influences, and the most wrongheaded beliefs, so that it seems almost as if we had drunk in error along with the milk of our wetnurses. And when we are returned to our parents, and then handed on to our teachers, we are steeped in such a variety of errors that truth gives way to foolishness, nature itself to hardened belief.   *3* ⟣   The poets come in as well, making a grand show of wisdom and erudition: we listen to them, read them, learn them by heart, and so receive a deep and lasting impression.

But it is when we meet with society at large—that is, with the people, who with one accord give approval to our faults, and are what I might call the greatest of all our teachers—it is then that we become thoroughly infected with corrupt beliefs and secede from nature absolutely. As a result, we think the meaning of nature best understood by those who have made up their minds that public office, military commands, and the glory of popularity are the best and most honorable goals a person can have. These things attract the noblest among us, so that, even as they pursue that genuine distinction which is the one chief aim of their nature, they spend their lives in great emptiness, chasing not a solid figure of virtue but only a shadow-shape of glory.

For real glory is a solid thing, clearly modeled and not shadowy at all: it is the unanimous praise of good persons, approval sounded without bias by those who know how to judge excellence of character. It is, as it were, the reflection or echo of such excellence, and there is no need for good men to disown it, since it is the regular accompaniment to right actions.   *4* ⟣   But there is another sort of glory, which pretends to imitate the first, and which is rash and ill-considered, frequently praising misdeeds and faults. This is popular acclaim, which offers a perverted caricature of the beauty that belongs to true distinction; and people are blinded by it, so that they do not know where to find or how to recognize the fine things they desire. This is why some have overthrown their governments, and others have ruined even themselves.

Yet these, at any rate, were striving for something good; they did not go astray voluntarily so much as they were deceived by the meanderings of the path. What about those who are carried away by a desire for money, or by longing for pleasures, whose minds are so troubled by emotion that they are not far from insanity? And this happens to everyone who is not wise. Are these not in need of healing? Shall we say that the infirmities of the mind are less harmful than those of the body? Or that bodies can be cured, but a medical science for the mind does not exist?

5 ⟣   No, the sicknesses of the mind are both more destructive and more numerous than those of the body. They are troublesome, in fact, precisely because it is the mind they attack; for, as Ennius says,

The mind distressed is ever astray,
can nothing bear, nothing endure;
unending its desire.

Distress and desire—what sicknesses of body could be more irksome than
these two of the mind? And I have not yet mentioned the others.

But surely we must admit that the mind is capable of healing itself. After
all, it was the mind that invented the science of medicine for the body. And
while bodily healings are largely dependent on the nature of the bodies
themselves, so that not all those who submit to treatment show any immediate improvement, of the mind there can be no doubt: once it is willing
to be healed, and heeds the precepts of the wise, it does indeed find healing.   6 ⁑   A medical science for the mind does exist: it is philosophy.
And unlike medicine for the body, the help of philosophy is something we
need not look to others to gain. Instead, we should make every possible
effort to become capable physicians for ourselves.

But I have already discussed this topic in my *Hortensius,* which concerns
the value of devoting oneself to philosophy in general; and what I said there
was, I think, sufficient. Since that time I have been almost continuously employed in discussing and writing about these great subjects. In these present
volumes, now, I have been setting forth the discussions I had with close
friends at my villa near Tusculum. And just as the two previous books related our talk about death and pain respectively, this third book will
comprise the discussions of a third day.

PART I: THE QUESTION TO BE ADDRESSED

A.   Is the Wise Person Subject to Distress?

7 ⁑   As we were going down to our Academy in the early afternoon, I
asked one of those who were there to suggest a topic for discussion. This is
what followed.

"It seems to me that the wise person is subject to distress."
Would you say the same about the other emotions, about the various
forms of terror, desire, and anger? For all such things are covered by the
Greek term *pathē*. A literal translation for *pathē* would be "sicknesses," but
that would run counter to normal Latin usage. For pity, envy, elation,

gladness, and so forth are all called by the Greeks "sicknesses," as being movements of mind not obedient to reason. But I think I was right to refer to these same movements of the mind when aroused as "emotions," since "sicknesses" would sound peculiar. Or do you prefer another word?

8 ₰   "My preference is the same as yours."

Well, then, do you think that the wise person is subject to these also? "Indeed I do."

I tell you, I wouldn't give much for your kind of wisdom. For all its fine name, it's hardly better than insanity.

B.   A Preliminary Investigation on the Basis of Latin Usage

"What? You think every emotion amounts to insanity?"

I'm not the only one to hold that opinion. It's a marvelous thing, but as I understand it, our ancestors held the same view many generations before Socrates, who was the originator of that whole branch of philosophy that deals with how we live and conduct ourselves.

"How on earth do you come to that conclusion?"

Because the term *insania* refers to an infirmity or sickness of the mind.   9 ₰   For they judged that *sanitas* or "health" for the mind consisted in having a serene and consistent temper. Consequently, the state of mind that lacked such a temper was called by them *insania* or "insanity," on the grounds that health cannot be present in a disturbed mind, any more than in a disturbed body.   10 ₰   It was with equal insight that they called that mental condition which lacks the light of thought *amentia*, "losing one's mind," or *dementia*, "being out of one's mind." From this terminology we may infer that those who invented it held the same view as has come down to us from Socrates in the scrupulous keeping of the Stoics, namely that all those who are not wise are insane. For a mind which is sick in some way cannot be healthy, just as a body cannot, and, as I said, philosophers apply the word "sickness" to all such emotional movements. This proves that wisdom is health for the mind, and the absence of wisdom is a kind of ill health, that is, insanity or being "out of one's mind." These things are much more clearly indicated by the Latin terminology than by the Greek—as is true in many other cases as well. But more on that elsewhere. Let's stick to the matter at hand.

11 ₰   So the very meaning of the word makes clear for us the whole nature and substance of the problem we are investigating. Since the word "sane" has to refer to those whose minds are not disturbed by any movement or, as it were, sickness, those who are in the opposite condition must

be termed "insane." Furthermore, nothing could be better than that usage by which we Latin speakers say that people have gone *ex potestate*, "out of control," when they are carried away by unbridled desire or anger. (Although really, anger is a species of desire, since it is defined as "a desire for revenge.") Thus when people are said to be "out of control," it is because they are not under the control of the intelligence, which nature appointed to rule over the mind as a whole.

Why the Greeks call this state "madness" *(mania)* I really cannot say. Our language makes clearer distinctions: we discriminate between *insania*, which has a wide application because its link with folly, and *furor* or "frenzy." The Greeks mean the same thing we do, but they do not have a good word for it. What we call "frenzy," they call *melancholia*, "biliousness," as if the mind were stirred up only by black bile and not by some more serious form of anger, fear, or grief, as happened with the frenzy (as we say it) of Athamas, Alcmaeon, Ajax, and Orestes. A person in such a condition is prohibited by the Twelve Tables from managing his own affairs. Hence the law reads not "if he be insane" but "if he be frenzied." For they judged that a person who is foolish and lacking in consistency—that is, in health—was still capable of handling ordinary responsibilities and of managing his life in the usual and customary way; but frenzy, they thought, was a complete darkening of the mind. This would seem to be worse than *insania*; nonetheless, frenzy is the sort of thing that can come upon a wise person, while *insania* cannot.

C. Distress Must Come First

But that is a different inquiry. Let us go back to our original question. **12 ☙** I believe you expressed an opinion that the wise person is subject to distress.

"Yes, and that is what I actually believe."

It's very human to think that way. After all, people are not made of stone; it's natural that there should be some soft and tender element in our minds, something that would be shaken by distress as by a storm. There is some sense in what Crantor says (he was one of the most eminent members of the Academy, to which I adhere):

> I cannot by any means agree with those who extol some kind of impassivity.
> Such a thing is neither possible nor beneficial. I do not wish to be ill, but if I
> am, and if some part of my body is to be cut open or even amputated, let me
> feel it. This absence of pain comes at a high price: it means being numb in
> body, and in mind scarcely human.

13 ᴥ   But let us be careful. It may be that these are the words of those who choose to indulge the weak and womanish parts of us. Let us be bold enough not only to prune away the branches of unhappiness, but to yank out its very roots, down to the last fiber. Yet so deep are the roots of folly that there will perhaps be something left over. But we will leave no more than is necessary. Of this one thing you must be assured: unless the mind is healed—which cannot happen without philosophy—there will be no end to our unhappiness. Therefore, since we have made a beginning with philosophy, let us entrust ourselves to her care. We will be healed, if we are willing to be. And I will go even a step further, to explain not only distress—though that must come first—but every emotion or, as the Greeks would have it, every sickness of the mind.

PART II: TWO WAYS OF PRESENTING THE STOIC POSITION

A.   Arguments in the Stoic Manner

If you don't mind, I will begin in the Stoic manner, with brief, compressed arguments. Later on, I will speak more freely, in my usual way   *14* ᴥ

[AI]   Anyone who is courageous is also confident (*fidens*).

I use the word *fidens* here, since *confidens* is applied by an unfortunate linguistic usage to the fault of overconfidence, even though the verb *confidere*, from which it is derived, has a positive connotation.

[A2]   Moreover, anyone who is confident does not become greatly frightened.

Assuredly not, since being frightened is incompatible with confidence.

[A3]   But anyone who is subject to distress is also subject to fear,

since the things we are distressed at when they are present are the very things we fear when they are impending. It follows that

[A4]   distress is incompatible with courage.

In fact, it seems likely that anyone subject to distress would also be subject to timidity and a broken spirit, which means that he would also submit to servitude, or admit to being vanquished, if it should come to that. And one who can be enslaved or vanquished must also be capable of timorousness and cowardice. So, since a courageous man is not subject to timorousness and cowardice, he is not subject to distress either.

[A5]   But no one is wise who is not also courageous.

[A6]   Therefore, the wise person will not be subject to distress.

15 Furthermore,

[B1]   Anyone who is courageous must also be great in spirit.

[B2]   A person great in spirit must also be indomitable.

[B3]   The indomitable person must be able to disregard the circumstances of human life as matters beneath his notice.

[B4]   But no one can disregard things that are capable of causing him distress.

[B5]   Therefore, the courageous man cannot ever be distressed.

[B6]   But everyone who is wise is courageous.

[B7]   Therefore, the wise person is not subject to distress.

And just as the eye, when it is troubled in some way, is not in a proper condition to perform its function, nor can the whole body or any of its parts function as it should when in an altered state, so also

[C1]   the troubled mind is not fit to perform its function.

[C2]   And the function of the mind is to make good use of its reasoning power.

[C3]   But the mind of the wise person is always in a fit condition to make the best possible use of reason.

[C4]   Hence, the wise person's mind is never disturbed.

[C5]   But distress is a disturbance of the mind.

[C6]   Therefore, the wise person will always be free of it.

16 Here is another plausible argument.

[D1]   Anyone who is temperate . . .

The Greek word here is *sōphrōn* ("self-controlled"), and this virtue is called in Greek *sophrosunē* ("self-control"), which I render sometimes as "temperance," sometimes as "self-control" or "moderation." It may be, though, that the best term for it is "frugality." The corresponding Greek term is too narrow in its application: they call frugal people *chrēsimoi*, that is, merely "useful." But *frugalitas* is a broader term, carrying with it not only *abstinentia*, "restraint" and *innocentia*, "harmlessness" (for which there is no Greek term in use, though *ablabeia* or "non-hurtfulness" might serve, since harmlessness is the disposition not to hurt anyone), but all the other virtues as well. If "frugality" had not been such a broad term, but had been restricted to that narrow meaning which many people assign to it, it would never have become the honored title of Lucius Calpurnius Piso.

17 ⁊   The soldier who abandons his post out of fear is not normally described as "frugal"; rather, this is a case of cowardice. Similarly, the banker who refuses to return a sum of money privately entrusted to his care is not "frugal," but unjust, and the investor who takes bad risks and loses his money is not "frugal," but imprudent. Hence "frugality" implies the three virtues of courage, justice, and prudence. But this, as you know, is a characteristic shared by all the virtues, that each is tied to the others. So let frugality itself be the remaining virtue, the fourth. For as we see, the defining characteristic of this virtue is that it regulates and placates one's impulses to act, and so preserves that well-regulated consistency which on every occasion is opposed to desire. The fault contrary to it is called *nequitia* or "worthlessness."   *18* ⁊   I believe that the word *frugalitas* is derived from *frux*, "fruit," the best thing that comes from the earth. As for *nequitia* (this will perhaps be a bit strained, but let me try, and take it as a joke if it is no good)—well, *nequitia* is derived from the fact that there is *nequicquam*, "no thing," worthwhile in such a person, which is why he is also said to be *nihili*, a "good-for-nothing."

Now then:

[D1]   anyone who is frugal (or, if you prefer, self-controlled and temperate) must also be consistent.

[D2]   But the person who is consistent is also calm.

[D3]   And the one who is calm is free from all emotional disturbance,

[D4]   and therefore from distress also.

[D5]   And the aforementioned qualities are characteristic of the wise person.

[D6]   Therefore, the wise person will be free of distress.

Moreover, there is good sense in the comment which Dionysius of Heraclea made upon Achilles' lament in Homer. The lines run something like this:

My heart swells deep within me, sad and angry,

when I remember how I have been stripped
of my prize and all my glory.

Dionysius writes,

19 ᴖ   Is the hand in its proper condition when it has a swelling? Or is there
any other body part which can be swollen and inflamed and not be in a condition of fault? Even so is the mind at fault when it is puffed out and swollen.

Now,

[E1]   the wise person's mind is always free of fault, never inflamed or swollen.

[E2]   That of the angry person, however, is just that way.

[E3]   Therefore, the wise person never gets angry.

For if he does grow angry, he must also be desirous, since the defining characteristic of the angry person is that he desires to inflict as much pain as he
can on the one he believes to have harmed him. But one who desires this
must necessarily be delighted if he achieves it, which means that he is rejoicing over someone else's misfortune. Since the wise person never does
that, he is not subject to anger either.

[E4]   But if the wise person were subject to distress, he would also be sub-
       ject to anger.

[E5]   Since he is free of anger, he will also be free of distress.

20 ᴖ   Besides, if the wise person were subject to distress, he would also
be subject to pity and envying. I use the word *invidentia*, "envying," rather
than *invidia*, "envy," since the latter would mean he was the object of envy.
By thus deriving another noun from the verb *invidere*, it is possible to avoid
the ambiguity in *invidia*. The root verb *videre* ("see") indicates an excess in
looking upon the good fortune of others. Hence in the *Melanippus* of Accius
we have

Who did envy my children's bloom?

Bad Latin, it appears, but Accius makes his meaning very clear: since *videre*
takes an accusative object, it is better for *invidere* to take the accusative *florem*
("bloom") rather than the dative *flori*. Where you and I are constrained by
normal usage, he, as a poet, has the right to speak more boldly.

21   Now,

[F1]   anyone who is subject to pity will also be subject to envy.

For a person who is pained by another's misfortune will also be pained by another's good fortune. For instance, while Theophrastus was mourning the death of his friend Callisthenes, he was simultaneously pained by the good fortune of Alexander. That was why he remarked that Callisthenes had fallen in with one who had great power and wealth, but who did not know how to make proper use of his advantages. In any case, just as pity is distress over another's misfortune, so envy is distress over another's good fortune. Hence anyone who is subject to pity will also be subject to envy.

[F2]   But the wise person is not subject to envy;
[F3]   therefore, he is not capable of pity either.
[F4]   But if the wise person had a tendency to be distressed, he would also have a tendency to feel pity.
[F5]   Therefore, the wise person is untouched by distress.

B.   A More Rhetorical Presentation

22   That is how the Stoics make their points, wrapping them up in tight syllogisms. I must now set forth these ideas at greater length and with more freedom. Yet I will continue to rely primarily upon Stoic views, since among philosophers their reasoning is the strongest and, if I may say so, the most virile. For although my friends the Peripatetics are the best of all for eloquence, for erudition, and for seriousness, their theory of "moderate amounts" in emotions or in sicknesses of mind does not seem to me very convincing. If a thing is bad, it is bad also in a moderate amount. We, however, are endeavoring to make sure that the wise person does not experience anything bad at all. For just as the body, when moderately ill, is not healthy, so also what they call "moderation" in the mind falls short of actual health.

Hence the speakers of our language make matters very clear, as they often do, when they reserve the word *aegritudo* ("distress") for sorrow, worry, or anxiety in mind, by analogy with bodies that are *aegri* ("ill"). *23*   The Greek equivalent applies to every emotion quite generally, since they use the word *pathos* or "sickness" for every turbulent movement of the mind. Our usage is better, in that distress is, of all the emotions, the one most similar to bodily illness. Desire does not resemble an infirmity, and neither does unrestrained gladness, which is excessive and wild delight of mind. Even fear is not particularly similar to a sickness, although it is closely related to distress. But *aegritudo* specifically suggests mental pain, just as *aegrotatio*, "infirmity," suggests bodily pain.

My task, then, is to explain the source of this pain, what it is that causes distress in the mind, just as one might explain the cause of some bodily infirmity. For when doctors have learned the cause of some sickness, they feel that they have found a remedy for it; and we, too, once we have found the cause of distress, will discover some means of cure.

24 ⁂   Now the cause of distress, as of all the emotions, is to be found entirely in belief. There are many species of emotion, but only four genera. For while every emotion is a movement of the mind which is apart from reason or heedless of reason or disobedient to reason, the stimulus for such a movement may be of two kinds: it may be a belief either about what is good or about what is bad. This yields a neat fourfold classification. Beliefs about what is good give rise to two emotions. One is wild delight, that is, gladness carried away to excess: it arises from the belief that some great good is present. The other is desire, which can also be termed "longing": it is an ungoverned reaching, not subject to reason, toward some great good that is anticipated.   25 ⁂   Thus two genera, wild delight and desire, are caused by beliefs about what is good. The other two, fear and distress, are caused by beliefs about what is bad. Fear is a belief that some serious evil is impending, distress a belief that a serious evil is present. Specifically, it is a fresh belief, and the evil is of such a nature that it seems right to be pained by it—seems so, at least, to the person who is suffering and who believes that it is appropriate for him to suffer.

These are the emotions which folly has stirred up against human life, unleashing them and setting them upon us like Furies. We must resist them with all our strength, if we truly wish to spend our allotment of life in peace and tranquility. But we can deal with the others elsewhere; for now, let us do what we can to drive away distress. In fact, let that be the point at issue between us. You said that you think the wise person is subject to distress. I strongly disagree. For distress is a terrible, sad, hateful thing, something we should avoid by every effort we can—oars and sails together, as the saying goes.

26 ⁂   What sort of man was Thyestes, do you think? He was

Tantalus's grandson and Pelops's son, who once
from Oenomaus won a captive bride,
Hippodamea.

A great-grandson of Jupiter, no less! Should he have spoken these despair-
ing words?

> Back, friends, stay back, do not draw near to me!
> Let not my shadow, nor the taint in me infect
> the good. For great is the power of this crime;
> it clings to my flesh.

Will you condemn yourself, Thyestes, and deprive your own eyes of light,
because of the power of someone else's crime?

And what about the Sun's own child, Aeetes? Was he not undeserving
of his father's light?

> Sunken my eyes, my body gaunt with hunger,
> my pallid cheeks are rutted deep with tears;
> neglected, bristling, my grimy beard
> darkens with filth the sores upon my chest.

Foolish man! You brought these evils on yourself. These were not among
the ills which chance forced upon you; no, that misfortune was an old one,
and the swelling in your mind had long subsided. For distress requires a
fresh belief, as I shall go on to demonstrate. Aha! Your sorrow is not for the
loss of your daughter, but for the loss of your kingdom! Well, you hated
her, and perhaps you were right. The kingdom, though, you could not do
without. That is a shameless grief indeed, when a person goes to rack and
ruin just because he cannot have dominion over a free people.

27 ⟩ The tyrant Dionysius, when he was expelled from Syracuse,
went to Corinth and became a schoolmaster, so deep was his attachment to
power. But the most shameless of all was Tarquinius, who made war on anyone who refused to tolerate his proud behavior. They say that when he
could not be reinstated by force of arms either at Veii or in Latium, he re-
tired to the city of Cumae, where distress and old age put an end to him.

Now, do you think this could possibly happen to the wise person, to
be subject to distress in this way? That is, to misery. For every emotion is
a misery, but distress is a very torture-chamber. Desire scalds us; wild delight makes us giddy; fear degrades us; but the effects of distress are
worse: gauntness, pain, depression, disfigurement. It eats away at the
mind and, in a word, destroys it. This we must shed; this we must cast
away, or else remain in misery.

Part III: Hedonist Approaches

A. Epicurus and the Cyrenaic Expedient

28 ⁂   This much, at least, is quite clear: distress comes about only when a person has the impression that some serious evil is present and weighing upon him. Now, according to Epicurus, it is "by nature" that this belief comes to be distress. That is, anyone who directs his attention toward some relatively great evil will immediately be distressed, if he believes it has happened to him. The Cyrenaics, for their part, claim that distress is not produced by every misfortune, but only by a misfortune which was not foreseen and anticipated. And it is true that unexpectedness makes our distress considerably worse, for everything seems more serious when it happens suddenly. Hence these lines, too, are much admired, and with good reason:

> I knew, when I fathered them, that they must die,
> and when I nurtured them, it was for this.
> More: when I sent them to Troy, defending Greece,
> I knew that it was to death-dealing war they went,
> not to a feast.

29 ⁂   This is called the "pre-rehearsal of future evils": one looks far ahead to misfortunes that are to come, and this makes their arrival easier to bear. Hence the general admiration for the speech of Theseus in Euripides—which, as is my custom, I take the liberty of translating:

> I learned this from a wise man: over time
> I pondered in my heart the miseries
> to come: a death untimely, or the sad
> escape of exile, or some other weight
> of ill, rehearsing, so that if by chance
> some one of them should happen, I'd not be
> unready, not torn suddenly with pain.

30 ⁂   But when Theseus says he learned this "from a wise man," this is actually Euripides' statement about himself. For he had been a pupil of Anaxagoras, who is supposed to have said, when he heard of his son's death, "I knew my child was mortal." These words make it clear that such things are bitter primarily to those who have not thought about them.

So this, at least, is not to be doubted, that all those things that are considered bad are worse when unforeseen. To be sure, unexpectedness is not the sole cause of great distress. Nonetheless, foresight and mental preparation can do a great deal to lessen the pain, and for this reason we who are human should always be rehearsing every event of human life. This indeed is wisdom in its noblest and most godlike form: to scrutinize human life and understand it deeply; not to be surprised by anything that happens; and never to think that something cannot happen merely because it has not happened yet.

> Therefore, when life is at its best, then most of all
> should we rehearse within how trouble may be borne.
> As you return from travel, think always of danger
> and loss: your son's done wrong; your daughter's ill,
> your wife is dead—remember such events are common.
> That way, no one of them can strike you unawares.
> And when your expectation is unmet, count it as gain.

31 ⚬   It was from philosophy that Terence drew this idea which he expresses so well. Since, then, it is from our wellsprings that it came, isn't it likely that we philosophers will express the same thought even more beautifully, and believe it even more firmly? This is why the countenance of Socrates never changed. For they say that Xanthippe used to remark how her husband always looked the same to her when he returned to the house as he had when he left. Nor was this merely a set expression, like that of Crassus the elder, who, according to Lucilius, laughed but once in his entire life. No, it was a tranquil, unclouded face, by all reports. And it is no wonder that the countenance remained unchanged, since there was no alteration in the mind, which is what shapes our expressions.

For these reasons I do accept from the Cyrenaics this method of daily pre-rehearsal, as a shield against misfortunes to break the force of their assault when it comes. But I also hold that the problem is one of belief, and not a matter of nature. For if the event itself were the problem, why would anticipating our troubles make them easier to bear?

B.   The Method of Epicurus

32 ⚬   But if I am to treat the matter with precision, I need first to examine Epicurus's own position. Epicurus holds that every person who believes he is in evil circumstances will necessarily be distressed. In his view it does not matter if those circumstances have been foreseen and anticipated, or if they have grown old, since evils are not diminished by the passage of time, nor made easier by pre-rehearsal. In fact, it is foolish to rehearse misfortunes which have not yet happened and may not happen at all. Each of our misfortunes is distasteful enough, he says, when it is already here: those who have constantly been thinking about what disagreeable things are on the way simply make their evils perpetual. And those things may not happen at all, in which case all their voluntary misery goes for nothing. The result is that they are always in anxiety, either from the evils they undergo or from those they anticipate.

33 ※ As for the means of easing distress, he holds that there are two: distracting the mind from the thought of suffering, and redirecting it to the contemplation of pleasures. For he claims that the mind is capable of listening to reason and following where reason leads. Reason forbids us to direct our attention toward what is troubling, draws us away from painful thoughts, and dulls the vision with which we contemplate our sufferings. From all of this it sounds the retreat and urges us rather to concentrate on pleasures of every sort, fondling them with the entire mind. With these pleasures, he says, the wise person fills his life—these, and the memory of others now past, and the expectation of those still to come.

I have expressed these ideas in my usual style; the Epicureans have a style of their own. But let us concern ourselves with what they say, not how they say it. 34 ※ First of all, they are wrong to criticize the practice of pre-rehearsing future ills. Nothing does so much to soften the impact of distress as this practice of thinking at all times that there is no misfortune that cannot befall us, rehearsing the regular restrictions under which we humans live and resolving to abide by them. The result is not that we are always sad, but that we are never sad at all. A person is not saddened by thinking about the nature of things, about the changefulness of life and the weakness of humankind; rather, it is in this, above all, that one gains the benefits of wisdom. For not only does one have the satisfaction of doing what a philosopher should (that is, contemplating human affairs), but also, in times of trouble, one has a threefold source of consolation and healing. First, everything that has happened is something one has thought about for a long time, and such thinking does more than anything else to lessen and dilute every kind of suffering. Second, one understands that troubles are part of human life, and that to endure them, as we must, is also human. Finally, one realizes that nothing is truly evil except individual wrongdoing, and that when no individual could have been responsible for what happened, there is no wrongdoing.

35 ☙   Epicurus recommends that rather than gazing upon our evils, we should "redirect" the mind away from them. But this is of no use at all. For it is not within our power to forget or gloss over circumstances which we believe to be evil, at the very moment when they are piercing us. They tear at us, buffet us, goad us, scorch us, stifle us—and you tell us to forget about them? That is contrary to nature! Meanwhile, you wrest from us the aid which nature has provided as our sufferings grow old. For the passage of time is itself a means of cure, a slow one to be sure, yet very effective.

C.   What Epicurus Means by "The Good"

You tell me to think about good things and forget the bad. That would indeed be a worthwhile thing for a great philosopher to say, if only the things you consider "goods" were the goods most worthy of a human being.   *36* ☙   Pythagoras, or Socrates, or Plato might say to me, "Why are you downcast? Why are you sad? Why are you giving in to Fortune? She can, perhaps, pinch or poke you, but surely she cannot have broken your spirit. There is great power in the virtues: arouse them, if they happen to be asleep. Courage, above all, will come to your aid, and will instill in you such a great spirit that nothing that can happen to a person will seem to you worth noticing. Temperance will stand by you as well (or, what is the same thing, self-control; a bit earlier I called it "frugality") and will keep you from doing anything shameful or depraved—and what is more shameful and depraved than womanish behavior in a man? Justice will not allow it either. For although it may seem that this virtue has but little role to play here, it does have something to say to you. Your behavior is unjust in two ways: first, you are trying to get something that is not your own, since, born a mortal, you are asking for the status of the immortals; second, you are complaining because you had to give back something which was yours only as a loan.   *37* ☙   And what answer will you give to prudence? For prudence teaches that just as virtue is all we need to live a good life, so also is it self-sufficient for happiness. Virtue arises from itself, returns to itself, embraces all that is its own, and asks for nothing else. If virtue were dependent on externals, then would it be right to praise it so extravagantly, to pursue it so eagerly? I do not know why anyone would think so."

If these were the good things to which you redirect me, Epicurus, I would indeed obey you, follow you, make you my captain and forget about bad fortune, as you bid me. It would be easy for me to do so, since I hold that bad fortune ought not to be considered bad at all. But in fact you are turning my thoughts toward pleasures. Which pleasures? Those of the body, no doubt, or those which the mind anticipates or remembers for the sake of the body.

Or is there anything else? Am I not interpreting your position correctly? For the Epicureans claim that our side does not understand what Epicurus means. 38 ❧   Yet here is what he says. I will give it to you in the very words of Zeno, a sharp-tongued old fellow, and the cleverest of all the Epicureans. I used to hear him when I was a student in Athens, contending in a loud voice as follows:

> The happy person is one who appreciates the pleasures that are at hand, and is confident that he will continue to enjoy them, believing that all or most of his life will be free of pain, or, if not, that any extreme pain will be brief, while in any lasting pain the pleasurable will outweigh the bad. Anyone who thinks on these things will be happy, especially if he is content with the good things he has already experienced and fears neither death nor the gods.

Here you have Epicurus' conception of happiness, as expressed by Zeno. He cannot deny any of it.

39 ❧   Now suppose Thyestes were to adopt this approach to life and think about these things. Would that be able to ease his distress? What about Aeetes, whom I mentioned before? What about Telamon, driven from his homeland into exile and penury—Telamon, of whom they said in wonder,

> Can this be Telamon, whose glory reached the sky,
> who drew the eye, who turned the heads of all the Greeks?

40 ❧   No, anyone who has found, as the same poet says, that

> the spirit falls along with circumstances

must seek a remedy from those ancient, serious philosophers, and not from these pleasure-lovers. For what do they mean when they speak of "an abundance of good things"? Let us concede that the greatest of all good things is not to feel pain. (That is not what the word "pleasure" means, but we need not refute them on all points at this time.) Will *that* relieve our sorrow, if we turn our thoughts toward it? Let us concede that pain is the worst of all evils: does that mean that the person who is not in pain is automatically enjoying the greatest of goods, just because he is free of what is bad?

41 ⚬   Why are we hanging back, Epicurus? Why don't we admit that the pleasure we are talking about is indeed what you sometimes unblushingly say that it is? Are these your words, or not? In that very book which contains the whole of your teaching (for I will now turn myself into a translator, so that no one will think I invented this) you say as follows:

> Indeed, I do not know what is meant by "the good," if you take away the pleasures that are experienced through taste, and the pleasures experienced in sex, and the sweet motions which are experienced by the ears through music and by the eyes through forms, and the other pleasures which are generated in the whole person by any of the senses. Nor is it possible to say that gladness of mind is the only thing that is good. For as I understand it, what it means for a mind to be glad is for it to have an expectation of possessing, naturally and without pain, all those things which I have named.

42 ⚬   This is what he says, and those are his words. Anyone can see what Epicurus means by "pleasures." And he continues, a little further on:

> Many times have I asked those who are called philosophers, "What have you got left to count as good, once you take away those things I have mentioned? Or do you wish to utter empty phrases?" But I have not been able to get anything out of them. If they choose to spout words like "virtue" and "wisdom," they will be naming nothing more than the means to bring about those pleasures that I spoke of earlier.

What comes after this is in the same vein; in fact, his entire book on the highest good is crammed with words and sayings of this kind.

43 ⚬   Once again: is this the life to which you would redirect Telamon, to ease his distress? And if you see one of your own friends or family afflicted with grief, will you give him a sturgeon, rather than a Socratic dialogue? Will you bid him listen to the notes of the organ, rather than the voice of Plato? Will you set out pretty colors and flowers for him to look at, or hold a bouquet to his nose? Burn incense? Tell him to garland himself with roses? Something even better? Oh, yes, *that* will surely erase all grief from his mind!

44 ⚬   Epicurus must admit all this, or else excise those passages from his book, which I have translated word for word. Better yet, throw away the entire book, since it is crammed with pleasures. I cannot help asking how we are to set free from distress the man who says,

By god, it is not lineage that fails me now,
but Fortune, by whose grace I once was king.
You see how high a place, how vast a wealth,
how great a fall was mine, and all through fortune.

Well? Will you thrust into his hands a glass of honeyed wine, or something
of that kind, to make him stop lamenting? Look, here is something else
from the same poet:

Once wealthy, I am now bereft, O Hector, of your aid.

We should help her, since she is asking for aid.

Where shall I find defense? On what support
shall I rely in exile? Where shall I flee?
Orphaned of tower and city now, at whose feet can I fall?
The ancestral altars of my home no longer stand;
broken and scattered they lie; the temple burnt
to earth, the high walls charred, timbers askew,
disfigured. . , ,

You are all familiar with the lines that follow, and these most of all:

O father, O homeland, O home of Priam, temple
guarded by high portals echoing!
I saw you once attended by the wealth
of foreign lands, your molded, paneled ceilings
decked out in gold and ivory, king-befitting.

45 ≈ O noble poet! despite the contempt of these latter-day tunesters,
these would-be Euphorions. He understands that sudden events are always
harder to bear. He heaps up the royal wealth, which seemed as if it would
last forever, and then what does he add?

Before my eyes did all these things take flame;
and Priam lost his life in violence,
God's altar fouled with blood.

46 ≈ What fine poetry! It is mournful not only in content, but in style

and meter as well. But let us take away this woman's distress. How? Let us put her on a feather cushion! Bring in a harpist! Give her some perfume! Light up a little dish of incense! Let's see about something for her to drink and eat—something on the sweet side, I think. For these, after all, are the goods that banish the most severe forms of distress. You said, just a minute ago, that you did not understand what other goods there could be.

So I might be in agreement with Epicurus that one should redirect one's thoughts from grief to what is good, if only we were agreed about what it is that is good. Someone will say, "Do you think that Epicurus had all those things in mind? Do you think his views were merely perverse?" No, I do not. I see that much of what he said was austere, and much was brilliant. That is why I am discussing his intellect, rather than his character, as I have said on more than one occasion. It may well be that he declines to participate in those pleasures he was just now praising. But I will remind you what it is that he regards as the highest good. For when he says "pleasure," he is not merely employing it as a term; he made it quite clear what he meant. "Tastes," he says, "and the embrace of bodies, and games and songs and shapes that make a delightful impression on the eyes." Am I making it up? Am I lying? I would be very glad to be refuted. Why do I work so hard, if not to bring out the truth in every inquiry?

D.   Response to Epicurus's Defenders

47 ❧   "But Epicurus also says that once pain is gone, pleasure does not increase; and that the summit of pleasure is to have no pain at all." Here are three serious errors within the space of a few words. First, he is at odds with himself. He has just said that he cannot even imagine anything being good if there is not some pleasurable tickling of the senses, and now he says that the summit of pleasure is to be free of pain. What could be more inconsistent? Error number two: of the three things possible in nature, namely gladness, pain, and that which is neither gladness nor pain, he thinks the first and third are the same, thus failing to distinguish between pleasure and the absence of pain. The third error is one he has in common with some others: he makes the highest good something other than virtue—which is the thing people want most, and the very reason philosophy was invented.

48 ❧   "But he often speaks highly of virtue." Yes, and Gaius Gracchus, after squandering the state treasury on massive handouts to the public, still defends that same treasury in words. But why should I listen to words when I have the facts? Lucius Piso "the Frugal" had consistently argued against Gracchus's grain legislation. Once the law was passed, however, he ap-

peared, ex-consul as he was, to collect his allotment of grain. Noticing him in the crowd, Gracchus asked him in front of all the citizens whether it was not inconsistent of him to ask for grain under a law which he had opposed. "I would prefer that you refrain from distributing my property to the people, Gracchus," he replied. "But if you do it, I want my share." Did he not make it eminently clear, this stern, wise man, that the patrimony of them all was being wasted by Gracchus's legislation? But read Gracchus's speeches, and you will declare him to be a defender of the treasury.

49 ꞏ "Epicurus says that it is not possible to live pleasantly except by the exercise of virtue, that fortune has no power over the wise person, that a simple diet is better than a lavish one, and that there is never a time when the wise person is anything but happy." All these statements are well worthy of a philosopher. But they are inconsistent with his claim about pleasure. "That is not the kind of pleasure Epicurus means." Whatever kind he means, it is clear that the kind he is talking about has nothing to do with virtue. But in any case, even supposing I do not understand the point about pleasure, at least I do know what pain is. I say, then, that anyone who speaks of the worst of evils in terms of pain has no business talking about virtue.

50 ꞏ There are some Epicureans (and they are good men, to be sure; nobody is less spiteful than they!) who say that it is partisanship that makes me speak against Epicurus. Partisanship? Are we contending against each other for public office, or for influence? I think the highest good is to be found in the mind; he thinks it is in the body. I think it is in virtue, he in pleasure. They are the ones who are fighting. They go around asking the neighbors for support—and in fact there are plenty of people who will flock to their banner. But I am one who says, "This does not trouble me; I will abide by your decision." *51* ꞏ For what are we discussing, after all? The Punic Wars? Though even there, when Marcus Cato and Lucius Lentulus had a difference of opinion, there was never any wrangling between them. These people, by contrast, become heated all too easily, especially considering that the view they are defending is hardly one to stir the blood, not one they would dare to proclaim in the Senate or assembly, or before the army or the censors.

But I will debate with them another time, and even then I will engage in no controversy, but will yield willingly to anyone who speaks the truth. I will ask only this: if what turns out to be most true is that the wise person refers everything to the body (or, to put it more respectably, that he does only what is expedient, or refers everything to his own utility), let them keep their satisfaction to themselves, and refrain from bragging. For such points do not deserve applause.

PART IV: THE STOIC POSITION DEFENDED

A.   The Belief That One's Misfortunes Are Serious Ills

Why the Cyrenaic Expedient Works

52 ⁂   We are left with the Cyrenaic view. They hold that distress arises when something unexpected has occurred, and at no other time. And as I said before, suddenness is indeed a major contributor. Chrysippus is of the same view, I know: what is unforeseen strikes us with greater force. But there is more to it than that. It is true that a sudden assault of the enemy creates rather more confusion than an expected one, and that a sudden storm at sea strikes more fear into those on shipboard than if they had seen it coming, and there are many similar cases. But if you were to study such events carefully and scientifically, what you would find, quite simply, is that when things happen suddenly, they invariably seem more serious than they otherwise would. There are two reasons for this. First, there is not enough time to gauge the seriousness of what is happening. Second, we sometimes think that if we had foreseen what was to happen, we might have been able to prevent it, and then our distress is keener because compounded with guilt. <Thus the cause of distress is not solely that the events are unexpected. Such an event may indeed strike a heavier blow, but what makes it seem more serious is not merely the unexpectedness of it. The reason is rather that the event is fresh in one's mind.>

Why Grief Diminishes over Time

53 ⁂   The proof of this is in the way our griefs are soothed by the passage of time. So great is this effect that in many cases time not only relieves our distress but actually removes it altogether, even though circumstances remain unchanged. Many of the people of Carthage became slaves in Rome, and so did many Macedonians after the capture of their king, Perses. When I was a young man, I also saw Corinthians working as slaves in the Peloponnese. Any of these people could have uttered that same lament from *Andromache:*

Before my eyes did all these things take flame . . .

and so on. But perhaps they had sung themselves out before I saw them. For their faces, their speech, their very gait and posture were such that, for all anyone could see, they might have been born in Argos or Sicyon. The ruined walls of Corinth had a greater impact on me, coming on them all of a sudden, than on the Corinthians themselves. For they had thought about the event for so long that their minds had become hardened with wear.

54 ⚬   There is a book by Clitomachus, which he addressed to his fellow Carthaginians after that city was destroyed, to console them in their captivity. I have read it. It contains a disputation by Carneades which Clitomachus took down in his notes. The opinion stated as the thesis is that the wise person would be grieved if his homeland were to be conquered in war. Then are recorded Carneades's arguments in the negative. Here we see the philosopher applying strong medicine in a case where the disaster is still in the present. Had it been long in the past, however, no such strong medicine would have been needed or even wanted. If he had addressed that same book to the captives some years afterward, he would have been tending to scars, not wounds. For gradually over time the pain grows less—not, usually, because the facts have changed or could change, but rather because experience teaches us the lesson reason ought to have taught, that what seemed so serious is not in reality very significant.

Speeches of Consolation

55 ⚬   Someone will ask, "Why, then, is there any need to reason with people, or to offer consolations, as we often do when we wish to ease a person's grief? For it is on such occasions that we are quick to point out how nothing should strike a person unawares. Or how does it happen that a person beset with troubles will bear them more easily if he realizes that such events are a necessary part of human life? For this remark does nothing to decrease our total amount of evil; it merely contributes the belief that everything that happened ought to have been anticipated. And yet it is not the case that consolatory speeches of this kind have no value; indeed, they may well be the most valuable thing of all."

56 ⚬   Consider: there are two means of bringing out the truth of our circumstances, not only when those circumstances seem to be evil but even when they seem to be good. The first is to inquire into the nature of the thing itself, what it is truly like and how serious it truly is. For instance, a disputation intended to lighten the burden of poverty will sometimes set out to prove that nature's demands are very few and simple. The second is to move away from subtleties of argumentation and turn to examples, mentioning Socrates at one point, Diogenes at another, and at another quoting the familiar line of Caecilius,

Often beneath the grimy tunic, too, is wisdom found.

The effects of poverty are always one and the same: why, then, was Gaius Fabricius able to endure it, and others say they cannot?   57 ⊷   Closely related to this second approach is that method of consolation which says that what happened was part of human life. For arguments of this kind do more than convey knowledge of human nature: they also prove that the circumstances at hand are indeed tolerable, since others have tolerated them and continue to do so. If the topic is poverty, one lists many persons who have endured it patiently. If it is disdain for public office, one singles out individuals who never gained office and were actually happier for that reason, and mentions by name many who have preferred the leisure of the private citizen to the busy life of the public servant, extolling their choice. One also quotes those familiar anapestic verses in which the most powerful king of all speaks in praise of an obscure old man, saying how lucky he is to be able to live the remainder of his life in obscurity.

58 ⊷   Examples are used in the same way when one is speaking about the loss of a child. When someone takes this unusually hard, it is comforting to hear about others who have had the same experience. For their endurance frequently makes what has happened seem less serious than is generally believed, with the result that in time, as one thinks the matter over, one realizes the extent of one's error. This is the same point that Telamon is making when he says,

I knew, when I fathered them, that they must die,

Also Theseus, when he says,

I pondered in my heart the miseries
to come,

and Anaxagoras, with "I knew my child was mortal." For all these speakers have thought long about the human situation and have come to understand that there is no reason for the degree of terror which popular opinion thinks justified.

In my view, the result for those who practice pre-rehearsal is very much the same as for those who are healed by time. The only difference is that the former are cured by method, the latter by the very nature of things, when they realize that what is generally thought to be the worst of evils is by no means serious enough to demolish that life which is properly called happy.

Is the Remedy Effective?

59 ᴥ   Now, while it does follow from this that misfortune deals us a heavier blow when unexpected, we cannot conclude, as the Cyrenaics do, that when two people are beset by equivalent misfortunes, only the one who did not anticipate it will feel distress. In fact, it is said that some people have actually sunk deeper into mourning when reminded of that regular restriction under which we are born, that no one remains free of trouble forever. I find something on this topic in the writings of my friend Antiochus. He says that Carneades used to object when Chrysippus would extol the following lines of Euripides:

No mortal lives who is untouched by grief
and sickness. Many have to bury children
and bear new ones; death is ordained for all.
And humans feel anxiety for this—in vain:
earth must return to earth, and life for all
be mowed, like wheat. Necessity insists.

60 ᴥ   He claimed that this kind of talk is of no value at all in easing distress, since the fact that we are subject to such cruel necessity is itself a reason to grieve. Only spiteful people, he said, would find consolation in a speech based upon the misfortunes of others. My own view is quite different. The fact that it is necessary for us to put up with human restrictions serves as a reminder that we, too, are human, and ought not to put ourselves in contention with god. Thinking of this does a great deal to lessen our grief. As for the list of examples, it is offered not to please the spiteful but to encourage the mourner to resolve on enduring his misfortune, when he sees that many others have endured the same thing with calmness and self-control.

61 ᴥ   We must do everything we can to shore up those who are falling apart. For deep distress causes people to disintegrate: that is why Chrysippus believes that the very word *lupē,* "distress," is derived from the "dissolving" *(luein)* of the person as a whole. But all of this can be eliminated, as I said at the outset, once the cause of distress has been laid open. For the cause is nothing but a belief, an opinion that some serious evil is present and weighing upon oneself. And just as the most biting physical pain is endurable when one has an expectation of some good thing before one's eyes, so also those who know that they have lived an honorable and illustrious

life have such a source of consolation that distress either does not touch them or, at most, stings them very lightly.

B.   The Belief That Grief Is Appropriate

But when our belief in the seriousness of our misfortune is combined with the further belief that it is right, and an appropriate and proper thing, to be upset by what has happened, then, and not before, there comes about that deep emotion which is distress.   62 ⚹   It is this latter belief that gives rise to all those despicable forms of mourning such as smearing oneself with dirt, scratching at one's cheeks like a woman, and striking oneself on the chest, head, and thighs. It is this that makes Agamemnon, both in Homer and in Accius,

> for grief tear often at his unkempt hair.

You know the witticism of Bion about this line: "How stupid it was for the king to tear at his hair in his grief! As if baldness were a cure for sorrow!"   63 ⚹   Yet those who do such things believe that it is appropriate that they do them.

Hence Aeschines criticizes Demosthenes for holding a sacrifice only six days after his daughter's death. And how polished and full is his rhetoric! What phrases he devises! What epithets he hurls! Declaimers can get away with anything, you know. But no one would give approval to such stuff, if it were not ingrained in our minds that a good person should always be terribly grieved at the death of a family member.

It is this belief that causes some people to seek out lonely places when their minds are grieved, as Homer says Bellerophon did:

> Sadly he wandered in the Aleian fields,
> eating his heart for sorrow, shunning every human track.

Niobe, too, observed a perpetual silence in her grief, and this is no doubt the reason she is supposed to have turned into stone. As for Hecuba, some think that a kind of savage bitterness took over her mind, and that this is the basis for the story that she turned into a dog. Other mourners take pleasure in soliloquy, like Medea's nurse in Ennius:

> A longing have I now, alas, to speak
> to sky and earth, telling Medea's troubles.

64 ✺   All such acts are done in times of grief because people think that they are genuinely right and appropriate. Clear evidence that they are doing what they judge to be right can be seen in this: when those who mean to be in mourning happen to catch themselves behaving too normally, or speaking too cheerfully, they make themselves go back to their sorrow and accuse themselves of misconduct in allowing their grief to be interrupted. Mothers and teachers even punish children for acting or speaking too cheerfully while the house is in mourning; they scold them or even beat them to make them weep.

C.   Why Grief Must Be Considered Voluntary

Now this: once grief has ebbed away, and we realize that mourning does no good, don't facts themselves make it plain that the emotion was altogether voluntary?   **65** ✺   Think of that character in Terence, "the Self-Tormentor."

> Chremes, I have decided: just as long
> as I continue miserable, the wrong
> done to my son is less.

This man actually decides to be miserable! A person can't decide unintentionally, can he?

> Whatever the ill, I'd think that I deserve it.

He thinks he would deserve ill if he were not miserable. You can see, then, that his trouble has to do with opinion, not with nature.

And what about those who are actually prevented from mourning by their situation? In Homer, the sheer number of killings each day causes their sorrow to abate, as one of them says:

> We see men fall in numbers every day;
> one would not ever cease to mourn the dead.
> With firm minds, rather, should we lay the dead
> to rest, and end our grief with this day's tears.

66 ✺   This shows that it is in your power to cast away grief whenever you choose, in obedience to the occasion. But given that it is in our power, shouldn't we give obedience to any and all occasions, and thus lay aside all our care and distress? All accounts have it that when Pompey's men saw him collapse from his wounds, shocking and sad as the sight must have been, they yet feared for their own lives (for they saw the enemy fleet all about them) and so did nothing at that moment but urge on the rowers and flee to safety. Only after they reached Tyre did they begin to sorrow and lament. It was possible, therefore, for them to be shielded from distress by their fear. How, then, would it not be possible for the wise person to be shielded by reason?

When a person realizes that grieving is futile and of no use, this more than anything else enables him to lay aside his grief. Since, therefore, it is possible to put grief aside, it is also possible never to feel it at all. Thus we cannot help but admit that distress is experienced voluntarily, through judgment.

67 ⋅ A further indication of this is the endurance of people who have suffered through numerous misfortunes and afterward take whatever happens relatively easily, feeling that they have steeled themselves against Fortune. There is the character in Euripides:

> If this had been the first sad dawn for me,
> if I had never sailed such troubled waters,
> there would have been some cause for grief. The bit,
> pulled sharply, spooks the colt: the feeling is new.
> But troubles broke me long ago—I have grown stolid.

Therefore, since being weary of troubles makes distress easier, we cannot help but realize that the cause and origin of sorrow is something other than the event itself.

68 ⋅ Philosophers who are great, but have not yet attained a state of wisdom, understand, do they not, that they are afflicted with the worst of evils? For they are not wise, and there is no evil worse than unwisdom. Yet they do not grieve. Why not? Because where this sort of evil is concerned, no one makes that additional supposition: no one believes it is right, proper, and appropriate to be grieved over not being wise. However, where it concerns the sort of distress involved in mourning (which is the greatest distress of all), we do make that supposition.   69 ⋅ Aristotle criticizes his predecessors for thinking that philosophy was made complete by their own ingenuity. "They were either very foolish or very vain," he says, "and yet so great are the advances made in recent years that I think the problems of philosophy will soon be completely solved." They say that Theophrastus, on his deathbed, reproached Nature for giving a long life to stags and ravens

but a short one to humans, since for us it would have made a great difference, while to them it makes no difference at all. For if humans had had a
longer lifespan, we might have perfected every discipline and schooled ourselves in every branch of knowledge. And so he complained about being
snuffed out just when he had begun to understand those things. What shall
we say, then? Don't all the best and most serious philosophers admit that
there are many things they do not know, and many things they have to learn
over and over?   70 ⁊   And yet, even though they recognize that they are
caught in the midst of folly, which is the worst thing there is, they feel no
distress. For they do not mingle with their other beliefs any notion that sorrow is appropriate.

What about those who feel that grieving is unmanly? Such was Fabius
Maximus at the funeral of his son, an ex-consul, and likewise Aemilius
Paullus when he lost two sons within a few days of each other; also Marcus
Cato on the death of his son, a praetor-designate, and all the others whom
I listed in my *Consolation*.   71 ⁊   What was their view of the matter, if not
that grieving and sorrow are not a man's part? Others give themselves over
to distress, believing that it is the right thing to do; they, however, rejected
it, believing it to be shameful. This demonstrates that distress is in belief,
rather than in nature.

D.   Peripatetic Objections Refuted

The Causation of Grief

Our opponents reply as follows. "Mourn voluntarily? Who would be
crazy enough to do that? Grief comes by nature, and look here, your own
Crantor says that one should yield to nature if to nothing else. For it presses
hard upon a person, and resistance is impossible." That is why Oileus, in
Sophocles's play, is unmanned by the news of his son's death, even though
he had made a speech of consolation to Telamon earlier in the play, upon
the death of Ajax. These words refer to his change of mind:

> No more than this is one man's share of wisdom.
> He tries with words to ease another's trouble,
> yet, when the blow of fortune shifts to him,
> he still may buckle at that sudden stroke.
> Then all his words and precepts are forgotten.

This argument is intended to show that it is impossible for a person to resist nature. Yet they admit that in some instances people experience distress

greater than nature requires. We may therefore ask them their own question: What madness is this?

72 ⨳   The fact is that the experience of distress has more than one cause. First, there is the belief that what has happened is a bad thing. Once a person has this impression, and decides that it is true, distress necessarily follows. Second, people also think that by being terribly grieved, they are doing something that is pleasing to the deceased. To this is added the womanish superstition that it will be easier for them to appease the gods if they profess to be completely crushed by the blow they have received.

Most people do not realize how illogical these beliefs are. They praise those who face their own death calmly, yet those who accept another's death calmly are considered blameworthy. As if that saying of lovers were for real— that a person can love someone else more than himself!   73 ⨳   There is a very fine saying, which, I might add, is also true and right, that when people have a very great claim on our affection, we love them as we love ourselves. But more than ourselves? That cannot be. Nor would it even be desirable in a friendship for my friend to love me more than himself, and I him more than myself. If that were the case, all our lives and every appropriate action would be thrown into confusion. But that is a topic for another day. Enough for now if we do not treat our unhappiness as a direct result of the loss of friends. For that would mean we loved them more than they themselves would wish, if they were aware of it, and more in any case than we love ourselves.

Neither is there any validity in their other two objections, that many people are not comforted at all by consolatory speeches, and that the would-be comforters will themselves admit to being miserable "when the blow of fortune shifts to them." For if people feel that way, it is not nature that is at fault, but their own shortcomings. Blame their foolishness for it, as much as you please. Those who are not comforted are inviting themselves to be unhappy, and those who bear their own misfortunes in a different manner than they have enjoined upon others are not suffering from any particular disability, but only from ordinary faults of character. They are no different from greedy people who criticize greed in others, or over-ambitious people who criticize others' ambition. That is just how foolish people behave: they observe the faults of others and forget their own.

The Diminishing of Grief over Time

74 ⨳   And here, indeed, is another point on which we must be very explicit. The disappearance of grief over time (a point on which all sides

agree) is not solely a matter of duration; rather, it comes of thinking for a long time about what has happened.

For if the facts are the same and the person is the same—if nothing has changed, neither the occasion of grief nor the one who feels it—then how can there be any change in the sorrow? What heals grief must be the length of time one spends thinking that no evil is in fact present. It can hardly be the passage of time in and of itself. At this point the Peripatetics put forward their teaching on "moderate amounts." But these moderate amounts must be determined either by nature or by opinion. If by nature, then nature itself will limit our grieving—and in that case, why do we need consolations at all? But if it is by opinion, then let us get rid of the opinion in its entirety.

I think I have stated adequately enough that distress is an opinion that some evil is present, involving also the belief that distress is appropriate in those circumstances.   75 ➤   To this definition, Zeno rightly adds a claim that the belief that an evil is present must be "fresh." The Stoics interpret this word as follows: a belief is "fresh" not only while the supposed misfortune is of recent occurrence, but for as long as it retains some force, some liveliness or, as it were, greenness. Consider for instance Artemisia, the wife of Mausolus, king of Caria. After she made a tomb for her husband (now famous as the Mausoleum at Halicarnassus), she spent the remainder of life in mourning and in the end died of grief. For her, the opinion remained fresh day by day. Only when it actually dries out and withers with age does it cease to be called "fresh."

PART V: CURES FOR GRIEF

A. Theory and Method of Consolation

Defining the Task

These, then, are the comforter's responsibilities: to remove distress altogether, or to cause it to subside, or to diminish it as much as possible, or to restrain it so that it cannot spread any further, or to divert it elsewhere.   76 ➤   Some hold that the comforter has only one responsibility: to teach the sufferer that what happened is not an evil at all. This is the view of Cleanthes. Others, including the Peripatetics, would teach that it is not a great evil. Still others, for instance Epicurus, would draw attention away from evils and toward good things, and there are yet others who

think it sufficient to show that nothing has happened contrary to expectation. And the list goes on. Chrysippus, for his part, holds that the key to
consolation is to get rid of the person's belief that mourning is something
he ought to do, something just and appropriate. Finally there are those who
bring together all these types of consolation, since different methods work
for different people. In my *Consolation,* for instance, I combined virtually all
these methods into a single speech of consolation. For my mind was
swollen, and I was trying out every remedy I could.

Timing

But with sicknesses of the mind, no less than with those of the body, it
is important to choose the right moment for treatment. Thus when a character in Aeschylus's play remarks,

> And yet, Prometheus, I think you know
> that reason may be doctor to your wrath,

Prometheus replies,

> Yes, if it chooses well the time for treatment,
> and does not probe the wound that is inflamed.

Argumentative Strategies Evaluated

77 ▵   Now, the medicines that can be given in speeches of consolation
are these. First, we may teach the sufferer that what happened either is not
a bad thing or is bad only in a very small degree. Second, we may speak
about the restrictions under which all humans live and about the mourner's
own situation, if there is anything to be addressed there. Third, we may say
that it is foolish to let yourself be overcome by pointless mourning, when
you know that nothing can be accomplished by it.

I pass over the method of Cleanthes, since that is directed at the wise
person, who does not need consoling. For if you manage to persuade the
bereaved person that nothing is bad but shameful conduct, then you have
taken away not his grief, but his unwisdom. And this is not the right moment for such a lesson. Besides, it seems to me that Cleanthes does not take
sufficiently into account the possibility that a person might be distressed
over the very thing which Cleanthes himself counts as the worst of evils. For
we are told that Socrates once persuaded Alcibiades he was unworthy to be

called human, and was no better than a manual laborer despite his noble birth. Alcibiades then became very upset, begging Socrates with tears to take away his shameful character and give him a virtuous one. What are we to say about this, Cleanthes? Surely you would not claim that the circumstance which occasioned Alcibiades' distress was not really a bad thing?

78 ⁑   And what of Lyco's method? He tried to make light of distress by saying that it is occasioned by small matters, mere inconveniences of the body or fortunes, and not by the evils belonging to the mind. But again, what about Alcibiades? Was he not suffering on account of evils and faults of the mind?

There is still the consolation of Epicurus, but I have said enough about that already.

79 ⁑   Nor is it a very dependable method of consolation—although it is certainly used a great deal and is often beneficial—to say, "You are not the only one to have this happen." This medicine is indeed beneficial, as I said, but not always or for everyone: some spit it out. However, the manner of administering it does make a difference: the point is not to list all the troubles people have experienced, but to describe the manner in which wise sufferers have endured them.

The most dependable method as regards the validity of its reasoning is that of Chrysippus, but it is a hard method to apply in time of distress. It's a big task to persuade a person that he is grieving by his own judgment and because he thinks he ought to do so.

It is clear, then, what we must do. Just as in our legal cases we do not always employ the same *status* (that being our term for the various argumentative strategies) but rather adapt our speeches to the needs of the moment, the nature of the case, and the persons involved, so also in soothing distress we must consider what sort of cure each hearer is able to accept.

B.   Conclusion: Let Us Do Everything We Can

80 ⁑   Somehow the discussion has strayed far afield from the topic you originally proposed. Your question concerned the wise person. To him, nothing which is free of shame can seem bad at all; or if it does, what is bad in it seems so trivial that wisdom eclipses it in importance and leaves it scarcely visible. Nor would he invent additional beliefs and add them to his distress, or think it right that he should be tormented and—most disgraceful of all—completely overcome by grief. For although it was not our purpose at this time to inquire whether anything is truly bad apart from that

which is called "the shameful," still, I believe, reason has taught us to recognize that what is bad in distress comes about not by nature but by voluntary judgment and mistaken belief.

81 ⚹   I have discussed that one type of distress which is the most
grievous of all. If that is removed, I do not think we need to inquire very
deeply into the others. For there are certain remarks which it is customary
to make about poverty, and others about living without office or esteem,
and then there are particular disputations for each of the various topics of
exile, destruction of one's homeland, servitude, physical impairment,
blindness, and every other occurrence that is generally regarded as unfortunate. The Greeks divide these up into individual disputations and treatises, as usual making work for themselves. Of course, the discussions are
pleasant enough to hear.   *82* ⚹   But just as doctors when they cure the
whole body also attend to pain in even the smallest of our limbs, so philosophy, in removing distress as a whole, also removes whatever errors may
trouble us on any particular point: the bite of poverty; the sting of public
disgrace; the darkness of exile; or the other things I have named, if any of
them happens to be the case. It is true that there are specific consolations
for each of these as well, and I will tell you about them, by all means, whenever you want.

But let us now return to the point from which we began. Distress of any
kind is far removed from the wise person, because it is an empty thing; because it serves no purpose; because it has its origin not in nature, but in
judgment and opinion and in a kind of invitation that is issued when we decide that grief is appropriate.   *83* ⚹   Once this entirely voluntary belief
is removed, distress will be eliminated—the real, unhappy distress, that is;
but the mind will still feel a bite, still be contracted a little from time to
time. This last they may indeed call "natural," provided they do not use the
name "distress." For that is a grim and deadly name, which cannot by any
means coexist or, as it were, dwell together with wisdom.

Yet how numerous are the roots of distress, and how bitter they are! The
trunk itself may have been cast down, and still they must be pulled out, every
one, by single disputations if need be. I have more than enough free time to
do so—if "free time" it can be called. For although all forms of distress have
the same explanation, they have many different names. Envy is a form of distress, and so are rivalry, jealousy, pity, anxiety, grief, sorrow, weariness,
mourning, worry, anguish, sadness, affliction, and despair.   *84* ⚹   The
Stoics have definitions for all of these. For although it may appear that the
terms I have listed all mean the same, they in fact refer to slightly different
things, as I may perhaps explain later on. These are those root-fibers I

mentioned at the start, the ones which must all be found and pulled out, so that none of them can ever arise again. No one would deny that this is a heavy and difficult task. Every great work is arduous, is it not? Yet philosophy promises that she will accomplish it, if only we take her for our physician.

But this is enough for now. The rest I am ready to tell you, as many times as you like, both here and elsewhere.

BOOK 4

PREFACE: THE HISTORY OF PHILOSOPHY AT ROME

1 & The intelligence and virtue of our people, Brutus, have always astonished me, and more remarkable than anything is the way that they sought out these present studies—after considerable delay, to be sure—and brought them over from Greece to this country. For while many of our institutions were wondrously well designed ever since the city first came into being, by customs under the kings and some of them by law as well—the practices of divination and religious ritual, the assemblies, the right of appeal, the Senate, the class-divisions, and the whole military establishment—still, it was not until after the state had been liberated from kingly rule that truly amazing advances were made in every field of endeavor. But this is not the time for me to speak of the customs and institutions of our ancestors, or of the order and balance of our constitution. I have already written in detail about these matters elsewhere, especially in my six-book treatise *On the Republic.*   *2 &*   In this work, though, as I turn to the study of philosophy, I see many reasons to think that our ancestors not only sought out this foreign import, but also preserved and cherished it.

For Pythagoras, a man of outstanding wisdom and nobility, was practically under their noses; he was in Italy at the very time when Lucius Brutus (he from whom your own noble family traces its distinguished ancestry) liberated the state. Since the teachings of Pythagoras were then spreading far and wide, I think they must have reached Rome as well. It is plausible as a matter of inference, and there is also some evidence for it.

There were in Italy at that time many large and powerful Greek cities, at the height of their power—the ones referred to as "Magna Graecia"— and the name of Pythagoras, and later of the Pythagoreans, was great among them. One can hardly suppose, then, that the ears of our people were deaf to such highly learned voices.   *3* ⋅   On the contrary, I am persuaded that it was because of their admiration for the Pythagoreans that later Romans believed King Numa to have been a follower of Pythagoras. For they were familiar with the teachings and customs of the Pythagoreans, and they had heard from their ancestors that Numa was a just and wise king, and consequently, not knowing the dates and lifespans for such an early period, they assumed that a man of such outstanding wisdom must have been a pupil of Pythagoras. All this is derived from inference.

As for evidence of Pythagoreanism, one could collect a great deal, but since this is not our topic for today, I will mention only a few items. It is said that the Pythagoreans were in the habit of using verses to convey their precepts in an arcane manner, and that they would bring their minds into a state of tranquillity after concentrated thought by the music of voice and strings. And Cato, the most reliable of sources, says in the *Origins* that our ancestors had a custom of singing in turn the praises of famous men, to the accompaniment of the flute, when they were reclining at feasts. This makes it clear that both verses and song had already been devised from the sounds of the voice.   *4* ⋅   Likewise the Twelve Tables indicate clearly that verses were already being composed at that time, since they contain a sanction against composing verses injurious to another person. Another proof of the culture of those times is that stringed instruments were played at the feasts of the gods and the banquets of the magistrates, something that was characteristic of the teaching I am discussing. In fact, I maintain that the poem of Appius Caecus, which Panaetius praises highly in a letter to Quintus Tubero, was Pythagorean in character. Many of our other customs are drawn from them as well, but I refrain from listing them, lest even those things we are thought to have invented ourselves begin to appear derivative.

5 ⋅   But let me return to my theme. What a number of poets appeared in that brief stretch of time, and what great ones they were! What great orators as well! It cannot be doubted, then, that our compatriots had the ability to achieve in all fields as soon as they conceived a wish to do so. But about those other studies I have often spoken, and will again, if need be, on some other occasion. As for philosophy, it is indeed ancient among us, but the earliest names I can give are from the time of Laelius and Scipio. For according to my sources it was when they were young men that a Stoic, Diogenes, and an Academic, Carneades, were sent by the Athenians as ambassadors to the Senate. Those men had never been involved in politics in any way; one was from Cyrene, the other from Babylon. Surely the Athenians would never have selected them for such a mission, rousting them out of their schools, had it not been the case that some of our leading citizens at that time had an interest in philosophy. Other matters they committed to writing—some their studies in civil law, others their orations, others the records of their ancestors—but this most comprehensive science, that of living a good life, they pursued in actions rather than in writing.

6 ⁓ And so of the true and elegant philosophy—the one which originated with Socrates and was preserved among the Peripatetics and among the Stoics (whose teaching is the same, though they say things differently), while the Academics acted as arbitrators in the controversies between them—of this philosophy, then, no records were preserved in Latin, or extremely few. The subject is large, and writers were otherwise occupied; or perhaps they thought that untrained minds would not be able to accept such things. Meanwhile, when these others were saying nothing, Gaius Amafinius came forward with his appeal. When Amafinius's books were circulated, the multitude was moved to adopt that teaching more than any other, either because it was extremely easy to learn, or because they were enticed by the sweet seductions of pleasure, or because nothing better had been offered, and they took what there was. 7 ⁓ After Amafinius came many others, adherents of the same system, and their numerous writings took over all of Italy. Their teachings are easily mastered and accepted by the unlearned, and this they take as confirmation of their views, although in fact it is a sure sign that they are crudely formulated.

But let each person defend his own position; after all, judgments are free. For my part, I will observe my usual custom: I will not be tied to the tenets of any single school as something I must obey in my philosophy, but will continue always to ask what is the most plausible answer to each question. This procedure I followed scrupulously in the disputations at Tusculum, as also on many other occasions. And so, since I have already recounted three days' worth of discussions, I will in this book tell of the fourth day.

PART I: THE QUESTION TO BE ADDRESSED

A. Does the Wise Person Experience Any Emotions at All?

We were going down to the lower of the two walkways, just as we had on the previous days, and our conversation went as follows.

8 ๛   Would someone like to propose a topic for discussion?

"I do not think it is possible for the wise person to be free of every emotion."

Yet it was settled in yesterday's discussion that he is free of distress— or were you agreeing with me only to save time?

"No, not at all; I found your speech highly persuasive."

You do not, then, believe that the wise person is subject to distress?

"Indeed I do not."

And yet if distress, as you say, cannot disturb the wise person's mind, then no emotion can. How could it? Would fear trouble him? But the objects of fear are the same as the objects of distress, except that in the one case they are not present to us, and in the other they are. Hence in getting rid of distress we also get rid of fear. Two emotions are left, wild gladness and desire. If it turns out that the wise person is not subject to these, then his mind will be tranquil at all times.

9 ๛   "That is indeed my understanding."

B. The Procedure to Be Followed Here

How, then, would you like to proceed? Shall we spread our sails at once, or shall we row for a bit, as if moving out from harbor?

"What do you mean? I don't understand."

I mean that when Chrysippus and the Stoics discuss the emotions, they concern themselves primarily with classifications and definitions, and the part of their discourse devoted to calming the mind and freeing it from disturbance is quite short. The Peripatetics, on the other hand, say many things to soothe the mind but leave out the thorny bits concerned with classification and definition. My question, then, was this: Shall I spread out the sails of rhetoric right away, or shall I first row forward for a bit with the oars of dialectic?

"The latter, by all means. My question will be answered more completely if we take in both methods."

10 ☙   Yes, this is the better way. But if anything is left unclear, you must ask me about it afterward.

"I will indeed, and you, for your part, must, as usual, explain these vexed questions more plainly than the Greeks do."

I will try. We must pay careful attention, though. If a single point gets away from us, the whole structure will fall apart.

PART II.   STOIC TERMINOLOGY EXPLORED

A.   Rational and Irrational Affect

The Twofold Division of Mind

Now, what the Greeks call the *pathē*, I prefer to translate as "emotions," rather than "sicknesses." In treating of these emotions, I shall preserve the familiar distinction made long ago by Pythagoras and later by Plato. They make a division of the mind into two parts, one of which has a share in reason, while the other does not. In the part which has a share in reason they put tranquillity (that is, a calm and quiet consistency); in the other, the turbulent motions of anger and desire, which are opposed to reason and inimical to it.   11 ☙   So let this be our point of departure. In describing these emotions, however, let us employ the definitions and classifications of the Stoics, who seem to me to proceed most acutely with this investigation.

The Four Generic Emotions and Their Objects

This, then, is Zeno's definition of an emotion (which he calls a *pathos*): "a movement of mind contrary to nature and turned away from right reason." Others say, more briefly, that an emotion is "a too-vigorous impulse," where "too vigorous" means "having deviated too far from the consistency of nature." The different classes of emotions, they say, arise from two kinds of things thought to be good and two thought to be evil. Thus there are four possibilities: those arising from goods are desire and gladness, gladness being directed at present goods and desire at future goods; while those arising from evils are fear and distress, fear being directed at future evils and distress at present ones. For the things we fear when they are in prospect are the very things that bring distress when they are upon us.   12 ☙   Gladness and desire, on the other hand, are concerned with beliefs about what things are good: desire catches fire from its attraction toward what seems good, while gladness is wildly excited at having obtained some longed-for object.

The Three Consistencies and Their Objects

By nature, all people pursue those things which they think to be good and avoid their opposites. Therefore, as soon as a person receives an impression of some thing which he thinks is good, nature itself urges him to reach out after it. When this is done prudently and in accordance with consistency, it is the sort of reaching which the Stoics call a *boulēsis,* and which I shall term a "volition." They think that a volition, which they define as "a wish for some object in accordance with reason," is found only in the wise person. But the sort of reaching which is aroused too vigorously and in a manner opposed to reason is called "desire" or "unbridled longing," and this is what is found in all who are foolish. *13* ⅰ Similarly there are two ways we may be moved as by the presence of something good. When the mind is moved quietly and consistently, in accordance with reason, this is termed "joy"; but when it pours forth with a hollow sort of uplift, that is called "wild or excessive gladness," which they define as "an unreasoning elevation of mind." And just as it is by nature that we reach out after the good, so also it is by nature that we withdraw from the bad. A withdrawing which is in accordance with reason is termed "caution," and this, as they understand it, is found only in the wise person; while the name "fear" is applied to a withdrawing that is apart from reason and that involves a lowly and effeminate swooning. Thus fear is caution that has turned away from reason.

14 ⅰ For present evil the wise person has no affective response, but the foolish person responds with distress. For those who do not obey reason lower and contract their minds in circumstances which they believe to be evil. Hence the first definition for distress is this: "a contraction of mind contrary to reason." Thus there are four emotions, but three consistencies, since there is no consistency which corresponds to distress.

B.   The Definition and Classification of Emotions

More Precise Definitions for the Genus-Emotions

They hold, moreover, that all the emotions come about through judgment and opinion. For this reason they give more careful definitions for them, in order to convey not only how faulty they are but also how much they are in our power. Distress, then, is "a fresh opinion that an evil is present in which one thinks it right to lower and contract the mind." Gladness is "a fresh opinion that a good is present in which one thinks it right to be elevated." Fear is "an opinion that an evil is impending which one thinks intolerable." Desire is "an opinion that a good is in prospect which it would be expedient to have present here and now."   15 ▲   Further, they say that it is not only the emotions which consist in the judgments and opinions which I have mentioned, but also the effects of those emotions. For instance, distress brings about a kind of biting pain, fear a sort of withdrawing and fleeing of spirit, gladness an outpouring of hilarity, desire an unbridled reaching. But they say that "opining" (the word used in all the above definitions) means "a weak assent."

Specific Emotions Belonging to Each Genus

16 ▲   Moreover, for each emotion there are several others of the same kind which are classified under it. Classed under distress, for instance, are envying (for instructional purposes I use the less familiar word, since "envy" may refer to the object as well as the subject), rivalry, jealousy, pity, anxiety, grief, sorrow, weariness, anguish, mourning, worry, sadness, affliction, despair, and whatever else is of that kind. Under fear are classified indolence, shame, terror, fright, panic, petrifaction, agitation, and dread. Under pleasure come spite (that kind of spite which rejoices in another's ills), enchantment, vainglory, and the like, while under desire come anger, heatedness, hatred, rancor, soreness of heart, need, yearning, and other things of this kind.

They define these as follows. Envying, they say, is "distress experienced because of the good fortune of another person," which does no harm to the one who envies.   17 ▲   For if a person is annoyed at the good fortune of someone because it is injurious to himself—for instance, if Agamemnon is aggrieved at Hector—what he feels is not properly called envy. The person who truly envies is the one who is annoyed at another's gains even though they do no harm to himself at all. Rivalry is used in two senses, as a term of praise or as a term of blame. For the imitation of excellence is termed "rivalry" (although that is not what we are referring to here, since it is a term of praise), and rivalry may also be "distress that another has obtained what one desired for oneself but does not have."   18 ▲   Jealousy (by which I mean *zēlotypia*) is "distress that another has likewise obtained what one desired for oneself." Pity is "distress over the misery of another who is suffering unjustly"—for no one is moved to pity by the punishment of a parricide or traitor. Anxiety is "oppressive distress." Grief is "distress at the untimely death of a person who had been held dear." Sorrow is "distress that is inclined to weep." Weariness is "toilsome distress." Anguish is "distress that involves torture." Mourning is "distress accompanied by sobbing." Worry is "distress accompanied by thinking." Sadness is "lasting distress." Affliction is "distress accompanied by bodily ailment." Despair is "distress that has no expectation that things will improve."

The ones classified under fear they define as follows. Indolence is "fear of impending work." **19**   < ... > Terror is "fear that strikes hard." Hence shame is accompanied by blushing, but terror by paleness, trembling, and chattering of teeth. Fright is "fear of imminent evil." Panic is "fear which unseats the mind," as in Ennius' line,

> then panic drove all wisdom from my breast,
> and I was petrified.

Petrifaction is "fear which follows upon panic"—panic's companion, as it were. Agitation is "fear which scatters one's thoughts." Dread is "long-lasting fear."

20   The species of pleasure they describe as follows. Spite is "pleasure arising from misfortune to another that brings no benefit to oneself." Enchantment is "pleasure which charms the mind through sweetness of sound," and similar to this pleasure of the ears are those of the eyes, and those of touches, smells, and tastes, all of which are alike in that they pour over the mind like liquids. Vainglory is "pleasure which exults and makes a display of arrogance."

21   The ones classified under desire are defined as follows. Anger is "desire to punish a person who is thought to have harmed one unjustly." Heatedness is "anger at its inception, when it has just come to be"; in Greek it is called *thumōsis.* Hatred is "inveterate anger." Rancor is "anger biding its time for revenge." Soreness of heart is "a more bitter anger which has its birth in the depths of mind and heart." Need is "desire which cannot be satisfied." Yearning is "desire to see someone who is not yet present."

A Grammatical Nicety

They also draw this distinction: "Desire" is directed at what is said about a certain thing or things (what dialecticians call *katēgorēmata,* "predicates"), for instance, to have riches or to receive honors; "need" is directed at the things themselves, the honors or the money.

How We Lose Control

22   But the source of all the emotions, they say, is "loss of control," which is a rebellion in the mind as a whole against right reason. This rebellion has turned away from what reason dictates to such an extent that there is no way the mind's impulses can be directed or restrained. Self-control soothes the impulses and makes them obey right reason, considering and maintaining the judgments of the mind; but loss of control is just the opposite: reason's enemy, it lays flame to every state of the mind, throwing it into disturbance and riot. Thus it is that all forms of distress, fear, and other emotions arise from loss of control.

C.   The Character of Individuals

Sicknesses and Infirmities of the Mind

23 ⁕   Just as sicknesses and infirmities of the body come into being when the blood is impure or when there is an excess of phlegm or bile, so also the confusion of crooked opinions and the conflict of one with another robs the mind of health and disturbs it with sicknesses. These disturbances or emotions produce, first, the conditions which the Stoics call *nosēmata*, "sicknesses," together with their contraries, each of which involves a wrongful aversion to some specific object—that is, a distaste. Next come infirmities, which they call *arrōstēmata*, and again the aversions which are their contraries.

At this point the Stoics, especially Chrysippus, expend a great deal of effort working out the analogy between the sicknesses of the body and those of the mind. But all that talk is not really necessary. Let us pass it by and devote our detailed discussion to the essentials of the matter.   24 ⁕   The point to be grasped, then, is that although emotion itself is turbulent and inconsistent, constantly in movement through shifts in belief, it sometimes happens that this simmering and agitation of mind becomes habitual, settling into the veins and marrow, as it were. It is then that the sicknesses and infirmities come into being, and also the aversions which are their contraries.

The conditions I have mentioned differ from each other in theory, but in reality they are closely linked. They arise from desire and from gladness. When a person has conceived a desire for money, and when there has been no immediate application of reason—the Socratic medicine, as it were, which might have cured that desire—then the evil works its way into the veins, and settles in the vital organs, and comes to be a sickness and an infirmity. Once it has become habitual, the sickness cannot be removed, and its name is "greed."   25 ⁕   It is the same with the other sicknesses, such as desire for glory or liking for women (if I may so translate the Greek *philogunia*), and the other sicknesses and infirmities, which arise in the same way.

The contraries of these are thought to arise out of fear. Examples include hatred of women, such as we see in the *Misogyne* of Atilius, and hatred of the whole human race, such as we have heard of in the case of Timon, who is called "the Misanthrope"; also hostility to guests. All these infirmities of mind arise from some kind of fear of those objects which the persons in question dislike and avoid.

26 ⁂   They define an infirmity of mind as "a vigorous opining that some object is worthy of pursuit which is in fact not worthy of pursuit, that opinion being deeply attached and rooted in the mind." The state arising from aversion they define as "a vigorous opinion, deeply attached and rooted, that some object is worthy of avoidance which is in fact not worthy of avoidance." "Opining" is when a person judges that he knows something which he does not in fact know.

Classified under infirmities are such things as greed, ambition, liking for women, stubbornness, gluttony, fondness for wine, covetousness, and so forth. "Greed" is "a vigorous opining, deeply attached and rooted, that money is very much to be pursued," and a similar definition is given for each of the others.   27 ⁂   Definitions for the aversions are like this: "hostility to guests," for instance, is "a vigorous opinion, deeply attached and rooted, that company is very much to be avoided." Similar definitions are given for "hatred of women," like that of Hippolytus, and for "hatred of the human race," like that of Timon.

Proclivities

But let me make some use of the analogy with bodily illness—more sparingly, though, than the Stoics do. Some people are more prone than others to contract certain sicknesses; for instance, we say that certain people "suffer from sinus" or "suffer from colic," meaning not that they are suffering from it now but that they often do. In the same way, some people are more prone to fear and others to other emotions. It is thus that we speak of "anxiety" in some people—that is, a tendency to become anxious—and "irascibility" in others. Irascibility is different from anger: it is one thing to be angry, another to be irascible. Similarly there is a difference between suffering from anxiety and feeling anxious. For not everyone who feels anxious now and then suffers from anxiety, nor are those who suffer from anxiety anxious all the time. It is like the difference between drunkenness and fondness for drink, or between being amorously inclined and being in love. The proneness of different persons to different sicknesses is used extensively, for it has application to each of the emotions and manifests itself also in many of the faults,   28 ⁂   although in that case there is no separate term for it. Hence people are "envious" or "spiteful" or "desirous" or "timid" or "pitying" not because they experience those emotions all the time, but because they are exceptionally prone to them.

It is permissible, then, to continue the analogy with the body and use the term "infirmity" to refer to these various proclivities, provided we understand it to mean "a proclivity to become infirm." Meanwhile, a tendency toward what is good may be termed a "facility." For one person is more inclined to one good quality, another to another. But a tendency toward the bad should be called a "proclivity," to suggest falling into error, while a tendency toward things neither good nor bad may be called by the former term.

Mere Faults

In the mind, as in the body, a sickness is one thing, an infirmity another, and a fault yet another. The Stoics use the term "sickness" for an infection of the body as a whole, "infirmity" for a sickness accompanied by weakness, and "fault"   *29* ⁱ»   when the parts of the body are at odds with one another, so that the limbs are crooked, twisted, or misshapen. Thus the first two, sickness and infirmity, come into being through some unsettling or disturbance in the health of the body as a whole; but a fault may be exhibited independently, even when the person's health is unaffected.

In the case of the mind, however, the distinction between "sickness" and "infirmity" is only theoretical, while "faultiness" is a condition or state of being inconsistent and out of agreement with oneself over one's whole life. There are, then, two sorts of infection in the beliefs, one of which gives rise to sickness or infirmity, the other to inconsistency and self-contradiction. For not every fault involves the same level of discrepancy. For instance, those who are drawing near to wisdom are in a condition which, as long as it falls short of wisdom, is indeed out of agreement with itself, yet not twisted or perverted.

Sicknesses and infirmities are species of faultiness, but whether the emotions are also species of it is open to question.   *30* ⁱ»   For faults are conditions that last, but emotions are in movement; hence they can hardly be species of lasting conditions.

Non-intellectual Virtues

The mind is analogous to the body in good qualities as well as bad. For there are in the body certain preferable traits—among them beauty, strength, wellness, toughness, quickness—and the same is true of the mind. When the body is in a balanced condition, with all its elements fitting properly together, it is called "health"; and there is also a "health" of the mind, when its judgments and beliefs are in harmony. Some say that this virtue of mind is just self-control itself, others that it is obedient to the dictates of self-control and that it follows upon it and has no independent aspect. Either way, it is found only in the wise person. But there is also another sort of "health" of mind which can be found also in the non-wise person, when some mental disturbance is removed by medication and the care of doctors.

31 ⊷   When used of the body, the word "beauty" refers to a nice configuration of the limbs together with a pleasant coloring, and similarly "beauty" of mind means an evenness and consistency in the opinions and judgments, together with a certain toughness and stability, either following upon virtue or identical with it.

Likewise, the quality which is analogous to muscular strength and power in the body is called "strength" of mind, and equivalent to rapidity or "quickness" of body is a laudable "quickness" of intellect. For the mind can travel through many things in a short time.

Further Observations on the Theory of Character

One difference between minds and bodies is that when minds are well, they cannot be assailed by any sickness; but bodies can. Also, bodily aversions do not necessarily incur blame, but it is not so with those of the mind. For the mind's sicknesses and emotions do not come about except through some spurning of reason. Thus they occur only in humans: animals do not have emotions, though they do have similar behavior.

32 ⊷   Moreover, there is a difference between clever people and slow-witted people. Just as Corinthian bronze tarnishes slowly and is restored quickly, so there are some persons whose natural endowments make them slow to submit to sicknesses and quick to recover, while with the slow-witted it is the reverse. Nor is the mind of such a person subject to every emotional sickness. For it is not subject to any that are savage and bestial. But some emotions have an initial semblance of humaneness—pity, for instance, and distress, and fear.

Also, the infirmities and sicknesses of the mind are considered more difficult to eradicate than those extreme faults which are the contraries of the virtues. For the faults can be eradicated and the sicknesses remain, since removing the one is quicker than curing the other.

An End to Exposition in the Stoic Manner

33 ⊷   You have now heard the meticulous disputations of the Stoics on emotion, which they call *logika*, "rational disquisitions," because the dis-

tinctions are so finely drawn. Now that my speech has moved out of these waters—away from the reefs of precision, as it were—let us proceed on our way with the remainder of the discussion. That is, provided my treatment of these difficult topics was sufficiently clear.

"Very clear indeed. But we will inquire into the points requiring more careful study at some other time. Right now I am waiting for those sails you mentioned a while ago, and for the sailing."

Part III.   Rhetorical Treatment

A.   The Best Life Is without Emotion

34 ⁌. My theme is virtue, as it has been on many previous occasions and must often be again. For most ethical inquiries take virtue for their wellspring and point of origin. Virtue, then, is a consistent and harmonious condition of mind, one which makes its possessors worthy of praise and which is worthy of praise on its own account, even without considering its utility. From virtue proceeds every honorable activity, whether in volition, speech, or action, and all right reasoning. Indeed, in the most concise formulation virtue may itself be termed "right reason."

Contrary to virtue, so defined, is *vitiositas* or "faultiness"—for I prefer to use this translation for the Greek term *kakia*, rather than *malitia* or "malice," since "malice" refers to one particular fault, whereas "faultiness" refers to them all. From this faultiness arise the emotions, which, as I said not long ago, are turbulent and agitated movements of the mind. These have turned away from reason and are great enemies to tranquillity of life and thought. For they bring distress, anxious and bitter, and they crush and weaken the mind with fear; they set it afire with excessive reaching, which we call either longing or desire. This desire is a kind of anarchy in the mind, greatly at odds with temperance or self-control.   *35* ⁌   If it should at any time gain its object, it is carried away with excitement, so that it "knows not what to do," like the man who thought that

extreme delight of mind is my worst error.

These, then, are ills whose cure is to be found in virtue alone.

What is more wretched—yes, and also more foul, more ugly—than a person afflicted, weakened, prostrated by distress? And next to him in wretchedness is the one who fears some approaching evil and is petrified with anxiety. It is to show the power of this evil that the poets portray Tantalus in the underworld with a boulder hanging over him

> for his crimes and his anarchic mind,
> and for his haughty speech.

This is the punishment shared by all the foolish. For some such terror is always hanging over those whose minds reject reason.   36 ⁖   And no less corrosive than these emotions of distress and fear are those other more cheerful ones—desire, always chasing after some object, and empty excitement or wild gladness. These are not far removed from witlessness.

This shows us what that person would be like who is variously described as "self-controlled" or "moderate" or "temperate" or "consistent and self-contained." I sometimes like to sum up all these terms under the heading of "frugality." For frugality carries with it all the other virtues; otherwise the saying "the frugal person does all things aright" would never have become so common as to be a proverb. Yet when the Stoics say the same thing about the wise person, their speech is thought to be too grand and paradoxical!   37 ⁖   That person, then, whoever it may be, whose mind is quiet through consistency and self-control, who finds contentment in himself, and neither breaks down under adversity nor crumbles with fright nor burns with any thirsty need nor dissolves into wild and futile excitement, that person is the wise one we are seeking, and that person is happy. Nothing in human life is so difficult for him to bear that he must be downcast, nothing so excessively delightful that he must be carried away by it. For what in human life would seem great to one who has grasped the magnitude of all eternity and of the entire universe? What concern within the brief lifespan of a human could seem important? So constant is his vigilance that nothing unforeseen can happen to him, nothing which he does not anticipate, nothing strange at all.   38 ⁖   So keen is his glance in every direction that he sees always some resting-place where he may live without sorrow or anxiety, and so he endures with calm and decency whatever mishap fortune may inflict. A person who acts this way will be free not only of distress but of all the other emotions as well. And it is the mind free of emotions that makes a person completely and absolutely happy, while the mind agitated by emotions and cut off from solid and secure reasoning loses not only its consistency but even its health.

B.   The Position of Our Opponents

The Doctrine of "Moderate Emotion"

For this reason we must regard as feeble and unmanly the position of
the Peripatetics, who say it is necessary that our minds should experience
emotion but set what they call a "limit" beyond which one should not proceed.   *39* ♦   Will you set a limit on something which is a fault? And
when one fails to obey reason, is that not a fault? Does not reason insist
quite strongly that the thing for which you burn with desire, or which you
are inordinately excited to possess, is not a good, and that the thing under
which you lie crushed, or are beside yourself with fear lest it crush you, is
not an evil? And that it is only through error that these objects become so
very awful or delightful? But this is an error which even the foolish find less
potent over time, so that although their circumstances are unchanged, they
bear them more easily when long familiar than when they are fresh. As for
the wise, they are not touched by it at all.

40 ♦   What limit could there possibly be? Let us inquire about the
limit on distress, a subject upon which they expend much effort. We find
in the writings of Fannius that Publius Rupilius was upset when his brother
was defeated for the consulship. No doubt he overstepped their "limit,"
since it was for that reason that he took his own life. He ought to have
reacted more moderately. But what if, while he was having this moderate
reaction, the death of his children had been added? A new distress would
have come into being. That, too, might have been moderate, yet still the addition of the two would have produced a large sum. What if he had then
suffered serious bodily pain, the loss of his property, blindness, and exile?
If distresses are to accumulate with every misfortune, then there could be a
total which would be unendurable.

41 ♦   To try to find a limit for this fault, therefore, is like believing that
one who hurls himself off the cliff at Cape Leucatas can check his fall whenever he wants. That is how impossible it is for the disturbed and agitated
mind to contain itself or to stop where it wants to stop. The general principle is that things which are destructive when they increase are to be faulted
even when they first come into being.   *42* ♦   Now, distress and the other
emotions are certainly destructive when amplified. It follows that even
when first begun they are already largely pernicious. For once reason has
been left behind, they move on under their own power: in our weakness, we
make allowances for ourselves, and without realizing it get carried out to
sea where there is no stopping-place.

Therefore it makes no difference whether they give approval to moderate emotions or to moderate injustice, moderate cowardice, moderate intemperance. He who sets a limit for our faults takes the part of fault. This is reprehensible in itself, and it is all the worse because emotions stand on slippery ground. One push, and they slide right down the slope. There is no way to stop them.

The Claim That Emotions Are Useful

43 ❧   And that is not all the Peripatetics have to say about the emotions. We say they should be eradicated; they say not only that they are natural, but even that nature gave them to us to serve some useful end. Here is a sample of their discourse.

First, they have many words of praise for anger. They call it "the whetstone of courage" and say that those who are angry are much more vigorous in attacking the enemy or the wicked of their own country. They do not give any weight to the possibility that a person might reason, "It is right that I fight this battle: it is appropriate that I defend our laws, our freedom, our country." With them such sayings have no force if courage is not also aflame with anger. Nor does their argument concern warriors alone. They hold that none of the sterner forms of command would be effective without what they consider to be the sharpness anger gives. Moreover, they disapprove of the orator who speaks for the prosecution or even for the defense without the stimulus of anger. They think that even if the orator is not angry himself, he should still make a show of anger in his words and gestures, so that his delivery may kindle anger in the hearer. Finally, they say that one who does not know how to become angry cannot be considered a real man. That trait which we call *lenitas*, "gentleness," they regard as a fault, calling it *lentitudo*, "sluggishness."

44 ❧   And anger is not the only one of the desires that they praise (anger is by definition a desire for revenge, as I said before). They say that desire or longing in general has been bestowed upon us by nature for a very useful purpose, since a person cannot perform any notable action if he does not have a desire for it. Themistocles used to walk about in the public square at night when he could not sleep. If asked the reason, he would answer that the trophies of Miltiades were keeping him awake. And who has not heard how Demosthenes used to stay awake all night? It was painful to him, he said, to be beaten out by the artisans, who were at work before dawn. Even in philosophy the best practitioners would never have been able to achieve as much as they did had they not been burning with desire. Pythagoras, Democritus, and Plato are said to have visited the most distant

countries, judging it worth their while to travel to every place where there was something to learn. Do we believe that they would have done this if they had not had a strong and ardent desire?

45 ✦ Even distress, which for us is a thing to flee like some huge and terrible monster, has in their view a useful purpose. Nature ordained it, they say, so that people would be pained at the rebuke or punishment or disgrace meted out to them for their own wrongdoings. For when people bear disgrace and disrepute without sorrow, then their misdeeds seem to go unpunished. It is better to feel the bite of conscience. Thus the familiar line of Afranius is true to life. When the dissolute son exclaims, "Woe is me!" the father says,

Let him grieve however much he will,
so long as he does grieve.

46 ✦ Other forms of distress, they say, are useful as well. Pity ensures that those who suffer undeserved calamities will be assisted and relieved. Even rivalry (when a person sees that he has failed to obtain what another has) and jealousy (when he sees that another has obtained the same as himself) are not without their uses. And if fear were eliminated, then people would no longer take care for their own life, as they do when they are afraid of the laws and magistrates, or of poverty, disgrace, death, or pain. Their view on all of these emotions is that they ought to be trimmed back, but that it is neither possible nor needful to root them out entirely. In every situation, they say, the moderate amount is usually the best.

The Stance of the Skeptical Academic

This is their position. Do you think there is anything in it?

"To me it seems that there is, and so I look forward to your response."

47 ✦ Perhaps I shall find one. But first this: do you notice how reserved the Academics are in this? They merely say what is relevant to the matter in hand. It is the Stoics who respond to the Peripatetics. Let them fight it out! Nothing is required of me except that I seek to discover what position has the clearest semblance of truth.

C.   The Stoic Position Defended

Excellence of Zeno's Definition

What, then, do we find in this inquiry which might give some access to the probable? For beyond that the human mind cannot go. Just this: the definition of emotion, which was given correctly, in my opinion, by Zeno. He defines emotion as "a movement of the mind turned away from reason and contrary to nature"; or, more briefly, "a too-vigorous impulse." By "too vigorous" he means an impulse which varies widely from the consistency of nature.   *48* ⚖   How could I possibly object to these definitions? Nearly all these points were worked out by thoughtful and acute dialecticians, while those phrases about "the flame of the spirit" and "the whetstone of the virtues" belong to the displays of the orators.

Anger Is Not Useful

Is it really true that a brave man cannot be brave if he does not become enraged? That is the way gladiators behave. And even in gladiators we often find an even temper: they "meet and converse, inquire and make requests" more like men at peace than like angry persons. Still, there could well be a gladiator whose frame of mind is that of Pacideianus, the character in Lucilius:

> Yes, I'll kill him; I'll win the fight, if that's what you ask.
> Here's how it will go: I'll take one on the face, then
> plunge my sword into his guts, or his chest, the scoundrel!
> I hate him, and I'm angry when I fight. I can hardly wait
> for someone to put a sword in my hand; that's
> how eager I am—how wild with anger—how I hate him!

49 ⚖   Yet we do not see any anger of this kind in Homer's Ajax, when he comes forward to fight with Hector. Indeed Ajax was quite cheerful when he took up arms: his coming brought "joy to his comrades, terror to his enemies," and Hector himself "trembled all through his chest," as Homer has it, regretting the challenge he had issued. Then, before the fight began, the two of them spoke calmly and quietly to each other, and even during the duel they did not act in anger or rage.

For my part I believe that even Torquatus, the one who first earned that name, was not angry when he snatched the torque from the Gaul, and that it was not out of anger that Marcellus acted so bravely at Clastidium.   *50* ⚖   About Scipio Africanus I am better informed, since he lived nearer to our own time, and can confidently assert that it was not anger that aroused him at that moment in battle when he protected Marcus Allienus Paelignus with his shield, at the same time driving his sword into the enemy's chest. And Lucius Brutus—did limitless hatred for the tyrant do anything to increase the ferocity with which he attacked Arruns? I am inclined to doubt it, since, according to my sources, the two of them fell in hand-to-hand combat, each struck down by the other. Why must you add anger to this?

Must courage go insane, or does it not have forces of its own? What of Hercules? Courage raised him to heaven! But you equate that same courage with anger. Was he angry, do you suppose, while he was combatting the Erymanthian boar, or the Nemean lion? Theseus, too: was he angry when he seized the bull of Marathon by the horns? Indeed, it may well be that courage is not a matter of rage at all, and that this anger of yours is a sham. For there is no courage which does not have some share of reason.   *51*   "Scorn human affairs; think nothing of death; remember that pain and labor can be endured." Once these beliefs are established as one's considered judgment, then and only then does real, sturdy, unwavering courage take hold.

Or do we perhaps entertain a suspicion that all actions performed in a vigorous, fierce, and spirited manner must have been done in anger? Take Scipio, the great Pontifex Maximus, who demonstrated the truth of the Stoic saying, "The wise person is never a private citizen." Even he, I would say, was not acting in anger against Tiberius Gracchus when he gave up on the do-nothing consul and issued as a private citizen the consul's command, "Let those who wish to save the Republic follow me!"   *52*   Whether I myself have performed any brave action for the Republic, I scarcely know. But whatever I have done was certainly not done in anger.

Ennius did well to call anger "the beginning of insanity." For surely it is the next thing to insanity. Its complexion, its voice, its breathing, its inability to control speech and actions: are these the signs of mental health? Think of Achilles and Agamemnon during their quarrel in Homer. What could be uglier? I need hardly mention how Ajax was driven by anger to madness and death. That is why courage does not require the aid of anger to take its battle-stations or to find its arms and equipment. For by their argument one could say that drunkenness, and even insanity, are useful for courage, since those who are out of their minds or drunk often behave more vigorously. Ajax was always brave, and bravest of all in his frenzy:

> A great deed he performed: when the Danaans
> were in retreat, his hand accomplished all.

53   Insane as he was, he turned the tide of battle. Are we therefore to say that insanity is useful?

If you study the definitions of courage, you will understand that it does not require a bad temper. Courage is "a condition of mind which is obedient to the highest law as concerns things to be endured," or "the preservation of a stable judgment in meeting and overcoming what seems alarming," or "the knowledge of things which are either alarming or the reverse, or which are to be ignored altogether, and the preservation of a stable judgment concerning these things." Chrysippus's definition is shorter—for the previous definitions are those of Sphaerus, whom the Stoics consider particularly adept at definition. All the definitions are pretty similar, but some go further than others in clarifying ordinary notions. Anyway, what is Chrysippus's definition? "Courage," he says, "is knowledge as concerns things to be endured" or "a condition of mind which is obedient without fear to the highest law with respect to suffering and endurance." Criticize them we may, just as Carneades used to do, and yet I suspect they are the only real philosophers. For does not every one of these definitions reveal to us that folded and buried notion of courage which we all possess? And once that has been revealed, who would ask anything more for the warrior, the general, or the orator? Who would deny that they can act courageously without being enraged?

54 ᴥ   It is cases like this, surely, that the Stoics are referring to in their claim that all fools are insane. Set aside the emotions, especially anger, and their position will become ridiculous. But they explain that when they say "all fools are insane," it is like "all bogs stink." Not always! But disturb the bog, and you will smell it. Even so the irascible person is not always angry—strike him, though, and you will see him go mad.

And what about when your warrior's anger goes home? What is it like with his wife and children? Is it useful then, too? Is there anything, in fact, that the disturbed mind does better than the consistent one? Or is there anyone who can get angry without having his mind disturbed by emotion? Our ancestors did well, then, when they reserved the term "morose" (morosus) for those who are irascible. For although all faults are failings in morals (mores), there is no failing uglier than irascibility.

55 ᴥ   It is most improper for an orator to become angry, although there is nothing wrong with his putting on a show of anger. You sometimes see me arguing my cases more vehemently than usual: do you think I am always angry on those occasions? What about when the case is over and done, and I write the speech down? Surely you don't think I am angry then!

Does no one punish this deed? Bind him!

Do you think that Accius was angry when he wrote this line, or that Aesopus was angry when he delivered it? Such things are excellent to perform (and the orator, if he is really an orator, performs them better than any actor), but they are performed calmly and with a tranquil mind.

Other Emotions Are Not Useful Either

What is this desire to praise desire? You mention Themistocles and Demosthenes to me, and then add Pythagoras, Democritus, and Plato. How is that? Will you call every form of eagerness a desire? Eagerness should be calm and tranquil, even when it is directed at the best objects, as in the examples you give.

And what kind of philosopher would praise distress, the most hateful thing of all? Yes, Afranius spoke aptly when he said, "Let him grieve however much he will, so long as he does grieve." For he said it about a reckless and dissolute youth. We, however, are asking about a man, and one who is wise and consistent. In fact, let the centurion have his anger, real anger, and likewise the standard-bearer, and others whom I had better not mention, lest I reveal the secrets of orators. For those who cannot employ reason may well find it useful to employ emotion. We, however, are asking about the wise person, as I have declared more than once.

56 ⟡ "But rivalry is also useful, and jealousy, and pity." Why pity someone when you might assist him? Or are we incapable of being generous without pity? For our obligation is not to feel distress on account of others, but to relieve the distress of others if we can. And what is the use in either jealousy or in rivalry, which is a fault similar to jealousy? For rivalry is when a person is upset that someone else has a good thing which he does not have; jealousy is when a person is upset that the good thing he has is possessed by someone else also. Who could approve of your feeling distress rather than trying to get what you want? And as for wanting to be the only one to have a thing, that is utter lunacy.

Only Extirpation Will Do

57 ⟡ How could it be right to praise "moderate amounts" of what is evil? If desire or longing is in a person, isn't that person necessarily desirous? If anger is in him, isn't he necessarily irascible? If anxiety, mustn't he be anxious? If fear, mustn't he be timid? Shall we then hold that the wise person is full of longing, irascible, anxious, and timid? I could make many long and elaborate speeches about the excellence of the wise person, but the briefest is this: wisdom is the knowledge of things divine and human, together with an understanding of each thing's cause. The consequence is that wisdom imitates things divine and ranks all that is human lower than

virtue. Did you really mean to claim that *this* is subject to disturbance, like a sea exposed to the winds? What could disturb such dignity and consistency? A sudden or unforeseen event? But what could be unforeseen by one who has rehearsed in advance every one of the things that can happen to a person? They say that what is excessive should be trimmed back, and what is natural should be left. But how on earth can a thing be natural if it has the potential to become excessive? No, all the emotions spring from the roots of error: they should not be pruned or clipped here and there, but yanked out completely.

PART IV.   CURES FOR THE EMOTIONS

A.   Introduction to Therapeutic Approaches

Turning Point: Philosophy Does Provide a Cure

58 ◦ But I suspect that your question has more to do with yourself than with the wise person. That he is free of emotion is something you merely believe: what you want is to be free of it yourself. Let us therefore look to see what remedies philosophy has to offer for the sicknesses of the mind. For there must surely be some curative art. Nature would have had to be very unkind, very unfriendly indeed to the human race, to invent so many means of cure for our bodies, and none for our minds! But in fact she has done our minds an even greater service, for the things that aid the body are applied to it from without, but the mind's healing is contained within itself. And it is precisely because of this godlike superiority to the body that our minds need more assiduous care. Reason, if properly applied, discerns what is best; if left untended, however, it becomes entangled in numerous errors.

59 ◦ So all my discourse should now be addressed to you. You may pretend to be inquiring about the wise person, but your real inquiry, perhaps, is about yourself.

Different Approaches Compared

The curative measures, then, for the emotions I have been discussing are of several different kinds. For even in the case of distress, not every form is soothed by the same method: one remedy should be applied for grief, a different remedy for pity or envy. Furthermore, one has to decide for each of the four emotions whether it is better to aim one's remarks at emotion in general or at each emotion individually. Should we be speaking in terms of "the spurning of reason" and "too-vigorous impulse," or in terms of fear, desire, and so on? And is it to appear that the object of one's distress is not a proper thing to be upset about, or that distress should be eliminated altogether?

For instance, if a person is upset about being poor, should you argue that poverty is not an evil, or that one should never become upset at all? Clearly the latter, since if you try to convince someone that poverty is not an evil, but fail, you will have to concede that distress is permissible, but if you direct your arguments specifically toward eliminating distress as we did yesterday, then the point about poverty will be gained along the way.   60 ~   To be sure, all emotions of that sort could be washed away by that form of consolation which teaches that the circumstances which give rise to gladness or desire are not goods, and those which give rise to fear or distress are not evils. But the specific and more reliable cure is when you teach that the emotions are wrong in and of themselves and have nothing either natural or necessary about them. We chide the mourner for being weak and womanish in spirit, and we praise those serious and consistent persons who endure without turmoil the events of human life. We see that when we do this, distress itself is relieved, even in those who decide that such events are bad but that one should bear them calmly. One person thinks that pleasure is a good, another that money is a good, and still it is possible to call the former away from his intemperance, the latter from his greed.

The other method of address, the one which eliminates the false belief and the distress along with it, is indeed more useful; however, it works only in rare cases and cannot be applied to the uneducated.   61 ~   Besides, there are some forms of distress which cannot be relieved by this medicine at all. Suppose a person is upset about his own lack of virtue—his lack of courage, say, or of responsibility or integrity. The cause of his anxiety is indeed an evil! In that case, some other remedy would have to be applied.

But that remedy could be the same for every school of philosophers, despite their disagreements in other areas. For all of them ought to agree that it is a fault when the mind is moved contrary to right reason. Even if the circumstances which arouse fear or distress really are bad, and those which arouse desire and gladness really are good, still the movement itself is a matter of fault. For when we say that a person is great-spirited or a brave man, we mean that he is consistent, calm, serious, and despises all human affairs. But no one who grieves or fears or desires or exults can be like that. Those feelings are limited to people who believe that the vagaries of human life are greater than their own minds.

62 ♠   So as I said before, there is one method of cure which belongs to all schools of philosophy, namely to speak solely about the emotion itself, saying nothing at all about the status of the things which arouse emotion. Take for instance desire. When one's sole purpose is to get rid of that emotion, the first thing to do is not to inquire whether the object which stirs longing is or is not a good; rather, one ought first to get rid of the longing itself. Some say the highest good is moral excellence, some pleasure, some a combination of the two, and some the "three classes of goods," yet all should make use of the same discourse to chase away the too-vigorous impulse, even if it is an impulse toward virtue itself.

B.   Arguments To Be Used against Individual Emotions

Distress and Fear

One fully comprehensive means of consolation is to set in view what it is to be a human being. In order to convey the point more effectively, the speech should develop the idea of certain regular restrictions under which all humans live.   63 ♠   This serves to explain an anecdote about Socrates. It is said that when Euripides was conducting rehearsals of his *Orestes*, Socrates asked for a repetition of the first three lines:

> No tale is so terrible to tell, no lot,
> no ill inflicted by the wrath of gods,
> that human nature does not bear its burden.

Another tactic that is useful in persuading people that they can and should endure what has happened is to list others who have endured it in the past. But the means of calming distress have been explained already, both in yesterday's discussion and in my *Consolation*, which I composed in the midst of sorrow and pain, not being a wise person myself. I did what Chrysippus says one should not do: applied a remedy to the mind's swelling while it was still fresh. I brought the force of nature to bear upon it, so that my great pain would give way to the greatness of the medicine.

64 ♠   Enough has been said about distress. I must now say a few words about fear. Fear is closely related to distress, for just as distress has to do with present evils, so fear has to do with future evils. For this reason some have called it a species of distress, and others have named it "foregrief," since it is a kind of precursor to the grief that is to follow. Therefore, the methods which enable a person to bear present afflictions will also enable him to think little of those in prospect. In both cases, we have to be careful not to do any-

thing base, anything servile, anything soft, womanish, or effeminate, anything at all that is beneath us. The speaker should talk about fear itself, what an inconstant, weak, and feeble thing it is; however, it is also very beneficial to speak contemptuously about the things which are objects of fear. It is very convenient, then, that our first two days' conversations happen to have concerned death and pain respectively—whether or not we did this on purpose. For these are the two things people fear the most. If those discussions win acceptance, then we shall largely be free of fear.

Emotions Derived from Apparent Goods: Some General Remarks

65 ☙ From beliefs about what is evil, let us now turn to beliefs about what is good: that is, to gladness and desire.

As far as I am concerned, the entire theory of emotion can be summed up in a single point: that they are all in our power, all experienced through judgment, all voluntary. It is this error, then, that must be removed, this belief that must be taken away. Just as when people believe their circumstances to be evil, we have to convince them that they are in fact endurable, so also when people believe their circumstances are cause for great gladness, we must convince them that they merit a calmer response. Good and bad circumstances have this at least in common: if it should prove difficult to convince people that none of the things which arouse emotion should be considered either good or bad, there are still methods of cure to be applied to each movement individually. There is one method for correcting the spiteful person, and another for the amorous person; one for those who suffer from anxiety, and another for the timid.

Gladness

66 ☙ I might have argued that a person who is not wise cannot ever feel gladness, because he can never possess anything which is good. That would have been easy, and it would be in accordance with the most plausible position on what is good and bad. But I am speaking now in a manner common to all the schools. Let us concede, then, that those things which people regard as good—public office, wealth, pleasures, and so forth—are in fact good. It is still shameful to feel a wild and exuberant gladness upon gaining possession of them, just as a loud guffaw might be objectionable even at some times when a laugh would not be inappropriate.

Pouring out the mind in gladness is just as much a fault as is contracting it in distress, and if desire shows a lack of moral seriousness in reaching for its object, so also does gladness in possessing it. When people are excessively downcast by affliction, we judge them to be lacking in moral worth, and rightly; so also with those who are too much carried away with gladness. Envy is a form of distress, while rejoicing over another's misfortunes is a form of gladness, yet both are usually corrected in the same way, by describing them as inhumane and, as it were, bestial. And just as confidence is proper, but fear improper, so also joy is proper and gladness improper—for we make a distinction between "joy" and "gladness" for the purposes of teaching.

67 ♣ I have already pointed out that while it can never be a right action to contract the spirits, it can be right to elevate them. For there is a difference between the joy of Hector, in Naevius's play:

Glad am I, father, to be praised by you, whom others praise,

and that of the fellow in Trabea's comedy:

The madam's greased with silver; she'll observe my nod,
my wish, my eagerness; I'll go and tap the door;
she'll open, and Chrysis, when she sees me suddenly there,
eager, will fly to meet me, longing for my embrace,
and give herself to me—

Does he think this a fine thing? Here are his own words:

—blessing above all blessing!

68 ♣ We have only to observe this gladness carefully to see quite well how shameful it is.

Erotic Love

Not only is it shameful to be carried away with gladness when enjoying the pleasures of Venus, but it is also disgraceful to have the mind aflame with desire for those pleasures. Indeed, speaking of what is popularly called love (not that I have any other name to call it!), all of it is so frivolous that I scarcely know what to compare with it. Caecilius says,

Love is the greatest god: he who thinks otherwise
is stupid, I think, or lacks experience of life.
It's in Love's power to choose who shall be mad, who sane,
who shall be healed, and who shall sink into disease,
whose love shall be requited, who be chased, who summoned.

69 ✦ What a fine moral guide is poetry! To think that love should be seated in the council of the gods—love, the instigator of frivolous and disgraceful conduct! I have been referring to comedy, which would not exist at all if we did not condone such behavior. What of tragedy? What does Jason say, the great leader of the Argonauts?

> You saved me for the sake of love, not honor.

And no wonder, for that was Medea's love. What a conflagration of miseries that stirred up! Yet in another poet she dares to say to her father,

> I had him for my husband. Love bestowed him,
> and love is stronger and more powerful
> than is my father.

70 ✦ But we see that in the tales of the poets even Jupiter is engaged in this scandal. Let us then leave the poets to their games and turn to the philosophers, the teachers of virtue. These say that the object of love is something other than illicit sex and argue the point with Epicurus, who in my opinion was not far from speaking the truth. For what do they mean by "a love whose object is friendship"? Why does no one love either an ugly youth or a handsome old man? If you ask me, this custom began on the exercise-grounds of the Greeks, where such loves were freely permitted. Ennius is right, then:

> Disgrace begins with nudity: the body
> naked before one's fellow-citizens.

Even if they are chaste, which I suppose could happen, they are still worried and anxious, and all the more so because they are restraining themselves.

71 ✦ I shall set aside the love of women, which nature has made more permissible. Which of us has any doubt as to what the poets mean by "the seizing of Ganymede"? Which of us fails to comprehend what Euripides' Laius is saying, or what he wants? What, in fact, do the most learned persons and the greatest poets give out concerning themselves, both in verses and in song? Alcaeus was known as a brave man in his own country, and look what he writes about the love of young boys! Anacreon's entire corpus is love-poetry. Ibycus of Rhegium is the most flagrant lover of all, as is evident from his writings.

But these men's loves are all of the desiring kind. We philosophers have arisen, on the authority of Plato himself (and the charges of Dicaearchus were not unfounded!) to give official sanction to love. 72 ♣ Indeed, the Stoics say that the wise person will fall in love. They give as their definition of love "an effort to form a friendship, due to an impression of beauty." If such a love exists in the world—one without worry, without need, without care, without sighing—then so be it! For that love is free from all desire. But this talk is about desire.

But if there is any love which is scarcely different from insanity—and you may be sure there is, like that of the lover in *Leucadia:*

> If there is any god who cares for me indeed—

73 ♣ What a thing for the gods to care about! Finding a way for this fellow to enjoy the pleasures of love!

> How wretched I am!

He never said a truer word. And the reply is also quite true:

> Are you of sound mind, to lament thus heedlessly?

He seems insane even to his own family. And what histrionics!

> You I invoke, Apollo, holy one,
> and you, Neptune omnipotent,
> and you, O winds: bring aid!

He thinks that all of heaven will devote its attention to furthering his love. Venus alone he excludes, on the grounds that she is unfair:

> For why should I name you, O Venus?

He says she cares for nothing but lust—as if lust were not the motivation for his own scandalous words and actions! 74 ♣ Here, then, is the cure that should be applied to a person thus affected. One should make clear to him the nature of the thing he desires, how slight, how contemptible, how completely worthless it is, and how easily one can get it somewhere else or in some other way, or else do without it altogether. He should also be distracted at times with other studies, worries, cares, or tasks, or cured by a change of place, like invalids who are not getting well.   75 ⚘   Some say also that the old love should be driven out by a new one, as one nail is knocked from its hole by another. But the most important thing is to warn him what frenzy there is in love. For of all the emotions, this is the most violent, so that even if you do not wish to condemn the actions themselves—illicit sex, seductions, acts of adultery, and even incest, all shameful acts which might well be condemned—even leaving these aside, the emotional disturbance of love is vile in and of itself.   76 ⚘   For even if I pass over its acts of frenzy, how capricious are its seemingly moderate behaviors!

> The wrongs, the suspicions, the quarrels, and the truces;
> war, and peace again! Would you seek by reason
> to make the uncertain certain? Wasted effort!
> As well attempt by reason to go mad.

Is there not sufficient deterrent in the very perversity of such an inconsistent and changeable state of mind?

Finally, one should prove to the person what we say about every emotion, that it is experienced only through one's own opinions and judgment and is voluntary. For if love were natural, everybody would be in love all the time and for the same object, but in fact one person is deterred by modesty, another by thought, another by satiety.

Anger

77 ⚘   As for anger: while this emotion lasts, there can be no doubt that it is insane. Under its influence even brothers may quarrel like this:

> *Agamemnon:* Is there anyone in all the world that's beaten you
>   for insolence?
> *Menelaus:* Or you for spite?

You know the rest: verse by verse, the brothers hurl at each other the most serious insults. One can easily believe they are the sons of that Atreus who plots an unheard-of penalty for his own brother:

> A greater weight, a greater ill I must contrive
> to bruise and crush his bitter mind.

Where then does this weight of ill burst forth? Hear Thyestes:

> My very brother bids me bite with my own mouth
> alas! my sons.

He serves up their flesh. For anger will go to any length, just as madness will. Thus we are right when we say that angry persons have gone "out of control"—that is, out of their intent, their reason, their conscious thought. For it is these things which ought to control the mind as a whole.

78 ⚹   When angry persons try to attack people, we must get the victims away from them until they collect themselves. (And what does it mean to "collect oneself," if not to bring the scattered parts of the mind back to their proper place?) Or, if they are in a position to exact revenge, we must beg and plead with them to put it off until their anger ceases to boil. For this reason we praise the remark Archytas made when he had become excessively angry at his overseer. "What a beating you'd have gotten from me," he said, "had I not been angry!"

79 ⚹   Where does this leave those who claim that anger is useful? Can insanity be useful? What of their claim that it is natural? How can a thing be in accordance with nature, when it is done against the objections of reason? If anger were natural, how could one person be more prone to it than another? How could it be that the desire for revenge sometimes ceases before revenge is exacted? How could anyone ever regret actions taken in anger? As an example of this we have King Alexander, who, after he had killed his comrade Clitus, could hardly keep from turning his hand against himself, so powerful was his regret.

If these things are taken into account, can there be any doubt that this emotion, like the others, is entirely a matter of belief and entirely voluntary?

C.   Conclusion to Book Four

Review of Essentials

Who would doubt that the infirmities of the mind, like greed and desire for glory, come about because one sets high value on the things from which the infirmity is contracted? This should enable us to realize that every emotion is likewise a matter of belief.   80 ⚹   If confidence, or a firm assurance of mind, is a form of knowledge, namely a serious opinion on the part of one who does not assent rashly, so also is fear an opinion that some anticipated evil is impending, and as hope is an expectation of good, fear is necessarily an expectation of evil, and so also with the other emotions. Thus a consistency is a matter of knowledge, while an emotion is a matter of error.

Some people are said to be irascible, pitying, envious, and so on, "by nature." These have, as it were, a poor constitution, and yet they can be healed. There is a story to that effect about Socrates. A certain Zopyrus claimed that he could discern a person's nature from his physiognomy. This man gave out a list of Socrates' faults in the midst of a gathering and was laughed at by all the rest, for they were aware that Socrates did not exhibit those faults. Socrates himself, however, supported Zopyrus, saying that they were indeed inborn in him, but that he had cast them out by reason. *81* ⚚ So minds can have a proclivity to one fault or another in much the same way that each person can appear to be naturally prone to some sickness of body even while the actual health is excellent.

Others are said to have certain faults not by nature but culpably. Faults of this kind consist in false beliefs about what things are good or bad, so that different people are prone to different emotional movements. And when an emotion has become habitual, this habit is harder to banish than the emotion itself, just as in our bodies a sudden swelling of the eyes is more quickly cured than a chronic inflammation.

The Value of Our Discussions Together

82 ⚚ We have now come to understand the cause of emotions, how all of them arise out of judgments and opinions and are voluntary. Let us now put an end to our discussion. But now that we have understood, insofar as humans can, the endpoints of good and evil, we ought to know that of all the things we might want from philosophy, nothing is greater or more useful than the things we have discussed on the last four days. For having already risen above death and made pain endurable, we went on to provide consolation for distress, which is the worst thing a person can feel. For although every emotion is burdensome and hardly different from insanity, still it is the case that when people experience fear, gladness, or desire, we call them merely "moved" or "disturbed"; but those who have surrendered themselves to distress we call "wretched," "afflicted," "suffering," or "ruined." *83* ⚚ So your proposal that we should discuss distress separately from the other emotions seems not to have been made by chance, but by design. For distress is the very wellspring of misery.

And yet the method of cure is the same for distress and for the other sicknesses of mind: to show that they are a matter of belief and are voluntary, and that we experience them because we think it appropriate to do so. It is this error which philosophy promises to eradicate, since it is, as it were, the root of all the evils.   *84* ✺   Let us therefore hand ourselves over to philosophy, and let ourselves be healed. For as long as these ills remain we cannot attain to happiness, nor even to health. Let us therefore either deny that reason can do anything—when in fact nothing can be done rightly without reason—or, since philosophy consists in comparing reasoned arguments, let us seek from it every form of assistance, so that we may live not only well, but also happily, if such is indeed our wish.

COMMENTARY

BOOK 3

ON GRIEF

The mind, like the body, suffers from disorders, but the medical science that might cure those disorders is little cultivated. The source of our troubles is in false beliefs imparted to us since. childhood by our families, by poetry, and by society in general: all of these teach us to value power, popularity, wealth, or pleasure above doing what is right. Such values cause people to behave badly, but also to live in emotional turmoil. The cure for this illness is to be sought in philosophy, which enables us to become our own physicians.

The preface to book 3 resembles most of Cicero's other philosophical prefaces in its formal style, in offering a dedication to a contemporary figure, and in exhorting the reader to take up the study of philosophy. It is unusual, however, in that it takes up a question which is of serious philosophical import and which is, moreover, indispensable to the argument of the remainder of the book. If nature has designed humans to be happy and to behave well, then why are we so often miserable? And why do we often harm others and ourselves? Cicero's treatment of the problem follows closely on solutions proposed in the writings of the early Stoics Cleanthes (331–232) and Chrysippus (c. 280–207).

1. Philosophy a Healing Art

The exhortation to study philosophy is based on an analogy between philosophy and medicine: as medicine is needed to cure the diseases of the body, so philosophy is a healing art for the mind. The analogy is broadly significant: it asserts that there is for the mind as well as the body a normative or healthy condition which those who do not make use of philosophy have little prospect of maintaining. Philosophy thus serves practical as well as intellectual ends. In this general sense, the medical analogy was widely used in Hellenistic philosophical writing, not only by Stoics (see the formulation of it by Chrysippus in Appendix C, passage [j]) but also by Epicurus (Porphyry, *To Marcella* 31, fr. 221 Usener) and others. In the way he expresses it here, however, Cicero is clearly thinking of the Stoic use of the analogy. For the preface goes on to describe the "sicknesses" of the mind in a manner exactly consonant with the Stoic analysis to be presented in 4.23–27. A mental "sickness," it emerges, is an improper, but deeply ingrained, ascription of value, as when one comes to believe firmly that some object not solely dependent on oneself—for instance wealth or public office—is completely and unqualifiedly worthy of pursuit or, in the analogous negative case, worthy of avoidance. It is these false values which predispose us to experience powerful feelings about the things valued or disvalued.

2.   The Origins of Error

But this analysis raises a theoretical problem which is especially pressing for Stoics. If, as the Stoics insist, the universe as a whole is a perfectly ordered system, and if humans are part of that system and base all their beliefs on it, then how does any human come to believe what is false? The answer given here depends on an account of human development which begins at birth. For humans are not born virtuous: all we have are "seeds" or "sparks" which have the potential to develop into virtue, if all goes well during the process of intellectual maturation. Cicero has written about these starting-points (*aphormai*; see on 3.2) in more detail in book 3 of *On Ends*. There he describes them as innate tendencies to prefer those things that are in accordance with our own natural state—things probably like wholesome food and companionship—and lays out in some detail the sequence of steps the maturing mind passes through as it develops the cognitive capacity to understand the rational principles of the universe and, eventually, to base its own impulses on that comprehensive understanding (*On Ends* 3.16–23).

Here, however, he is concerned with the intrusion of false belief into that sequence. This seems to happen in two different ways. Many errors

come to us through the influence of those around us, when we accept un-
critically the opinions of others as to what is to be valued and pursued.
Nurses, parents however well-intentioned, teachers, and even works of literature are all likely sources of corruption. Even without such influences,
however, we might still fall into error, because in our immature state we are
not able to distinguish between certain kinds of impressions which resemble one another closely but are in fact importantly different. Cicero's
chief example of this second kind of error concerns the difference between
popular acclaim, which is the praise generally accorded to one's public actions; and glory, which is praise accorded by the wise. Only the latter sort
of praise is well-grounded and reliable: the non-wise may indeed praise
those who have acted rightly, but they may also fail to do so, or praise misdeeds along with good deeds. The two sorts of praise are in theory always
distinguishable—for persons whose ethical understanding is fully developed. But those who have not yet reached this stage of development may
not be able to tell on any given occasion what sort of praise they are receiv-
ing: they are "deceived by the meanderings of the path." Even the noblest
among us, remarks the class-conscious Cicero, may thus be led astray; others, less noble perhaps, are corrupted by the persuasiveness of wealth or of
bodily pleasure.

At least the second part of this answer, the part which makes humans
misinterpret similar impressions, appears already in Cleanthes' *Hymn to Zeus*
22–31 (*SVF* 1.537). There it is asserted that "although humans yearn to possess the good, they often do not see or hear the natural order correctly" and
so base their actions on love of fame, wealth, or pleasure. The resemblance
between fame and glory is also an early Stoic theme. But both parts of Cicero's answer appear together in some Stoic texts, for instance in the summary by Diogenes Laertius: "A rational being is corrupted sometimes by
the persuasiveness of external circumstances, and sometimes by the influence of associates, since the starting-points which nature provides are un-
corrupted" (7.89). This "twofold" explanation was the one offered by
Chrysippus in his treatise *On Emotions* (Appendix C, passage [n]), and
Cicero must have encountered it there; see the discussion of Chrysippus's
influence on the present work in Appendix C. An unusually full account of
the twofold cause in a late source (Appendix C, passage [o]) resembles Cicero's version closely: it includes, for instance, the point about the messages
given to us by wet-nurses, parents, and books of poetry, and it elaborates as
Cicero does on the resemblance between fame and glory. If this report is
reliable, then Cicero must have drawn nearly everything in 3.2–4 from

Chrysippus or another early source, only adapting it to suit his prefatory
context. For this possibility see further Appendix C.

3.   The Influence of Literature

Cicero mentions with some emphasis the influence that literature may
have on the young. This is again a theme taken up from the philosophical
tradition. The substance of the complaint is clear enough: poetry, whether
memorized in the schoolroom or absorbed in the theater with all its accou-
trements of music, dance, and spectacle, presents us with memorable scenes
of humans and even gods suffering and rejoicing in accordance with values
which philosophers would call into question. For this reason, its cultural
preeminence was challenged not only by Plato in the *Republic* (2.376e–3.403c),
but persistently by philosophers of the Hellenistic period. The challenge at
first appears inconsistent, since many of these same philosophers, again like
Plato, also make liberal use of examples and quotations from Homer, Euripides, and other canonical authors to illustrate their own points. The *Tusculan Disputations* quote poetry more frequently than any other Ciceronian
work, sometimes in a hostile spirit, as at 4.69, but often with deep appreciation (3.45) and as a source of psychological insight. The implied claim is that
while the uncritical reading of literature is indeed a cause of moral error, this
pernicious influence can be neutralized by thoughtful and selective use of the
same material, and that teaching such critical reading is an important task of
philosophers. For explicit statements of this claim see Plutarch's treatise *How
the Young Should Listen to Poetry*, which draws upon Chrysippus's work of the
same name, and compare the reading of Euripides's *Medea* put forward by
Epictetus in *Discourses* 1.28.7–9, 2.17.19–22.

The implications of the medical analogy in ethics, and its use in the Hellenistic schools, are
explored in depth in Nussbaum 1994; see also Sorabji 1997. On moral development and
corruption, see Gill 1998, 120–21; Scott 1995, 179–86, 201–10; Annas 1993, 178–79, 219–20. Stoic
uses of poetry are treated in detail in Nussbaum 1993, esp. 121–45; in Long 1992; and with
particular reference to *Medea* in Gill 1983 and Dillon 1997. On Brutus see Rawson 1985, 285–86;
Reid 1885, 104–5. On the *Hortensius*, MacKendrick 1989, 109–13; the fragments are assembled in
Grilli 1962.

3.1   **Brutus:** The direct address in the opening sentence follows the usual
formula for book dedications. M. Junius Brutus was a long-time friend
of Cicero and, like him, an amateur philosopher writing in Latin. He
had recently dedicated to Cicero a treatise *On Virtue*, to which the present work, like the preceding *On Ends*, is in some ways a response (*Tusc.*

5.1, 5.121; *On Ends* 1.8). Brutus's own philosophical views were Antiochan; see p. xxiv–xxv.

3.2   **the tiniest sparks … seeds of the virtues:** Stob., *Ecl.* 2.7.5b3 (62.9–12 W) reports that "one has from nature starting-points *(aphormai)* toward discerning what is appropriate, toward stabilizing the impulses, toward enduring, and toward fair distributing"; in other words, toward the cardinal virtues of prudence, temperance, courage, and justice; cf. D.L. 7.89, quoted above. The metaphors used here are apt: "sparks" *(igniculos)* suggest the Stoic designing fire, seeds the seminal principles (Aetius 1.7.33 (*SVF* 2.1027); Cleanthes, *Hymn to Zeus* 9–13 (*SVF* 1.537); D.L. 7.136). Cicero uses the two metaphors together with similar content also in *On Ends* 5.18 and 5.43.

hardened belief: Our temporary errors—typically mistakes of evaluation, such as believing that money is a genuine good—become, through repetition, deeply ingrained values. Compare 4.26, where it is the fact that a false value is "deeply attached and rooted" that makes it a sickness.

3.3   **The poets come in:** Compare *Tusc.* 2.27, together with 4.69–70.

the glory of popularity: Stoic texts distinguish fame *(doxa)*, a preferred indifferent (Stob., *Ecl.* 2.7.7e, 83.4–7 W), from glory *(timē)*, which is a genuine good restricted to the virtuous (Stob., *Ecl.* 2.7.5l, 11i (73.16–19, 103.4–9 W)). Cleanthes wrote separate treatises on each (D.L. 7.175). Cicero had already touched on the distinction in *On Ends* 2.48–49 and *Tusc.* 1.109–10, 2.63–64 (see further on 3.61, p. 110). He was to revisit it the following year in a separate treatise *On Glory:* see the fragment in Jerome, *On Galatians* 5.26 (fr. 6 Garbarino), and compare *Off.* 1.65.

chasing not a solid figure … but only a shadow-shape: The imagery is surprisingly complicated. Although true glory is only a concomitant of virtue, and is thus called a "reflection or echo" of it, it is nonetheless a solid thing, of which popular acclaim is in turn only a shadow-shape *(adumbratam imaginem)*. Popular acclaim is thus a shadow of a reflection, the multiple image-original relations strongly recalling Plato's analogy of the Cave in *Republic* 7.514a–16d. The language of mirroring and echoing appears to be Cicero's own embellishment on the Stoic point.

the regular accompaniment to right actions: As at *Tusc.* 1.91, 109. Compare Stob., *Ecl.* 2.7.11i (103.6–7 W), "the deserving of a reward, that being the prize for virtue which does good"; Calcidius (Appendix C, passage [o]) "the testimony to virtue."

3.4   **did not go astray voluntarily:** Cicero speaks loosely. In Stoic ethics, all human error will count as voluntary, since it is the product of one's own judgment. See comm. 3, IVc (on 3.64–71).

    by a desire for money, or by longing for pleasures: "Love of money" *(philarguria)* and "love of pleasure" *(philēdonia)* are included along with "love of fame" *(philodoxia)* among the "sicknesses" of Stoic theory. Compare Cleanthes' *Hymn to Zeus* 27–29 *(SVF* 1.537), and see comm. 4, IIc (on 4.23–33), section 1.

    are not far from insanity: In fact, the persons described are already insane in Stoic terms, since insanity is just that unsound condition of mind which renders us subject to emotion. See 3.10 with comm. 3, IB (on 3.8–11).

    this happens to everyone: Not everyone is greedy or pleasure-loving (4.24–25), but all the non-wise are troubled by emotions.

    bodies can be cured, but a medical science for the mind does not exist: Compare Appendix C, passage [j], from the "therapeutic" book of Chrysippus's *On Emotions.*

3.5   **Ennius:** Ennius (b. 239) was the most influential of the older generation of poets writing in Latin. Cicero makes every effort to promote appreciation of his work.

    The mind distressed: Ennius, fr. 174 Jocelyn. Ennius uses *aeger,* literally "ill," with the meaning "distressed"; this helps Cicero to establish a further connection between sickness *(morbus)* and distress *(aegritudo).* See further on 3.23.

3.6   **my** *Hortensius:* An exhortation to the study of philosophy, defending its claims against those of rhetorical training. Judging by the mention of it in *On Ends* 1.2, it, too, may have been dedicated to Brutus.

    I have been ... employed: In the *Academics* and *On Ends.* For the chronology see p. xiv, xxxii.

PART I: THE QUESTION TO BE ADDRESSED

A.   Is the Wise Person Subject to Distress? (3.7–8)

The topic of the third day's discussion is to be whether one who is truly wise can experience distress. Distress must be treated in the context of mental disturbances generally; the Greeks speak of pathē or "disorders," but "emotions" is a better term.

In accordance with the usual disputation format, the first section sets out a "thesis" or topic for discussion which will be at issue throughout the

book. This is stated not by the principal speaker, but by an unnamed interlocutor who claims it as his personal view. (The speaker-designations "A"
and "M" which appear in some manuscripts are not authorial and have been
omitted here.) In his initial response, the principal speaker (hereafter "Cicero") establishes that grief may be treated as a representative of the broader
class of emotions in general, thus signalling the relation between the subject matter of books 3 and 4. He then expresses his own opposition to the
thesis, claiming that in Greek even the very word for emotion refers to an
abnormal and undesirable state.

Cicero overstates his case somewhat when he insists here and in 3.23 that
the very word *pathos* might appropriately be translated as *morbus*, "sickness."
It is true that *pathos* is sometimes used in medical contexts to refer to the
symptoms or condition of an afflicted person (see LSJ s.v. *pathos* 1.2c). But
pathos is often a broad and colorless term, roughly equivalent to "experience" in English. By bringing out this particular semantic possibility, Cicero scores a preliminary rhetorical point against those who would treat the
emotions as normal and natural experiences.

But this small rhetorical advantage is gained at the expense of some confusion of categories. For Cicero will later use the same word *morbus* to render the Stoic term *nosēma*. A "sickness" in this second sense is not the same
thing as a *pathos*, although the two concepts are related: the *nosēma* is a particularly strong evaluative belief which predisposes some individuals to
have emotions toward certain objects, and is a condition *(hexis)*; while a
pathos is normally an actual episode of emotion, a movement or mental event
(kinēsis). Cicero has already made some use of the former concept in the
preface to book 3, and he is later to explain it in some detail (4.23–26). It
should be noted that the same misuse of *pathos* in the sense of *nosēma* occurs
in older Stoic material. On this see further comm. 4, IIc (on 4.23–33), section 1, and Appendix C.

On the disputation format, see esp. Douglas 1995. On "A" and "M" the standard discussion is
that of Pohlenz 1911, more briefly Dougan 1905, 13; Pohlenz and Heine 1957, 1.22. On the rendering of *pathos*, cf. Inwood 1985, 127–28.

3.7   **our Academy:** One of two exercise-grounds or promenades (*ambula-*
        tiones, 4.7) at Cicero's villa at Tusculum; the other was called the
        Lyceum (*On Divination* 1.8). *Tusc.* 2.9 indicates that the Lyceum was used
        particularly for practice in rhetoric, which Cicero associated especially
        with Aristotle and his followers, while the Academy was used for
        philosophical discussion.

is subject: For the Latin expression see *OLD*, s.v. *cado* 22b. The claim is that the wise person may sometimes be the subject of a true proposition of which "is distressed" is the predicate.

emotions: Cicero's phrase *perturbationes animi*, literally "disturbances of mind," is chosen to suggest violence and disarray, and he will occasionally make use of the underlying metaphor in his argument, e.g. at 3.15, 3.18, 4.54. Compare *On Ends* 3.35, where he remarks that emotion "is shown by its very name to be a fault." But the term did not always draw attention to itself: *turbare*-derivatives were already standard in the Latin vocabulary of emotion, and *perturbatio* here and in *Acad.* 1.38–39 is in accordance with Cicero's own regular usage (e.g. *On the Orator* 2.214; *Acad. Pr.* 2.135 has *permotio*). A somewhat blander term, *adfectio*, was also available to him (*On Invention* 1.41, 2.17), but *adfectio* is also his rendering for *hexis* ("condition"); it will be pressed into service only once, for an even broader genus of feeling, at 4.14. Later authors generally prefer to use *habitus* for "condition" and render *pathos* by *adfectio* or *adfectus*.

various forms of terror, desire, and anger: It is assumed that emotions, properly so called, constitute a natural class. See comm. 4, IA (on 4.7–9).

movements of mind not obedient to reason: This form of the definition, which does not specify that emotions are contrary to nature (cf. 4.11, 4.47), is one which Peripatetics, as well as Stoics, might well accept. Compare the definition offered, probably at a slightly later date, by Andronicus of Rhodes (see comm. 4, IB (on 4.9–10)). But the implication that emotions are contrary to nature has already been made clearly enough in the equation of them with "sicknesses."

B.   **A Preliminary Investigation on the Basis of Latin Usage (3.8–11)**

Ordinary Latin usage can be pressed to yield the view that anything which upsets a serene and calm state of mind is tantamount to insanity—not the frenzy of madness, but a more general unsoundness of mind. This, surely, was the view of our ancestors, who established our linguistic patterns. Here as elsewhere, Latin is clearer and more logical in the way it speaks of psychological matters than is Greek.

Cicero claims for his own position the support of the earliest speakers of Latin, drawing evidence for their views from the origins of certain Latin terms, from features of contemporary Latin usage, and from the Twelve Tables. If it can be made convincing, the appeal to ancestral Roman attitudes will forestall the objection that the Stoic position is so alien to ordinary moral intuitions as to have no chance of being right.

Cicero explains that the Latin word *insania* is literally "unsoundness" or the absence of *sanitas*, which can be either "health" in the usual sense or "sanity," i.e., health of mind. Given a particular norm for mental health ("a serene and consistent temper," 3.9), this yields the conclusion that anything which deviates from that norm can reasonably be called "insanity." To be sure, Cicero can hardly expect to prove that early speakers of Latin had a norm for mental health matching that of later Stoic philosophers. He can show, however, that the sense Stoics give to *mania* can be attached to *insania* without putting any undue strain on Latin usage. His interest in showing this is reminiscent of his program in the *Stoic Paradoxes*, which likewise deals with insanity (see further comm. on 3.10).

The last paragraph of the section indicates that Cicero's Greek sources made a distinction between two kinds of madness. Although the Stoics argue, somewhat rhetorically, that "all the non-wise are insane," they also recognize a category of insanity in the sense of complete derangement, characterizing it by the reception of false or erratic impressions (D.L. 7.118; Aetius 4.12.5–6 (*SVF* 2.54); Sextus, *AM* 7.244–49). Thus Ajax, when he slaughtered a flock of sheep in the mistaken impression that they were fellow-Achaeans, was not merely "insane" as all those not wise are insane, but actually "frenzied." Cicero notes that his Greek sources offer two different terms, *mania* for the madness of all non-sages and *melancholia* for derangement like that of Ajax.

But although the two conditions are distinct, they are not unrelated. Much of the present work will be devoted to establishing the point that all the emotions result from mental unsoundness, i.e. from false and inconsistent beliefs. Madness *(mania)* is defined as "fluttery ignorance" (Stob., *Ecl.* 2.7.5b13, 68.23 W), the condition which disposes us to experience "flutters" or erratic impulses. And an emotion is a "flutter" (Stob., *Ecl.* 2.7.10, 88.11–12 W). But Cicero also asserts that episodes of extreme emotion can actually unseat the mind, producing what he calls "frenzy." This is what happens in the case of Ajax (see further on 4.52). Seneca was to argue the same point in a Stoic context in *On Anger* 2.4–5. (But the assertion is not only Stoic; see the aphorism attributed to Ennius in 4.52, and Seneca, *Ep.* 18.14, attributed to Epicurus.) Thus Cicero objects to the term *melancholia*, literally "black-biliousness," on grounds that it implies mental derangement is caused only by an imbalance of humors (of brain chemicals, we would say) and not by a person's whole emotional history.

For antiquarian and linguistic interests in the late Republic see Rawson 1985, 117–31, 233–49. On the *Stoic Paradoxes*, MacKendrick 1989, 87–93, with the edition by Ronnick 1991. On drunkenness and *melancholia* (3.11), Rist 1969, 17–19.

3.8–9   After **sickness of the mind** I have omitted from the translation some three sentences of choppy and repetitive Latin which appear in the manuscripts, but which add nothing of substance to the discussion. These probably have their origin in a marginal note by some early copyist. See Dougan's concise note on the passage (in Dougan and Henry 1934). For a defense of the received text, see Lundström 1964, 33–45.

3.10   **all those who are not wise are insane:** The fourth of the "Stoic paradoxes" (literally "statements contrary to popular opinion") which Cicero had listed a year earlier in a set of rhetorical exercises bearing that title; its treatment there is unfortunately truncated. Its Socratic credentials are supported only by Xenophon, *Memorabilia* 3.9.6. Compare also *Acad. Pr.* 2.136, *On Ends* 4.74. The point is developed in a rather different way in 4.54.

3.11   **we Latin speakers:** But Greek had a similar expression, *parēllachōs,* used in this context by Chrysippus (Appendix C, passage [1]). "Carried away" and "unbridled" should likewise be compared with Chrysippus's discussions of how the undivided mind can sometimes act against its own best judgment. See Appendix C, passages [c]–[e], with comm. 4, IIB (on 4.14–22), section 2.

    anger is a species of desire: See 4.21.

    the intelligence: The intelligence *(mens)* is here the directive faculty or *hēgemonikon.* Cicero's choice of terms matches that of Lucretius at 3.94–95.

    Athamas, Alcmaeon, Ajax, and Orestes: Orestes is the usual Stoic example of derangement (Aetius 4.12.5–6 (*SVF* 2.54); Sextus, *AM* 7.244–45). Athamas killed his son in a fit of madness sent by Hera. Alcmaeon (on whom see also *Acad. Pr.* 2.52, 89–90) was the son of Amphiaraus and Eriphyle; like Orestes, he killed his mother to avenge his father and subsequently became insane, pursued by the Furies.

    the Twelve Tables: The old Roman code of law. Cicero assumes that his readers know the continuation of the law: "then let his family-members and relatives have control over him and his property" (Warmington 3.450–52).

    capable of handling ordinary responsibilities: In the view imputed to the old Roman legislators, "ordinary responsibilities" would be just the regular care of one's person and property. But the same phrase, *mediocritas officiorum* (*mesa kathēkonta*, more literally "intermediate appropriate acts"), also had a technical usage within Stoic ethics, where it refers to appropriate actions performed on the basis of true opinion only. See for instance *On Ends* 3.58, *Off.* 3.14–16. Cicero is hinting that Roman jurisprudence is unwittingly congruent with Stoic theory.

frenzy ... can come upon a wise person: Some Stoics, including Chrysippus, held that although the ideal state is inherently stable, it is not such as to be impervious to the effects of alcohol or madness-inducing drugs; see D.L. 7.118, 127; Simplicius, *Commentary on Aristotle's Categories* 402.22–26 Kalbfleisch (*SVF* 3.238); Seneca, *Ep.* 83.27.

C.   Distress Must Come First (3.12–13)

The view that the wise person can experience grief is appealing; it is in fact the view of the Academic Crantor. But the mind's real healing is to be found in the bolder negative position.

Returning now to distress in particular, Cicero restates the thesis and concedes its appeal, then proceeds to identify sides in the debate. The interlocutor's view is identified as that of Crantor (c. 335–275), an important member of the Academy, whose larger position, sometimes labeled "Peripatetic," will be criticized in large portions of book 4 as well as book 3. In taking exception to this view, Cicero makes himself an advocate for the Stoic ideal of impassivity (*apatheia*), even though he, too, professes a formal adherence to the Academy.

Crantor's treatise *On Grief*, which is quoted here, was much consulted by writers of consolatory treatises. Cicero knew it well: he cites it also in *Tusculan Disputations* 1.115, and in *Prior Academics* 2.135 he praises it as "a small book, but made of gold, and worth learning by heart." According to Pliny (*Natural History pref.* 22), he also named Crantor as a major source for his own self-directed *Consolation*, composed a few months earlier than the *Tusculans*. See Appendix A.

But Crantor also represents a particular strain of philosophical thought. The Academy with which he was connected was what Cicero sometimes calls the Old Academy, philosophers of the first two generations after Plato, before the school took a skeptical turn under the leadership of Arcesilaus (316–242). His views on emotion, also ascribed in the *Prior Academics* to the Old Academy in general, are indistinguishable from those of the Peripatetics who appear as opponents in 3.22, 3.71–74, and 4.38–47. Positing the existence of a natural "limit," he holds that emotion in "moderate amounts"

is not incompatible with wisdom and argues also that each emotion is ordained by nature to serve a useful purpose. See further comm. 3, IVᴅ (on
3.71–75), section 1.

It should be noted that while Cicero in 3.12 does not hesitate to associate
himself with Crantor as a fellow-Academic, the Academic stance which he
himself adopts in 3.50–51, 4.7, 4.47, and elsewhere in his philosophical works
does not by any means commit him to the position he reports for the Old
Academy. His own Academic stance—one well suited to his role as expositor—is a matter of avoiding dogmatism, making no claim to certain
knowledge but merely "yielding to the plausible" (the *probabile*, Gr. *pithanon*;
mentioned at 4.7 and 4.47; see *Acad. Pr.* 2.99–102). This is meant to be the
stance of the skeptical Academy in the tradition of Arcesilaus, Carneades
(214–129), Clitomachus (187–110), and Cicero's own teacher Philo of Larisa
(159–84). Thus he is free to examine Crantor's position on its own merits
and even to side against it where it is found wanting. For Cicero's engagement with the skeptical Academy in this work, see further 3.54, 3.59, 4.53.

For the history of the Academy after Plato, see Dillon 1996; sources in Long and Sedley 1987,
chs. 68–70. On Crantor see Appendix A, together with Dillon 1996, 40, 42–43; Scourfield 1993,
15–17; Gregg 1975, 83–94. For Cicero's knowledge of the Academy and Peripatos, see Barnes
1997b, Long 1995, Classen 1989; for his own contribution to the Academy, Gersh 1986, 1.53–54,
with the comments of Dillon 1996, 426.

3.12   **I cannot by any means agree:** See Appendix A, passage [b] for what
       appears to be a fuller version of the same remark of Crantor. Crantor's
       Greek distinguishes between the absence of emotion (*apatheia*, "impas-
       sivity") and absence of bodily pain (*anōdunon*), but the point he is mak-
       ing depends to some extent on a blurring of this distinction. Cicero's
       translation is interpretive insofar as he uses equivalent terms for both
       concepts (*indolentia . . . non dolere*).

3.13   **the weak and womanish parts of us:** The charge of effeminacy (*mol-
       litudo*) is levelled especially at Peripatetic opponents. For the gendered
       language cf. 3.22, 4.38.

       that there will perhaps be something left over: Here, as occa-
       sionally elsewhere, Cicero makes a rather inadequate summary refer-
       ence to a point which will be explained more fully later on. The treat-
       ment of this issue at the end of book 3 makes it clear that the "roots of
       folly," i.e. the deep-seated beliefs which are a necessary condition for
       emotions to occur, are in fact to be distinguished from the residual
       "bitings" which cannot be completely eradicated from the sage. The

latter do not depend on the presence of vice; see comm. 3, VB (on
3.80–84) and on 3.83 and 3.84.

PART II: TWO WAYS OF PRESENTING THE STOIC POSITION

A.   Arguments in the Stoic Manner (3.13–21)

*I present first a series of arguments compressed into bare syllogisms in the Stoic manner.
Such arguments can be premised on the wise person's courage, reasoning power, temperance
(which might be better called "frugality"), freedom of anger, and freedom of envy. Each of
them demonstrates that the wise person cannot possibly be susceptible to distress.*

Cicero's first presentation of the Stoic position is in the dialectical manner which he associates with actual Stoic treatises. Accordingly, it consists
almost entirely of a string of syllogisms, interspersed with some less formal
remarks and with several digressions on matters of etymology and semantics. No doubt it is the syllogisms themselves which represent the style of
discourse which he regards as specifically Stoic. If these do not carry conviction, it is perhaps because of an excessively schematic presentation, but also
because of the premises employed, many of which depend for their validity
on characteristically Stoic analyses of the virtues and mental processes.

Cicero is impressed with the conciseness and rigor of the syllogism as
used by the Stoics, and here and elsewhere he finds for it many metaphors
expressive of all that is careful and precise: tight wrapping, sharp instruments, small weights, separating bones from flesh (see on 3.13 below). At the
same time, he complains about its inadequacy for effecting any real change
in the hearer; see esp. *On Ends* 4.5–7, quoted on p. xxvii–xxviii. Here, he accepts the arguments as valid but clearly does not expect the reader to derive
much benefit from them, since he proceeds in later sections to restate the
same case and never refers again to the conclusions established here.
Abruptly introduced, and as abruptly dropped, the arguments in this manner function chiefly to provide a foil for the more expansive treatment of
this same position in 3.22–27 and thereafter.

The arguments do have some intrinsic interest, however, as specimens
of Stoic argument-types. There is no reason to doubt their genuineness: although Cicero does not name his source, and no extensive parallels are ex-
tant, he is unlikely to have devised these syllogisms himself. At one point
(3.15), we have a close correspondence of detail with material preserved in
Stobaeus, which suggests direct adaptation of older material. For the syllo-

gistic mode of presentation, there are many comparison texts; see for instance D.L. 7.76–82. Seneca in particular echoes Cicero's complaints about its efficacy as moral suasion (*Ep.* 82.9).

All six of the arguments are premised on characteristically Stoic ways of thinking about the mind and its interactions with the world. Two basic notions come into play: first, that our ways of interpreting and responding to states of affairs are determined by our mental states, so that a mind in its optimal epistemic state will always respond in optimal, and hence (in theory) predictable, ways; and second, that all the virtues interentail, so that anyone who has one virtue necessarily has all the others.

1.   Impression and Assent

The first of these points is fundamental to much that follows in these two books of the *Tusculans* but is never fully explained in them, no doubt because Cicero had already devoted much of the *Academics* to the issues in question. It concerns the process of belief-formation, explained in *Acad.* 1.40–42 and in other sources (see esp. Origen, *On Principles* 3.1.3 (*SVF* 2.988); D.L. 7.45–54; Stob., *Ecl.* 2.7.11m (111.18–113.11 W)). The impressions that occur in adult humans as we become aware of objects in the world (putative states of affairs, 4.21) regularly have some propositional content. That is to say, we collect, compare, and evaluate information in mental sentences (propositions, *lekta*) which can be stated verbally if we have occasion to do so. The mental event in which I become aware of a proposition can be distinguished from a further mental event in which I either accept that proposition as true or reject it as false: the former is called in Stoic texts an "impression" *(phantasia)*, the latter an "assent" *(sunkatathesis)*. The manner in which we assent has ethical as well as epistemological significance, since only propositions accepted as true can become the basis for action. For this reason, assent, rather than impression, is identified as the locus of responsibility.

The key point here is that our assents are themselves fully determined by our moral character. The propositions we accept as true are just those which we recognize as fitting with beliefs we already hold, for as rational beings we understand that some propositions follow from others, and we favor the creation of logically coherent subsets among our beliefs (Sextus, *AM* 8.275–76 (*SVF* 2.223)). Only subsets, for in ordinary cases the belief-set as a whole is never fully coherent: practically all of us are in error on some points, and our assents are accordingly classed as "weak" assents (see on 4.15). In theory, however, a person could possess a fully coherent belief-set containing only true beliefs. In this case, which is that of the wise person or sage, assent can only be given to propositions which are in fact true and will always be given to those (Stob., *Ecl.* 2.7.5l, 11m (73.19–74.3, 112.1–12 W)). The wise person, then, can be expected not to think that an object merits a particular response unless it really does merit that response. And it is an axiom of Stoic ethics that the kinds of objects which in ordinary flawed humans are objects of fear, distress, envy, and other emotions do not in fact merit such responses. This line of thought supplies key premises for the arguments here labeled [A], [B], and [F].

2.   The Unity of the Virtues

The second point mentioned above supplies key premises for arguments [A], [B], and [D]. This claim, sometimes labeled "the unity of the virtues," asserts that a person who possesses any one of the virtues necessarily possesses all the others as well. Thus if any virtue, properly so called, is shown to be incompatible with distress, then every other must be incompatible with it also. The different virtues come near to being the same thing: each of them is only an alternative description of that condition of logical coherence among all one's beliefs which Stoics call simply virtue or knowledge (D.L. 7.126; Stob., *Ecl.* 2.7.5b5 (63.6–25 W)). Differences among the virtues are defined as differences in the matters to which each is chiefly related, its "own principal task" *(idion kephalaion)*. That is to say, the epistemic state which disposes a person to behave prudently is exactly the same state as that which disposes her to behave courageously or temperately, and yet we can still speak of her prudence in knowing what to do or of her courage in facing danger. Compare Cicero's mention in 3.17 of the "defining characteristic" *(proprium)* of frugality or temperance.

3.   Linguistic Digressions

The several digressions on etymology and semantics (*frugalitas* in 3.16–17, *nequitia* in 3.18, *invidere* in 3.20) may recall a feature of some Stoic treatises; compare the etymology of *lupē* attributed to Chrysippus in 3.61. As the terms in question are all Latin words, however, the etymologies themselves must be Cicero's own or borrowed from a Latin source. The most extensive argues the appropriateness of *frugalitas*, a word richly resonant of ancestral Roman morality, as a translation for *sōphrosunē*. *Frugalitas*, as Cicero correctly opines in 3.18, is the abstract noun derived from *frux*, "fruit" or "harvest"; it refers both to the judicious management of one's resources and to one's own worth or merit as a family member and citizen. Cicero reasons that as ordinary usage restricts the adjectival form *frugi* to cases in which justice, courage, and prudence are also present, and as interentailment characterizes the cardinal virtues, it is linguistically reasonable to give *frugalitas* the status of a cardinal virtue. Despite his elaborate plea here, he will not in fact make use of *frugalitas* as a standard rendering for *sōphrosunē*, though he does refer back to the discussion here at 3.36 and 4.36.

On the formation of beliefs, see Long and Sedley 1987, 1.321–23, 1.256–59; Inwood 1985, 18–101; Engberg-Pedersen 1990, 142–69; Annas 1980; on 'weak' assent, Görler 1977. Connections between Stoic logic and Stoic ethics are explored in Barnes 1997a and Long 1978. On Stoic etymologies see Long and Sedley 1987, 1.195, also Long 1992.

3.13   **with brief, compressed arguments:** The Stoics habitually "compress" or "constrict" their arguments; compare *On Ends* 3.26, "the Stoics' brief, sharp-pointed syllogisms"; *Stoic Paradoxes pref.* 2, "tiny little questions like stingers"; *Brutus* 120, "too compressed and concise for a general audience." For additional observations on the Stoics' argumentative style see 3.22, 4.9, 4.33.

3.14   **In fact, it seems likely . . . timorousness and cowardice:** This remark is not needed to advance the argument and seems to be parenthetical. Cicero might have wished to include it as an illustration of argument-type called the *sōritēs* or Heap, in which he was interested; see *Acad. Pr.* 2.49, 92–93.

3.15   **great in spirit:** "Great-spiritedness" or largeness of view is that quality that enables a person to perceive the larger natural order and understand how one's own affairs fit into it. Cicero speaks of it in two particular and slightly different contexts: as a virtue associated with courage here and in 3.36, and as a quality developed through pre-rehearsal (but not specifically connected with courage) in 3.30 and 3.34. The account in Stobaeus similarly offers two clearly distinct senses for *megalopsuchia*. At *Ecl.* 2.7.5b2 (60.21–22 W), it is a virtue subordinate to courage, defined as "knowledge making one superior to what naturally happens among both the wise and the base." A page earlier, however, at *Ecl.* 2.7.5b (58.9–14 W), great-spiritedness is listed as one of the "virtues which are neither forms of knowledge nor crafts"; this classes it as one of the capabilities (*dunameis*) which supervene upon virtue in *Ecl.* 2.7.5b4 (62.17–20 W). Compare Cicero's discussion of such "non-intellectual virtues" at 4.30–31, and see further on 3.30.

3.16   **Anyone who is temperate:** The word "temperate" occasions a lengthy excursus on the semantics of *frugalitas*. The argument will not be resumed until 3.18.

the honored title of Lucius Calpurnius Piso: L. Calpurnius Piso Frugi was a prominent political figure of the previous century; see on 3.48.

3.17   **prudence:** Prudence or foresight *(phronēsis)* is that excellence of mind which enables a person to reason properly about what to do in any situation; it might also be called intelligence or good sense. It is not the same as the foresight of 3.30.

regulates and placates one's impulses to act: The defining characteristic of *frugalitas* is seen to be the same as Stoic theory assigns to *sōphrosunē*. So Stob., *Ecl.* 2.7.5b5 (63.15–17 W): "Temperance has as its own principal task to render the impulses stable and to oversee them." See also comm. 4, IIB (on 4.14–22), section 2. For "impulses" *(hormai)*, Cicero here employs an awkward periphrasis *motus animi adpetentes;* in book 4 he will generally use *adpetitus,* but at 4.22 *adpetitio.*

3.18   **take it as a joke if it is no good:** The joke is in fact here, since *nequitia* actually means "being no good." The derivation Cicero offers is essentially correct: *nequitia* is the substantive form of the indeclinable adjective *nequam,* which is equivalent in meaning to *nihili.* There is some strain, however, on Latin usage; although *nequicquam* is formed correctly enough as a negation of *quicquam,* "anything," it is never used in the pronominal sense required here, but only adverbially (= *nequiquam*). The derivation of *nequam* was to be discussed in much the same way in Varro, *On the Latin language* 10.81; had Cicero known this (for Varro's work was not circulated until the following year), he might have been less diffident in introducing the point.

Dionysius of Heraclea: This Dionysius belonged to the first generation of Stoics under Zeno but later defected to the Cyrenaics, supposedly convinced by his own experience of pain that pleasure and pain could not be indifferent (*Tusc.* 2.60, *Ends* 5.94, *Acad. Pr.* 2.71). The comment on *Iliad* 9.646–47 quoted here might belong to either period of his career.

3.19   **the mind . . . when it is puffed out and swollen:** The language of inflammation and swelling refers to the period of greatest emotional disturbance; see further comm. 3, VA (on 3.75–79).

3.20   **envying:** Cicero here coins the word *invidentia* "envying" as a way of resolving a linguistic ambiguity. It is not possible to use the expression *incidere in invidiam* in parallel to the terms already used, since *cadere in invidiam* regularly means to incur envy, rather than to feel it. The new term is based on the verb stem and is thus more suggestive of agency; Cicero uses it again at 4.16, repeating the explanation given here.

Accius: Latin tragedian (170–c. 86); Cicero had met him in his youth (*Brutus* 107). The fragment is known also to Nonius, who identifies the speaker as Oeneus, the father of Tydeus (Warmington 2.470).

3.21   **the death of his friend Callisthenes:** The historian Callisthenes, a nephew of Aristotle and companion of Alexander the Great, was executed by Alexander in 327 for insubordination. Theophrastus wrote a work called *Callisthenes, or On Grief* (*Tusc.* 5.25, D.L. 5.44).

he would also have a tendency to feel pity: Because distress is the genus to which pity belongs (4.16), a capacity for distress implies a capacity for pity.

B.   A More Rhetorical Presentation (3.22–27)

Although I favor the Peripatetics in many areas, the Stoic view of distress is better reasoned than theirs. It is not logical to speak of "moderation" in emotional response if emotions are actually sicknesses, and of all the emotions, distress most clearly resembles a sickness, as indeed its name suggests. In fact, distress and the other emotions are dependent on certain types of belief: they are the result of our unwisdom and our skewed values. Besides, grief is a very painful emotion: how could it be part of an ideal state?

In contrast to the Stoic style of argumentation used in the preceding section, Cicero now presents in his own more expansive manner what is still a Stoic understanding of grief. Although he admires the philosophers whom he calls "Peripatetics" for their preeminence in rhetoric, he cannot accept their position on grief. That position is presented here only in summary form, as a claim that emotions in "moderate amounts" (*mediocritates*) need not be excluded from an account of the best human life. A fuller account of Peripatetic views, and of the reasons for rejecting them, will be given in 3.71–74 and 4.38–57. For the present, Cicero is concerned only to note that there is a difference of view, and to set forth the essentials of the Stoic position.

1.   Causal History of Distress

The claim that the wise person is not subject to distress is made plausible in an initial and general way by reminders of what grief is like: how can anything so terrible be a part of what is supposed to be the best human life? To support the position adequately, however, Cicero needs to show, among other things, that humans have a choice about whether they experience distress or not. For if this is not established, then his opponents will be free to argue that, terrible as distress may be, it is still a part of the life which is the best possible for humans. The discussion here thus gives a brief account of the causal history of distress, the same account Cicero will later defend for emotions in general. This account seeks to establish that the feelings we identify as distress are caused by certain kinds of beliefs which in our best and most natural state we would not hold—and are caused only by these, so that if we do manage to correct our beliefs, we will also eliminate distress.

More particularly, the cause of distress is identified as the agent's belief that some serious evil is present, that evil being of such a kind that it would be appropriate for him to be pained by it. A report in Stobaeus (*Ecl.* 2.7.10b, 90.14–16 W) confirms that this is indeed the Stoic account: "The cause of distress," it says, is "a fresh believing that an evil is present toward which it is appropriate to be contracted." In other words, the explanation for my distress lies in my belief that some present circumstance—something I have learned of very recently and which is still fresh in my mind—is an evil for me, coupled with a further belief that when presented with an evil of this kind, it is appropriate for me to experience mental pain (i.e., to contract the mind-material; see comm. 4, IIB (on 4.14–22), section 1).

This seems a complicated sort of belief to have, and in fact the power of the analysis lies in a further breakdown of it into the occurrence itself—say, a bereavement—and two different beliefs to which one must be antecedently committed in order to experience distress in connection with some class of objects. These components can be laid out as a kind of practical syllogism:

COMPONENT #1: "The death of my child is an evil for me."
COMPONENT #2: "When something which is an evil for me has just occurred, it is appropriate for me to feel mental pain."
OCCURRENT BELIEF: "My child has just died."

CONCLUSION: "It is now appropriate for me to feel mental pain."

Properly speaking, the emotion of distress is just that mental event in which I assent to the conclusion of such a syllogism. For the conclusion always takes the form of an "impulsory" impression, one which indicates what action it is appropriate for me to take at this very moment (Stob., *Ecl.* 2.7.9, 86.17–18 W). Assent to this sort of impression constitutes an impulse (*hormē*), in this case an impulse to feel mental pain. And if one seeks an explanation for such a judgment, the proper place to look is in my adherence to the three premises listed above. For my believing the premises is a necessary condition for accepting the conclusion and will also be sufficient for it, unless other beliefs are present which seem to me more salient (for this possibility see comm. 3, IVc (on 3.64–71)). No other causes need be identified.

Moreover, there is a distinction to be made among the three premises in terms of causative force. For the third premise, the one here labeled "occurrent belief," is a simple matter of fact. It is perfectly correct to treat it as a cause of the distress-impulse; after all, it is what sets things in motion. But it is not what Stoics call a *principal* cause. A push may start a log rolling, but the reason it rolls is that it is round. In the same way, an occurrent impression is the immediate or proximate cause of the impulse, but the best explanation for that impulse lies in the agent's own character (*On Fate* 41). Thus we cannot explain why someone is grieving merely by stating that he is recently bereaved. We must also say what beliefs he holds about bereavement and about appropriate responses to it.

But if it is the case that emotions are caused in this principal sense only by beliefs, then they are also in our power or, as Cicero's predecessors might have said, "up to us" (*eph' hēmin*). For it is a basic principle of Stoicism that one's beliefs are under one's own control in a way that the lives of one's children are not. This is not to deny that the experience of emotion is frequently one of losing control and being carried away against one's better judgment. Stoics merely claim that their causal analysis can explain this aspect of emotion as well; see further comm. 4, IIb (on 4.14–22), section 2. But their theory does assign full responsibility for the emotional movement to the rational mind as a functional unity. So Thyestes has "condemned himself" through his belief that Atreus's crime is a great evil for himself, and Aeetes has brought upon himself the signs of mourning through his beliefs about the importance of kingly rule. This claim, which can also be stated as a claim that grief is *voluntary*, will be developed more fully in 3.64–73.

This interesting causal analysis does not by itself give adequate support to the Stoics' claim that distress is never in accordance with nature, or (what is the same thing) that the wise person is completely free of it. But that conclusion follows easily for Stoics, since within their ethics, ascriptions of value—the class of proposition to which component #1 belongs—are false for all circumstances not under one's own control. And circumstances not under our control, like bereavements or the loss of property, status, or reputation, are the very kinds of circumstances that ordinarily constitute the objects of distress. If we believe them to be evils, it is only because our minds are epistemically flawed: we hold many beliefs which are at variance with one another, and our assents are never thoroughly justified in the way that they would be if we lived up to our fullest potential as rational beings.

The only kinds of circumstances which can be truly said to be evils for us are our own moral failings, and about these we rarely experience distress (3.68–70; cf. the case of Alcibiades, 3.77).

2.   The Fourfold Classification

In 3.24, as later in 4.11–15 and elsewhere, Cicero says firmly that this causal analysis of distress is on the same outlines as the analysis given by Stoics to the three other possible types (*genera*) of emotion, and thus to all emotions, since all can be described as species (*partes*) of the four genera. The types are defined by two kinds of variation in the underlying beliefs: we may think of objects either as evils or as goods, and the impression concerning them may be either that some such circumstance has recently become the case (and so is "present") or that it is about to become the case (and so is "in prospect"). This yields the classification shown in figure 1. This often-repeated fourfold classification constitutes an implicit denial that the two kinds of variation it identifies (good/bad, present/prospective) need make any difference in the causal account. The denial is perhaps ill-judged, since it is only fear and desire which have immediate and obvious implications for action; accordingly it is these two genera which are regularly associated in ancient accounts with the basic impulse-types of pursuit or "reaching" (*orexis*) and avoidance or "withdrawing" (*ekklisis*). Delight and distress are more easily linked to felt sensation, especially as the Greek terms *hēdonē* and *lupe* can also refer to pleasure and pain of body. Some scholars argue that the Stoic account does not, in fact, treat the four generic emotions uniformly but makes fear and desire "primary," with delight and distress "supervening" upon them. Evidence supporting this analysis is gleaned from Stob., *Ecl.* 2.7.10 (88.16–21 W), which says that

THE GENUS-EMOTIONS

	PRESENT	IN PROSPECT
GOOD	DELIGHT	DESIRE
EVIL	DISTRESS	FEAR

FIGURE I

desire and fear come first, one toward the supposed good, the other toward
the supposed evil; delight and distress follow upon these, delight when we
obtain the thing we desired or avoid what we feared, and distress when we
fail to obtain what we desired or when we encounter what we feared.

If the term "follow upon" *(epigignesthai)* is understood to mean "supervene,"
a sense which it carries in some Stoic contexts, then the Stoic position will
be that we are distressed or delighted *only* at circumstances about which we
have previously experienced desire or fear. Compare *Tusc.* 4.12: "gladness is
wildly excited at having obtained some longed-for object." But Cicero's repeated insistence on the fourfold nature of the analysis tells against such a
stringent reading of the evidence. The point of the Stobaeus passage may
be only to establish the sameness of object-type, as at *Tusc.* 4.11: "The things
we fear when they are in prospect are the very things that bring distress
when they are upon us."

For the Peripatetics of the first century see Dyck 1996, 61–64; Moraux 1973, 217–56; and the
works cited under comm. 3, IVᴅ (on 3.71–75). On the causal analysis, Annas 1992, 103–20 provides a useful introductory account, and see further the works cited under comm. 4, IIᴀ (on
4.10–14) and 4, IIʙ (on 4.14–22). On the status of circumstances not under our control (the
Stoic "indifferents"), see the works cited in note 34 to the introduction. On the four genera:
Inwood 1985, 146; Price 1995, 147–49; Nussbaum 1994, 386; Long and Sedley 1987, 1.421.

3.22   **my friends the Peripatetics:** Although the position to be criticized
is already represented by Crantor of the early Academy (3.12), the
phrase *Peripatetici familiares nostri* almost certainly refers to contemporary
figures. Cicero claims to have known more than one Peripatetic
philosopher personally, but the one for whom he expresses the most
admiration is Cratippus, to whose tutelage he had entrusted his son
Marcus in May (*On Divination* 1.5, *Timaeus* 1–2, *Off.* 1.1–2).

   the best of all for eloquence: Cicero's enthusiasm for the school is
directly related to what he sees as its special excellence in rhetoric; see
p. xxvii–xxviii.

3.23   *aegrotatio* ... **suggests bodily pain:** Both *aegritudo* and *aegrotatio* are
simply abstract nouns built on the stem in *aeger* ("sick, feeble"); however, the second of these was restricted in ordinary usage to illness of
body. For specialized uses of the term *aegrotatio* (= "infirmity") see
comm. 4, IIc (on 4.23–33), section 1.

3.24   **belief:** The Stoic *doxa,* sometimes translated "opinion," usually referring, as here, to insufficiently justified belief in non-sages. But Cicero will sometimes use the same word *opinio* for the result of assent in the normative case; see 4.31, 4.80.

There are many species: These are listed in 4.16–21.

apart from reason or heedless of reason or disobedient to reason: All three expressions are equivalent. They indicate, first, that the emotions involve false judgments, contrary to right reason, but they also acknowledge that emotions sometimes seem to run counter to the intentions of the agent, so that one is tempted to think of them as involuntary. This is the same point as is made by "ungoverned," just below, and by "too vigorous" in the standard definitions for emotion and the genus-emotions. See further comm. 4, IIA (on 4.10–14), section 2.

an ungoverned reaching ... anticipated: Cicero's phrase *opinati boni* can mean either "an anticipated good" or "a supposed good." But the notion of futurity is needed here, to establish the correspondence between desire and fear. Compare the definitions at 4.14. For the term "reaching" see further comm. 4, IIB (on 4.14–22), section 1.

3.26   **Thyestes:** Thyestes is the first of four examples showing thoroughly unattractive characters grieving for bad (but psychologically plausible) reasons. Thyestes usurped the throne of Mycenae from his brother Atreus and was later exiled by him. Eventually recalled, he was deceived by Atreus into eating the flesh of his own sons. His reaction betrays his unstable character. Both quotations are usually assigned to Ennius's *Thyestes* (fr. 149 Jocelyn).

Aeetes: Aeetes, the father of Medea, was a son of Helios, the sun god. His grief at being ousted from the throne of Colchis is treated as a clear example of emotional upset occasioned by false values. The quotation is usually assigned to the tragedy *Medus* by Pacuvius (220–c. 130); see Warmington 2.260.

the swelling in your mind had long subsided: The intensity of Aeetes' grief makes it all the more likely that he is grieving for the loss of kingly rule, a recent event, rather than for the loss of his daughter, now long in the past. For "swelling," see comm. 3, VA (on 3.75–79). The evidence of the calendar is not conclusive, since freshness is not strictly a matter of time; compare 3.74–75. But Aeetes is hardly an Artemisia.

3.27   **The tyrant Dionysius:** Dionysius II, Plato's one-time patron, ruled Syracuse 367–357. For the story see also Valerius Maximus 6.9 ext. 6. Cicero wrote to Paetus in the summer of 46 that he meant to follow Dionysius's example himself, as an alternative to suicide (*Fam.* 9.18).

Tarquinius: Tarquinius the Proud ruled as Rome's last king 534–510. The emphasis laid on his expulsion from Rome functions as a compliment to the addressee, who claimed descent from the revolutionary leader L. Junius Brutus. See also 4.2, 4.50.

PART III: HEDONIST APPROACHES

A.   Epicurus and the Cyrenaic Expedient (3.28–31)

There is general agreement that distress takes for its object some circumstance seen as evil. But there is a difference of opinion on the way that object produces distress: Epicurus holds that the response arises when one fixes one's attention upon the misfortune, while the Cyrenaics hold that it arises when one is presented with a misfortune which one did not expect. Consequently the Cyrenaics suggest using the method of "pre-rehearsal" to make oneself aware of all possible misfortunes before any of them can happen. And in fact this method does lessen distress considerably.

Temporarily abandoning his main line of argument, Cicero now considers the contribution of two hedonist schools, those of Epicurus (341–270) and of the Cyrenaics (late 4th–early 3d centuries). Both of these share with the Stoics the view that we do not experience distress unless we become aware of some present circumstance which we regard as a serious evil for ourselves. But they differ from the Stoics and from one another as to the exact sort of awareness that is required, and consequently as to the remedies to be used. Epicurus is especially interested in the manipulation of attention, while the Cyrenaics insist that the key is to remove the element of surprise.

Cicero does have some points to make against all the hedonists equally. He is soon to express strong objections to Epicurus's position on value, and although he does not say so explicitly, we know from the more detailed treatment of the same issues in *On Ends* that some points in his attack are meant to apply to Cyrenaic ethics as well. Also, he intends to argue against the claim made by both hedonist schools that grief arises "by nature" (see on 3.28), a claim which puts them temporarily in the same camp as his Peripatetics opponents of 3.71–74. As a point of entry into these topics, however, he chooses a controversy *between* the two hedonist schools. This concerns the "pre-rehearsal of future ills" (*praemeditatio futurorum malorum*), an old expedient for removing the sting from misfortune by pondering every possible untoward event long in advance. This he represents as the principal

Cyrenaic method for controlling mental pain. As he, too, means to argue for the efficacy of pre-rehearsal, he now sides with the Cyrenaics against Epicurus, who finds the expedient counterproductive.

Although Aristippus and his followers may have defended pre-rehearsal, they can hardly have invented it. Familiarity with the practice is implied already in the quotation from Euripides, and a Pythagorean text (Iamblichus, *Life of Pythagoras* 31.196) suggests that it was known also in southern Italy from an early period. Much of what Cicero says about it occurs together with the same supporting examples and quotations in various consolatory treatises, especially in the pseudo-Plutarchan *Consolation to Apollonius* (Appendix A, passage [g]) and in Seneca's consolations (*Consolation to Polybius* 11, *Ep.* 91.3–12). Some of the same material was used also by earlier Stoic authors as a source of psychological insight. The clearest attestations are for Cicero's older contemporary Posidonius and for Posidonius's teacher Panaetius (Plutarch, *On the Control of Anger* 463d = fr. 115 van Straaten), but the point was probably discussed also in Chrysippus's treatise *On Emotions;* see the evidence cited in Appendix C and D.

The prominence given to the Cyrenaics here must therefore be on account of their differences with Epicurus. By showing that Epicurus's fellow-hedonists hold the "right" position on pre-rehearsal (although they have stumbled on it for the wrong reasons, 3.31), Cicero puts himself in a better position to argue in the next section that Epicurus's approach to consolation is flawed even on its own terms. Having served this purpose, the Cyrenaics will then drop out of the discussion entirely, although pre-rehearsal itself will continue to be of interest even after 3.52.

We have, unfortunately, very little evidence as to how the recommendation reported here might have fitted into the Cyrenaics' overall position on pleasure and pain. Such evidence as survives is best studied in context with the related Epicurean material and has accordingly been reserved for Appendix B.

On pre-rehearsal see esp. Hadot 1969, 60–63. On the Cyrenaics, see the overview in Annas 1993, 227–36; more specialized work is cited in Appendix B.

3.28   **by nature:** Although attributed specifically to Epicurus here and in 3.32, the appeal to nature was made by the Cyrenaics as well: see 3.31, and compare D.L. 2.91: "The wise person will experience fear and grief, since these come about by nature *(phusikōs)*." For Epicurean versions of the claim see Appendix B, passage [b] on natural desires, together with

the material on natural anger cited in comm. 4, IVʙ (on 4.62–79). Motivation for the claim is in part epistemological; see Appendix B.

I knew, when I fathered them: The speaker is identified in 3.58 as
Telamon, but the source of the quotation is unknown (though the
lines are often assigned to Ennius; see Jocelyn, 394–95). Telamon was
the father of Ajax and Teucer; here, he responds to the news of Ajax's
death.

3.29   **I learned this from a wise man:** Euripides fr. 964 Nauck, perhaps
from his *Pirithous.*

a death untimely: Cicero's word *acerbus* regularly carries the meaning "untimely" or "unripe" and is thus an appropriate translation for
aōros here and in 4.18. But the word's usual meaning "bitter" must also
have been felt, especially in this context.

3.30   **Anaxagoras...**"**I knew my child was mortal**": The same anecdote is
told also of Pericles, Xenophon, and Solon (Valerius Maximus 5.10 ext.
1–3, D.L. 2.13).

we who are human ... every event of human life: Cicero connects
the practice of pre-rehearsal especially with this reflection on what it is
to be human. The theme is attested for Crantor, and its association
with pre-rehearsal is likewise traditional; see Appendix A, with passages [c] and [d]. Cicero's polyptoton (*sint omnia homini humana meditata*)
occurs also in ps.-Plutarch (Appendix A, passage [i]; see Appendix A).
Compare also 3.34, "part of human life ... and to endure them is also
human" (*humana humane ferenda*).

wisdom in its noblest and most godlike form: This may be great-
spiritedness as a non-intellectual virtue; see on 3.15 and comm. 4, IIc (on
4.23–33), section 3. Cicero repeatedly associates this quality with pre-
rehearsal and with the argument from the human lot (3.34, 4.62–63).

Therefore, when life is at its best: Here and at 3.65 Cicero quotes
from the comic poet Terence (2d century). In these lines from *Phormio*
(lines 241–46), Demophon reflects, in a context more humorous than
philosophical, that the anguish he now feels over his son's improper
marriage might have been prevented.

3.31   **the countenance of Socrates:** The same anecdote as in Seneca, *On
Anger* 2.7.1.

Crassus the elder: M. Licinius Crassus Agelastos ("the Laughless,"
On Ends 5.92) was a contemporary of the satirist Lucilius (180–102). For
the quotation see Warmington 3.422.

daily pre-rehearsal, as a shield against misfortunes: The importance of a daily routine is stressed also by Seneca also; see *Ep.* 16.1, *On Anger* 3.36.

B.   The Method of Epicurus (3.32–35)

Epicurus holds that the connection between distress and evil circumstances is necessary and immediate. For him, the principal means of eliminating grief lies in manipulating our attention, distracting the mind from evil circumstances and redirecting it toward goods. By his lights, then, the Cyrenaic cure is counterproductive. But he is wrong to deny the efficacy of pre-rehearsal, and wrong also to deny that grief diminishes over time. Meanwhile his claims about "redirecting" are unrealistic. How can one simply forget what one believes to be a serious evil?

Epicurus's position on the causation of mental pain has already been stated in 3.28. Distress occurs when a person comes to believe that some evil is present to him, provided only that the object is a "relatively great" evil *(maius malum)*, i.e., one greater than any goods measured against it, and that the person "directs his attention" toward it *(intueri)*. Given these conditions, mental pain is a natural and necessary result of events in our lives. Nonetheless, we can always prevent even the most serious of perceived evils from causing us pain, since it is we who control where we direct our attention. When troubling circumstances are present, we have the power to disregard them and to concentrate instead on pleasures of various kinds, either those we now have or others available to us through memory or anticipation.

This recommendation for the management of distress runs counter to the method of pre-rehearsal attributed to the Cyrenaics. Pondering in advance on all possible misfortunes would mean directing the mind toward evils, rather than goods, increasing our total experience of pain and decreasing our happiness. This would be "voluntary misery," suffering which we not only could have avoided, but have actually brought upon ourselves through our own efforts. Epicurus also contradicts a Cyrenaic claim when he insists that mental pain is not diminished by the passage of time. For the Cyrenaics are supposed to have held that all movements of the mind diminish with time. It is for this reason that they claim we do not derive pleasure from the memory or expectation of goods (Appendix B, passage [i]). Epicurus must argue against this claim if he is to maintain his own view that remembered pleasures can be used to counterbalance present distress. But if pleasures can continue to be felt through memory, then pain can do so as well. This leaves Epicurus the odd man out among all the schools treated here, for Peripatetics and Stoics will also assume that grief diminishes, though their treatment of the matter is otherwise quite different. See 3.52–54, 58, 74–75.

The account that Cicero gives here should be compared with what he says elsewhere concerning Epicurus's views on memory and attention. Note especially *On Ends* 1.57:

> It is in our power both to bury adversity in lasting forgetfulness and to remember what is favorable with sweet pleasure. When we fix the mind's attention sharply *(acri animo et attento intuemur)* on past events, the result is distress if those events were bad, but if they were good, then gladness.

The emphasis on events of the past and future is maintained also in the answering passage in *On Ends* 2 (2.104–6) as well as here (3.33) and more explicitly in *Tusc.* 5.96. The question raised here, though, is whether the mind's power to disregard certain objects is sufficient to soften the impact of *any* serious misfortunes. The Epicureans appear to be serious in claiming that it is; see further Appendix B. Cicero disagrees. Compare his exclamations about the difficulty of controlling memory in *On Ends* 2.104–5 and, on a different but related point, his teasing of Cassius in *Fam.* 15.16.1–2.

The evidence for Epicurus's position is treated in Appendix B, with references to the secondary literature.

3.33   **distracting … and redirecting:** Cicero repeats "redirecting" as a kind of refrain; see 3.35, 3.37. This is his usual manner when attacking a term favored by his opponent; compare his handling of "limit" and "moderation" when dealing with the Peripatetics in 4.40–41. But the surviving Epicurean texts do not supply us with any *pair* of terms used in quite the way indicated here for *avocatio* and *revocatio* (although *epiballein* is a reasonably close equivalent for the second; compare Appendix B, passage [g]). Cicero perhaps has in mind some catchwords of the Latin-speaking Epicureans mentioned at 4.6–7.

   the Epicureans have a style of their own: Stylistic inelegance is one of Cicero's regular complaints against the Epicureans, especially those writing in Latin (*On Ends* 1.15, *Tusc.* 1.6, 2.7–8). See also 4.6–7.

3.34   **the regular restrictions:** Unlike the immortals (3.36), humans have life under a sort of contract, which stipulates that we do not keep it forever, and also that each of us must encounter some suffering in life. The

language is reminiscent of Cicero's consolatory letter to Titius, *Fam.*
5.16.2, which calls such arguments "much-used."

>   **part of human life, and ... to endure them ... is also human:** See
on 3.30.

3.35   **contrary to nature ... which nature has provided:** The first "nature"
refers merely to consistently observed facts, which Epicurus's theory
contradicts; the second adds the providential notion that the diminishment of grief is in our best interests.

C.   What Epicurus Means by "The Good" (3.35–46)

*Moreover, in redirecting us toward goods, Epicurus can only be thinking of bodily plea-
sures, since—whatever Epicureans may say—that is his notion of the good. But it is absurd
to think of consoling extreme distress by means of bodily pleasure.*

While Cicero has grave doubts about the viability of Epicurus's method
of consolation, his real objection is to the hedonist's account of the good.
For Epicurus differs both from the Stoics and from the old Academy insofar as he bases his ethics on the assumption that humans have no intrinsic
good except pleasure. In instructing sufferers to direct their minds away
from evil and toward the good, Epicurus can only mean "toward pleasure."
Moreover, Epicurus derives all pleasures from movements and conditions
of the body: there are no strictly mental pleasures. His recommendation
thus amounts to saying that we should remedy our most devastating griefs
by replacing them with simple creature comforts.

Cicero is unusually careful in this section to bolster his description of
Epicurus's views with evidence drawn from actual Epicurean sources. There
is some reason for this caution, since it is by no means obvious that that
philosopher would subscribe to the position on grief which Cicero here attributes to him. The most widely known Epicurean texts deny that happiness can be derived solely or reliably from the pleasures of the flesh (*Ep. Men.*
131–32, *KD* 8, 10), and the personal austerity of their founder was clearly a
point of pride for latter-day Epicureans (See for instance D.L. 10.11, with
Appendix B, passage [f], an anecdote repeated in many sources). Epicurus
does say that mental pleasures depend on those of body, and that terms like
"goodness," "virtue," and "wisdom" have no meaning except insofar as
they specify certain means of acquiring pleasures of body or mind. But he
also holds that mental pleasures, though referred to the body (3.41), are
both different in kind from pleasures of body and greater than any bodily

pleasure (Appendix B, passage [h]). It is most unlikely, then, that that he would in fact have recommended honeyed wine as an appropriate cure for grief; indeed, he too should expect this to be ineffective.

But it is not from ignorance of Epicurus's actual views that Cicero credits him with this absurdity. He knows perfectly well what Epicurus says about the mind's overriding the body, since he has recently treated this very point in *On Ends* 1.55–56. His claim is that in grounding all pleasure in bodily sensation, Epicurus has *in effect* offered Andromache the honeyed wine, whether he admits to it or not. The aim of the attack, then, is to expose a weakness in Epicurus's position. The hedonist is charged not with what he says specifically on this topic, but with what he can consistently say given his other views on the nature of the good (compare *Tusc.* 5.26–28). If mental pleasures are reducible to pleasures of body, then some version of the honeyed-wine consolation emerges; but if they are not reducible, then it is up to Epicurus to provide some account of the distinctive nature of mental pleasures which will not make any use of the broad teleological claims which he finds so distasteful. Whether or not Epicurus himself attempted a solution, Cicero clearly believes that the Epicureans among his contemporaries have not confronted the issue: they will be unhappy with the implication he draws but unable to show why their system does not commit them to it.

Recent accounts of Epicurus's position include Striker 1993; Annas 1993, 236–44; Mitsis 1988; see also Long and Sedley 1987, 1.121–25 and, for the intellectual context, Gosling and Taylor 1982. On Zeno of Sidon, see Sedley 1989, 103–7, together with the evidence collected in Angeli and Colaizzo 1979. For Cicero's handling of the issues, see the judicious assessment by Stokes 1995.

3.36   **Courage . . . will instill in you . . . a great spirit:** For this connection between courage and greatness of spirit see on 3.15.

3.37   **self-sufficient:** Self-sufficiency (*autarkeia*) was listed as a necessary feature of the best human life since Aristotle (*NE* 1.7).

3.38   **Zeno, a sharp-tongued old fellow:** Zeno of Sidon, Epicurean scholarch at the beginning of the century and a voluminous writer. Cicero mentions having learned from him also in *Acad.* 1.46 and *On Ends* 1.16. In *ND* 1.59, he describes his speech as "clear, grave, and elegant," but this impression is counteracted by the report that he used to call Socrates a *scurra* ("gadabout") and referred to Chrysippus as "Chrysippa" (*ND* 1.93). As the occasion of his hearing Zeno in person was over thirty years earlier, and as he claims a high degree of accuracy, we should probably infer that Cicero supplements his memory with a written source, perhaps Zeno's own *On Ends*.

The happy person: The content of the quotation, though not the wording, is similar to Epicurus, *Ep. Men.* 133. See also *Vatican Saying* 33, and the fragment of *On the End* quoted by Plutarch in *That a Follower of Epicurus Cannot Live Pleasantly* 1089d (fr. 68 Usener).

3.39   **Thyestes . . . Aeetes . . . Telamon:** See on 3.26 and 3.28 **I knew.**

Can this be Telamon: This quotation and the one following must come from one of the several old Latin dramas which dealt with the legends of Telamon and his sons Ajax and Teucer. See Jocelyn, 395.

3.40   **That is not what the word "pleasure" means:** The point is argued at length in *On Ends* 2.10–16, 30.

turn our thoughts: *Animum traducere,* an alternative phrase for "redirecting" as in 3.33.

3.41   **that very book which contains the whole of your teaching:** Epicurus's work *On the End;* Cicero means the ethical teaching.

Indeed, I do not know: The first portion of the fragment (down to "forms") appears also in Athenaeus 12.546e (fr. 67 Usener) and in D.L. 10.6.

3.42   **Empty phrases . . . to spout words:** The contemptuous tone is as in *On Ends* 1.42 "the glitter of the word" and 2.48 "they are making an empty noise." For the thought, compare Athenaeus 12.546f (fr. 409 Usener), "The beginning and root of every good is the pleasure of the belly: what is 'wise' and 'extraordinary' have reference to this."

3.43   **a sturgeon:** The sturgeon (*acupenser*) had become proverbial as a luxury fish, especially in association with one Gallonius, satirized by Lucilius as a gourmand (Warmington 3.62–65). Thus in *On Ends* 2.23–25, 90–91, Epicureans are taunted with promoting the tastes of such as Gallonius, or simply with indulging a fondness for sweets, while Epicurus himself is charged with "living like Gallonius, but talking like [L. Calpurnius] Piso Frugi."

the notes of the organ: The hydraulic organ, invented at Alexandria in the third century.

Something even better? Sexual indulgence; cf. 3.41. Cicero was not above a private joke on Epicurus's own sexual activities (*Fam.* 7.26.1) but in his public works is generally more circumspect.

3.44   **By god, it is not lineage:** The title of the play is unknown; see Jocelyn, 394–95.

Once wealthy, I am now bereft: This and the three following quotations are from Ennius's tragedy *Andromache* (fr. 27 Jocelyn). Andromache suffers the worst that can happen to a human being: having lost home and family (whom she here laments) in the fall of Troy, she is now about to witness the brutal murder of her infant son, then to be carried off into sexual slavery.

3.45   **would-be Euphorions:** The learned and allusive poetry of the third-century scholar Euphorion was admired and imitated by some of Cicero's younger contemporaries, notably Cornelius Gallus and Helvius Cinna.

He understands that sudden events are always harder to bear: To be sure, the fall of Troy was hardly sudden. But the luxury surrounding Ennius's Andromache had made destruction seem less likely than it really was.

3.46   **some perfume . . . something on the sweet side:** Cicero mocks a regular Epicurean usage. Gr. *hēdonē*, "pleasure," is built on the same root as the adjective *hēdus*, "sweet," and the latter frequently appears in Epicurus in reference to any pleasurable sensation; so also, in Lucretius, the Latin equivalents *suavis* and *dulcis* (e.g. Lucretius 2.1–7). The word meaning "perfume" (*heducrum*, Gr. *hēduchroun*) is literally "sweet-skin." "Tastes, and the embrace of bodies": Paraphrased from 3.41.

D.   Response to Epicurus's Defenders (3.47–51)

Epicurus's claim that the absence of pain is the limit of pleasure is just wrong; and his statements about virtue, although they sound very noble, do not represent any real philosophical commitment. It is not partisanship that makes me criticize him in this way: such feeling has no place in philosophical discussion, and I myself am not committed to any dogma.

An unnamed interlocutor, introduced already in 3.46, now expresses two objections to Cicero's handling of Epicurean ethics: first, that he has not given a correct account of what Epicurus means by pleasure; and second, that he has not given Epicurus credit for his stand on the conventional virtues. Cicero dismisses both claims briskly, and the argumentation is much less patient than in book 2 of *On Ends*. To the first, he replies that while he is aware of Epicurus's views on pleasures of state ("katastematic" pleasures), he finds them self-contradictory and unconvincing: a pleasure which is not a movement (a "pleasurable tickling") cannot properly be called a pleasure at all. To the second, he replies that while Epicurus's claims about virtue are indeed attractive, they cannot be rendered consistent with his hedonistic premises. They are nothing more than philosophical window-dressing.

Both these points have already been treated in much more detail in *On Ends,* and neither bears more than tangentially on the subject now in hand.

Why then does Cicero see fit to raise the same issues again here? The answer must have to do with the rhetoric of his attack in the preceding section. Courtesy requires an acknowledgment that his opponents are morally serious individuals who adhere to Epicurus's ethics not because they are addicted to the pleasures of the table or of sex but because they respect his analysis of human motivations and share his commitment to decent and upright conduct. Compare *On Ends* 1.25, where Cicero insists that *KD* 5, Epicurus's endorsement of conventional morality, is the chief reason for the popularity of his system at Rome. Thus the Cyrenaics do not come in for criticism here. Their account of the good is by Cicero's standards even more reprehensible than that of Epicurus (*On Ends* 2.39–41), but they do not make any particular claim to uphold conventional morality and are for that reason less dangerous.

The response to imagined criticism at 3.50–51 is a transparent rhetorical ploy, giving the author an opportunity to reassert his official neutrality after this foray into polemic. The aggrieved animosity of his putative self-defense contrasts markedly with the respectful good humor of the letters to Roman Epicureans of his own class: Trebatius Testa (*Fam.* 7.12), Papirius Paetus (*Fam.* 9.25–26), Cassius (*Fam.* 15.16), Atticus himself (*Att.* 1.17.5, 4.6.1, but 14.20.5 voices real hurt). Greeks are a different matter: see the controversy surrounding Epicurus's house in Athens, recorded in *Att.* 5.11.6 and *Fam.* 13.1.

For Epicureans at Rome see Griffin 1997 and 1995, together with Castner 1988.

3.47   "**once pain is gone, pleasure does not increase**": Epicurus, *KD* 3 and 18; cf. *On Ends* 1.37–39, 2.10–11.

3.48   **Gaius Gracchus:** G. Sempronius Gracchus, tribune 123–122; his legislation provided grain to citizens at a subsidized price. L. Calpurnius Piso Frugi was consul in 133, during the tribunate of Gaius's brother Tiberius.

3.49   "**it is not possible to live pleasantly except by the exercise of virtue**": The virtues are instrumental goods (*KD* 5, *Ep. Men.* 132); cf. 3.42 "the means to bring about those pleasures." Cicero repeatedly criticizes the doctrine: *On Ends* 2.44–74, *Tusc.* 5.26–27, *Off.* 3.116–19.

3.51   **Marcus Cato and Lucius Lentulus:** M. Porcius Cato "the Censor" (234–149) met some senatorial opposition in his campaign for the destruction of Carthage. Nothing further is known of his disagreements with L. Cornelius Lentulus Lupus (consul 156); for the latter's checkered political career, see Valerius Maximus 6.9.10.

not one they would dare to proclaim in the Senate: The same challenge is put to Torquatus in *On Ends* 2.74.

will yield willingly to anyone who speaks the truth: That is, to anyone who speaks what has a plausible claim to be the truth, as at 4.7 and 4.47. This is Cicero's usual philosophical stance; see comm. 3, Ic (on 3.12–13).

PART IV: THE STOIC POSITION DEFENDED

A.   The Belief That One's Misfortunes Are Serious Ills (3.52–61)

Although the Cyrenaic expedient is effective against distress, only an analysis in terms of belief can provide a satisfactory explanation for that effectiveness. In reality, pre-rehearsal works because those who have pondered events in advance do not see them as serious evils. Similarly, grief diminishes over time because we change our estimate of the seriousness of the misfortune as other life-experiences assume a position of salience. The standard consolatory arguments and examples are effective because they convince the sufferer that the misfortune is more endurable, and thus less serious, than originally thought. Chrysippus's Academic critics are wrong to deny this.

Cicero now returns to the efficacy of Cyrenaic pre-rehearsal and to two other observed phenomena of grief: its tendency to diminish over time and its responsiveness to certain standard forms of consolation. All these can, in his view, be accounted for by alterations in the sufferer's belief that a serious evil has occurred—the first of the two components identified in the Stoics' causal analysis; see comm. 3, IIb (on 3.22–27), section 1. If, as the Stoics claim, this belief is a necessary condition for distress, then it is no surprise if arguments or expedients which lessen our commitment to it prove to be effective in consolation. It does not follow, of course, that the evaluation-belief is also sufficient for distress to occur in any given circumstance. The Stoic position is that it is sufficient only if conjoined with a corresponding belief about appropriateness, to be discussed in the section following.

In revisiting the point about pre-rehearsal, Cicero seeks to show that while those who have not used the method do experience distress in greater degree than those who have, this is not because of some mysterious element of "suddenness," but because they hold different opinions: they have never revised their estimate of the seriousness of the kind of misfortune they are encountering, and they perhaps think that they are themselves to blame for failing to act in some way which would prevent it. An explanation in terms of belief is also attempted for the phenomenon of diminishment. Diminishment in distress, as exampled by the former citizens of Carthage, appears to present a case in which an emotion disappears even while the complex belief posited as a sufficient cause for it remains in force. Cicero argues that the belief does not, in fact, remain the same: when the events are no longer recent or "fresh," we cease to regard them as serious evils. A third phenomenon to be considered is the efficacy of certain standard consolatory arguments. As these are addressed primarily to our beliefs, the very fact that they are effective—provided it *is* a fact—will tend to support the Stoic analysis. On all these points, Cicero is likely to have derived at least some of his argumentation from Chrysippus's treatment of the causes of grief. For evidence on this point, see Appendix C and D.

We see in this section how the composition of consolatory epistles and treatises might itself become an object of study. Such works were undoubtedly not intended as serious philosophy on their own account: surviving examples seem deliberately to soften any doctrinal commitment so as not to alienate those in need of consolation. For philosophers, however, the works might still hold considerable interest, not only in that they recorded a body of accepted views on grief, but also insofar as an analysis of the arguments to which grief responds provides evidence for the cognitive structure of grief. A lively episode in this ongoing discussion is reported in 3.59–60, where a question is raised between philosophers of different schools concerning the efficacy of one particular consolatory tactic. Significantly, the challenge is made against Chrysippus by Carneades, an Academic philosopher and regular critic of Chrysippus's views, who is known to have argued the very claim Cicero attacks in 3.52. As a skeptic, Carneades may be engaged solely in a destructive venture, but Chrysippus himself must be defending a positive view as to the efficacy of the tactic in question.

The section also provides some historical information on the form and content of various kinds of consolatory treatise. The most extensive report is about a work by Clitomachus (Hasdrubal), addressed to his fellow-Carthaginians to console them for the loss of their city. Recording a disputation given orally by his own teacher Carneades, Clitomachus organized his work around a thesis stated as the interlocutor's own view, with the principal speaker giving arguments in the negative. The resulting treatise must have been similar in format to the *Tusculan Disputations* themselves. Poverty and failure to gain public office are also mentioned as standard topics for works of consolation. See 3.81, which gives a longer list and indicates that the one-book *schola* was in fact the standard format.

Ioppolo 1980 gives a constructive account of Carneades' position, but cf. Glucker 1978, 393–94. Scourfield 1993, 15–23, gives an overview of the consolatory tradition in antiquity; see also 113–21. More detailed treatments include Johann 1968 and Kassel 1958. Hutchinson 1998, 49–77, comments on consolatory letters by Cicero and his correspondents.

3.52   **what is unforeseen strikes us with greater force:** The remark was also known to Posidonius; see Appendix D, passage [g].

    Thus the cause of distress ... one's mind: These words appear in the manuscripts at the end of 3.55, where they are clearly out of place. I have followed Dougan in locating them here because they are needed to provide the right referent for *quod* at the beginning of 3.53. Given the content of 3.53–54, "the proof of *this*" ought to mean "the proof of the importance of freshness, as opposed to unexpectedness"; without the inserted lines, however, "this" must refer to the heightening of distress by guilt, which is no longer at issue in the section following.

    the cause ... is not solely that the events are unexpected. Carneades argued the reverse, that "in significant misfortunes ... it is unexpectedness that is the sole and entire cause of distress and dispiritedness" (Plutarch, *On Tranquillity of Mind* 474ef).

3.53   **the people of Carthage ... many Macedonians ... Corinthians:** Macedon was conquered in 160, Corinth and Carthage both in 146. As Cicero's visit to Greece took place in 79–77, the length of time required to obliterate grief may, for all we learn here, be very great indeed. Argos and Sicyon are cities in the Peloponnese.

3.54   **Clitomachus:** His Carthaginian birth-name was Hasdrubal. D.L. 4.67 reports that he taught philosophy at Carthage before coming to Athens, where he studied under Carneades and eventually succeeded him as head of the Academy. For negative argumentation in the skeptical Academy compare *Tusc.* 5.11, 5.83, and see note 17 to the introduction. But Carneades might also argue in favor of a position, still without being committed to it (*Acad. Pr.* 2.139). Compare Cicero's own philosophical stance, comm. 3, Ic (on 3.12–13).

    The opinion stated as the thesis: The expression used here *(ita positum esset, videri)* matches Cicero's own phraseology for the interlocutor's statement of the thesis at *Tusc.* 1.9, 3.7, 4.8, 5.12.

    experience teaches us the lesson: Works of consolation regularly urge the mourner to do for himself by reasoning what time will eventually do in any case; so *Fam.* 5.16.5–6. This need not imply that time in and of itself effects the cure; rather, experience brings about a change in our beliefs.

3.55   **Why, then, is there any need:** The interlocutor's point is that if it is primarily the passage of time which causes distress to vanish, then consolations will presumably be unnecessary or ineffective, but this is not the case. The efficacy of consolations is at this point assumed; it will not be seriously challenged until 3.73.

nothing should strike a person unawares: The mourner is reminded that the circumstances over which he is distressed are a regular part of human life (whether or not he himself has actually anticipated them), and is thus encouraged to take the larger view.

3.56   **Socrates at one point, Diogenes at another:** Both are mentioned as examples of satisfied poverty. Diogenes of Sinope (4th century) was the earliest of the "Cynic philosophers"; he demonstrated his independence of conventional norms in part by living with a minimum of material possessions.

the familiar line of Caecilius: Caecilius Statius (d. 168) was a comic playwright, cited also in *Tusc.* 1.31 and, with less approval, at 4.68.

Gaius Fabricius: As censor in 275, he expelled a man from the Senate for possessing excessive amounts of silver tableware. Thereafter he became a favorite example of frugality in high station: see for instance Seneca, *Ep.* 120.6, *On Providence* 3.6.

3.57   **those familiar anapestic verses:** The content is that of Euripides, *Iphigenia at Aulis* 15–18 (Agammemnon speaks). But Cicero is probably paraphrasing a Latin version of the play, perhaps that of Ennius; see Jocelyn, 322.

3.58   **Telamon ... Theseus ... Anaxagoras:** The examples are repeated from 3.28–30.

3.59   **my friend Antiochus:** Cicero had studied with Antiochus of Ascalon (on whom see p. xxiv–xxv) for six months in 79 (*Brutus* 315). For Carneades see on 3.54. Antiochus cannot have known him in person, but many such anecdotes must have been preserved orally and in the writings of such as Clitomachus.

No mortal lives: From Euripides's *Hypsipyle,* fr. 757 Nauck, a warhorse of the consolatory tradition. For a literal rendering of the Greek see Appendix A, passage [f].

in vain: Cicero's *nequiquam* has no equivalent in the Greek.

3.61   **the ... word *lupē* ... is derived from ..."dissolving":** The same etymology appears in Plato, *Cratylus* 419c; Stobaeus attributes it to Cleanthes (*Florilegium* 108.59 Meineke = *SVF* 1.575). For Chrysippus's use of etymologies to explore psychological concepts, see also Galen, *PHP* 3.5.25–28.

an honorable and illustrious life: This restates in abbreviated form an argument from *Tusc.* 1.109–10. The point made there is closely connected with the argument of 3.3–4: True glory, which is the praise of the wise and not that of the many, is a concomitant of right actions, "virtue's shadow, as it were," and either this or the actions themselves may be a powerful source of consolation to those who have earned it. Much if not all of this is Stoic material; see the commentary to book 3 preface, section 2, and Appendix C, passage [o].

or, at most, stings them very lightly: Refers to the same vestigial feelings as mentioned in 3.13 and 3.83.

B.   The Belief That Grief Is Appropriate (3.61–64)

Most people are of the opinion that it is appropriate to grieve when one is experiencing some serious misfortune, in particular the death of a family member. Grief depends on this belief just as much as on the one discussed above.

The second of the two belief-components posited in the causal analysis of 3.24–25 always includes the predicate "it is appropriate for me" (*kathēkei moi*). It is this component which enables an evaluative belief ("my present circumstances are evil for me") also to suggest an action, the action of grieving. Cicero now seeks to show that this theoretical construct, like the first, is an accurate description of beliefs people actually hold. It may be true that most people are not aware of holding any such view; nonetheless, patterns of behavior regularly observed in times of grief betray that the commitment to it is nearly universal.

The inclusion of beliefs about appropriateness helps to fit the analysis of emotional impulses into the general Stoic theory of action. In general for Stoics, every action is the result of assent to an "impulsory" impression as to what it is appropriate for oneself to do (Stob., *Ecl.* 2.7.9, 86.18 W). Thus walking, for instance, is the direct result of assent to the proposition that "it is now appropriate for me to walk." This can hardly mean that I walk *only* out of a sense of duty (i.e., against my own inclinations); rather my inclination itself results from my believing (rightly or not) that walking is suitable to my own nature at this time. If this belief happens to be true, the result is an "appropriate action" (*kathēkon*). But the action-syllogism which generates distress can never produce a true conclusion, since at least one of its premises will always be false. In most cases, the first or evaluative component is false: we are wrong to think that events outside our own control can be serious evils for us. And as we learn later (4.61, 4.67), the theory Cicero is following made the appropriateness component always false where present evils are concerned. Thus grieving can never be an appropriate action.

What kind of action is distress? What is it that the grieving person believes it is appropriate for her to do? There seem to be two answers. The passage here, with its talk of scratching one's cheeks and smearing oneself with dirt, strongly suggests that component #2 directs us to perform such externally observable actions as are regularly practiced in one's own culture. That is, the bereaved person believes, consciously or not, that "when an evil occurs of the kind I have recently experienced, it is appropriate for me to smear myself with dirt." Cicero takes rhetorical advantage of the fact that in the ancient Mediterranean such "despicable" displays of grief were largely restricted to women, while the audience for which he writes consists primarily of males of the upper classes. But some less extravagant displays were expected of men as well: they might, for instance, refrain from appearing in public, and they might weep for a time (Seneca, *On Tranquillity of Mind* 15.6, *Ep.* 63.1–3).

But this way of describing the action that is grief may not seem to us to grasp what is most important about our emotional experience. Even if Demosthenes does not cancel his dinner party, he might still be expected to grieve inwardly; that is, to experience mental pain. This understanding of what it is to grieve is better described by the formulation of component #2 given in 3.25 ("that it is appropriate for him to suffer") or later in 4.67 ("it can never be a right action to contract the spirits"). For "contracting the spirits" is the Stoics' regular description in psychophysical terms of the inner feeling which we identify as distress. See further comm. 4, IIB (on 4.14–22), section 1, and on 3.83 and on 4.14–15.

See esp. Inwood 1985, 42–101, more briefly Brennan 1998, 28–29; also Engberg-Pedersen 1990, 126–40.

3.61   **it is right, and an appropriate and proper thing:** As at 3.25, Cicero renders *kathēkein* more than once, here not only as *oportere* but also as *rectum esse* and *ad officium pertinere*. The impression created is perhaps overly emphatic.

3.62   **for grief tear often:** *Iliad* 10.15. Cicero quotes from the *Night-Alarm* of Accius (see on 3.20), Warmington 2.490.

       the witticism of Bion: Bion of Borysthenes, the third-century satirist and wit. Diogenes Laertius, who reports a number of similar anecdotes about him, says that he was for a time a Cynic philosopher and as such favored impassivity (*apatheia*, D.L. 4.50).

3.63   **Aeschines criticizes Demosthenes:** *Against Ctesiphon* 77. The passage is quoted at more length by ps.-Plutarch, Appendix A, passage [k].

Bellerophon: *Iliad* 6.201–2. Bellerophon grieves after becoming "hated by all the gods."

Niobe: Niobe serves as an example of parental grief already in *Iliad* 24.602–17. The rock formation suggestive of a weeping woman was a familiar landmark in Magnesia in Asia Minor (Pausanius 1.21.3).

Hecuba: After the fall of Troy, Hecuba witnesses the death and enslavement of her children. Her transformation is mentioned in Euripides, *Hecuba* 1265.

Medea's nurse: From Ennius's *Medea in Exile* (fr. 106 Jocelyn), adapted from Euripides, *Medea* 57–58. Cicero's fondness for Ennius's *Medea* plays may be compared with that of Chrysippus for the Euripidean version; D.L. 7.180, Galen *PHP* 3.3.13–22, 4.6.19–23.

C.   Why Grief Must Be Considered Voluntary (3.64–71)

Grief is in fact up to us: we choose to feel it, and we can also choose to lay it aside. It is not caused by the event itself, but rather by particular beliefs which we can and should eliminate. This is proven by the fact that people do not always grieve over their misfortunes: special circumstances may occupy their thoughts, or a person may not have the belief that sorrow is appropriate.

Having established a near-universal commitment to the two belief-components identified as causes in 3.24–25, Cicero is ready to insist that distress is fully a matter of choice. Again, humans do not necessarily realize that grief is something they undertake voluntarily, and yet a careful study of conduct in times of distress will show that the occurrence or non-occurrence of grief is in fact dependent on our beliefs and these only. For even the most grievous of situations is not always met by a grieving response: where even one of the necessary belief-components is lacking, or is outweighed by competing considerations, distress does not arise. Thus the principal cause of the emotion will always be attributable to us, and what is attributable to us may also be called in Latin *voluntarius* or voluntary.

Although Cicero's argumentation in this section is not as lucid as we might wish, his principal contention is firmly in accordance with Chrysippus's general position on moral responsibility (see esp. *On Fate* 39–43). This position gives voluntariness (in Greek "what is up to us," *to eph' hēmin*) quite different implications from what the same expression might have in the context of an argument against determinism. For those arguments as we know them from Lucretius (2.251–93) are premised on the capacity of humans to generate uncaused volitional movements. Neither Cicero nor Chrysippus will grant that we have any such capacity. If our impulses are up to us, it is because we assent to impulsory impressions in accordance with our own moral character (as described in comm. 3, IIA (on 3.13–21), section 1). And if our moral character is the cause of impulse, then we ourselves are the cause, for the person herself is not to be distinguished from that set of beliefs, experiences, and predispositions which make up her character. But emotion is a species of impulse. The Stoic position is thus that an agent is responsible for having "willed" her grief just because she is the owner of certain beliefs which tend to give rise to grief. Attempts at therapy must accordingly address themselves to the underlying beliefs.

To render Greek *eph' hēmin* ("up to us" or "in our power"), Cicero uses either the ablative of the noun *voluntas* or the equivalent adjective *voluntarius*, both of which are here translated "voluntary." *Voluntas* already had a long history in Latin; in particular, Cicero will have been familiar with its use in legal contexts, where it regularly means "intention." Already in Lucretius it refers to a mental event or faculty, that in us which enables us to move ourselves, exempting ourselves from the causal nexus. But this latter notion is not required here, where the relevant faculty is that of judgment (*iudicium*; cf. Seneca, *On Anger* 2.3.5 *voluntate et iudicio*). The philosophical notion associated with the term is clearly somewhat variable at this period. Compare Cicero's use of *voluntas* (in the nominative) for the well-reasoned affect *boulēsis*, at 4.12 and 4.34.

The first of Cicero's examples of grieving behavior establishes that humans are at least sometimes aware of their own decision to grieve. Menedemus, the "self-tormentor" of Terence's comedy, can even verbalize his decision to grieve and the obligation-beliefs which lie behind it. To be sure, the example does not prove that grief is always a conscious choice. It does suggest, however, that there are no necessary conditions for grief which lie outside the agent's own control.

Other examples in 3.65–67 are chosen to support the slightly different claim that nothing outside the agent's own control is sufficient to produce distress. What is needed for this are instances in which people fail to experience grief despite being in the kinds of circumstances which might be expected to compel that emotion. Thus the Greek warriors at Troy are able to lay aside their grief for fallen comrades because it is in their wartime interests to do so, and the followers of Pompey concentrate on securing their own safety before reacting emotionally to his death. Others fail to grieve because their extensive experience with misfortune has made them less responsive or, in the last example of 3.66, merely because they "realize that grieving is futile." In none of these cases is the absence of distress a matter of sheer resolution on the part of agents determined to suppress it. Rather, the persons involved do not experience the expected emotion (or do not experience it at the expected time) because of differences in their beliefs or in their manner of evaluating competing considerations. In nonsages this may mean experiencing a different emotion, as did the adherents of Pompey. But the theory does not require that one emotion be driven out by another. In fact, the wise person will learn to attend to "any and all occasions" in such a way that no emotional impression can strike him as true.

A question then arises about the sufficiency of the beliefs identified in the causal account. If mere beliefs are enough to generate emotion, runs the objection, then anyone who believes that his circumstances are very bad for him should be deeply distressed. But philosophers are known to believe that lack of wisdom is a serious evil. Why, then, do they not become upset when they consider that their own wisdom is defective? This astutely framed counterexample turns out to serve the Stoics' own case, for Cicero uses it to insist upon the importance of the second of the two belief-components. Both, it emerges, are necessary: if the belief that grief is appropriate is lacking, or can be removed, then the belief that one's ills are serious will indeed not be sufficient for grief. See further comm. 3, Va (on 3.75–79) and, for earlier Stoic uses of this argument, Appendix D.

The examples from Roman history in 3.70–71 appear at least initially to support the same contention. Again, it is the second belief-component which is lacking. As aristocrats and military commanders, the men named—all familiar models of staunch Republican morality—have been schooled to believe that grief is never appropriate for them. Thus, it is argued, they do not and indeed cannot generate that emotion, even in the most compelling circumstances. As at 3.62, however, we may wonder whether Cicero is thinking of grief as inner experience or as public display. The observation that grieving and sorrow are "not a man's part" would appear to indicate the latter, since it is the public display which was the special province of women. But it is primarily the inner experience which might be thought injurious to the function of the commander or magistrate.

Chrysippus's position on moral responsibility and causal determinism has recently been treated in detail in Bobzien 1998; see esp. 234–89. See also Long and Sedley 1987, 1.392–94, which also gives the relevant texts, and Inwood 1985, 42–66, 129–32. For the usage of *voluntas* and related words see Dihle 1982, 133–42. Runia 1989 and Classen 1989 comment on Cicero's handling of Aristotle and Theophrastus in 3.69.

3.65   **Chremes, I have decided:** Terence, *Self-Tormentor* 147–48 and 135, the same quotation as in *On Ends* 5.28.

This man ... decides: Cicero assumes that Menedemus's words are sincere and his thought processes psychologically plausible.

We see men fall in numbers: *Iliad* 19.226–29; the speaker is Odysseus, consoling Achilles for the death of Patroclus.

one would not ever cease: Assume "if one were to begin." The subjunctive *possit* represents a potential optative in the Greek.

3.66   **Pompey's men saw him collapse:** When the fugitive Pompey arrived in Egypt, he was met and killed by agents of the boy king Ptolemy in full view of his family and followers (Dio Cassius 42.3–4; Livy, epitome 112).

3.67   **people who have suffered:** Not the same point as at 3.53–54. Rather than the diminishment of an old grief, these unfortunates undergo a deadening of their capacity to respond to further occasions of distress.

If this had been the first sad dawn: From Euripides' *Phrixus,* fr. 821 Nauck. The passage is cited by Posidonius in connection with pre-rehearsal; see Appendix D, passage [g].

3.69   **Aristotle ... Theophrastus:** The choice of names has some point. Both these philosophers would concede that vice is a serious evil, but neither is prepared to insist, as do the Stoics, that it is the only evil. They can therefore safely be named under Stoic standards as non-sages who recognize their own state as evil.

They were either very foolish: The remark is not otherwise attested.

Theophrastus, on his deathbed: Similar deathbed speeches are attributed by Diogenes Laertius to Theophrastus (5.40–41) and by Seneca to Aristotle (*On the Brevity of Life* 1.2); however, neither makes explicit the point which is here essential, that the philosopher admits his knowledge is incomplete.

3.70   **Fabius Maximus:** Q. Fabius Maximus (consul 233, 228, 214, 209), the opponent of Hannibal. Cicero claims in *On Old Age* 12 to have read the funeral oration which he delivered for his son. Fabius, Paullus, and Cato are mentioned together also in a letter to Servius Sulpicius Rufus on the subject of Tullia's death (*Fam.* 4.6.1). "I hold them up for myself as models," Cicero writes, "and am almost overwhelmed with sadness that the source of consolation which served them well in similar circumstances is of no use to me. . . . For they lived in a time when it was possible for them to find consolation for their grief in the esteem they had earned from the Republic."

Aemilius Paullus: L. Aemilius Paullus (consul 182, 168). The loss of his sons occurred within a few days of his triumph in 168 (Livy 45.40.7–41.12). The exemplum is similarly used by Seneca, *Consolation to Marcia* 13.3–4.

Marcus Cato: M. Porcius Cato "the Censor." His elder and only adult son died in 152, just three years before Cato's own death at the age of 85. In *On Old Age* 84, Cicero makes Cato say that while others admired his fortitude, he was indeed troubled by the loss, consoling himself only with the thought that the separation could not be for long.

my *Consolation:* The *Consolation* made extensive use of exempla from Roman history (*Att.* 12.20.2, 12.22.2, 12.24.2; Jerome, *Letter* 60.5.3); compare the recommendation of 3.56 and 3.58.

D.   Peripatetic Objections Refuted (3.71–75)

Thus it is a mistake to believe, as do the Peripatetics, that distress comes "by nature" and cannot be eliminated. For the beliefs which lie behind it are demonstrably false. If people do not respond to consolatory arguments, or if having comforted others they are subsequently overcome by their own misfortunes, it is their own foolishness that is to blame. It is true that grief diminishes over time in a way that beliefs do not. But this is because the relevant belief is no longer "fresh." The freshness of a belief is not solely a matter of time: witness the grief of Artemisia, which lasted for the remainder of her life.

If the Stoics are going to treat grief as a kind of voluntary action, they will need to respond to certain commonsense objections. Cicero represents these objections as Peripatetic (3.74), and they do bear a clear relation to views attested for Peripatetics and for the early Academic Crantor (3.71; see comm. 3, Ic (on 3.12–13). But whether or not they were actually formulated by Peripatetic opponents, these particular objections are ones which Stoics can find it useful to discuss as a means of clarifying their own position.

1.   Grief and Nature

The broadest objection, and the one most often reported elsewhere, is that grief is, after all, natural. This claim is specifically attributed to Crantor here and in *Prior Academics* 2.135, and it is part of the "ancient" view of emotion as challenged by Zeno in *Academics* 1.39. Seneca, like Cicero here, regards it as especially a Peripatetic claim (*On Anger* 1.9–17; compare also *Consolation to Marcia* 7–8). Of course, there is a sense in which everything humans do is part of human nature, but Cicero understands his opponents to mean more than this. "Natural" in this context must mean, first, that distress in humans is part of a larger world order which is, on the whole, beneficent, so that it would not be desirable to eliminate it even if that were possible. It is on the basis of this positive understanding of what is natural that the Peripatetic interlocutors will later attempt to establish that distress serves a useful purpose in human life (4.38–46). Such grieving behaviors as may be obviously undesirable are dealt with by admonishing the mourner to limit her grief. This admonition Cicero finds flatly self-contradictory: "What madness is this?" (For this argument see further comm. 4, IIIB (on 4.38–47).)

But the claim about "nature" is also taken to imply that distress is a given and intractable feature of human behavior: in certain circumstances we cannot do otherwise, so that it is not wrong to say that we grieve against our own inclinations, made to do so by events beyond our control. It is this more negative understanding of what is "in nature" that is shared with the hedonists (3.28, 3.31), and it is this claim that Cicero chiefly wishes to dispute. For from a Stoic point of view, the representation of any emotion as "natural" in this sense amounts to an evasion of responsibility for what may be very questionable kinds of behavior. It is better to insist that grief is indeed voluntary, meaning not (as the opponents seem to think) that one chooses to suffer, but that the emotion is caused by beliefs which we are not constrained to hold, and which we would not hold if we pressed harder for consistency of view. In particular, grief for a friend implies that we think the friend's well-being more important than our own; and this involves us in self-contradiction, for our most fundamental commitment, and the basis for all appropriate action, is loyalty to the self.

2.   Freshness and Related Issues

The discussion again gives special attention to observed phenomena of emotional behavior. For it is a key contention for Stoics that the account they are seeking to overturn has not given us adequate reasons for thinking that grief is inevitable. They will maintain that there is nothing in emotional experience which cannot be satisfactorily explained within their own causal account, as a consequence of choices which humans have made and could have made differently. Two phenomena are especially at issue here. The first of these is the failure of even the best consolatory arguments to have the desired effect in all cases, or to forestall grief in the consolers themselves, as they presumably would if distress were caused by belief alone. This point Cicero deals with in short order as a straightforward instance of inconsistency. His point seems to be that those concerned may indeed have accepted the beliefs expressed in the consolatory speeches but may experience grief just the same because of other beliefs they hold, at variance with themselves.

The second phenomenon is the diminishing of grief over time, mentioned already in 3.53–54 in connection with the belief about seriousness. When carefully considered, this phenomenon might seem to present a real difficulty for the Stoics, since they must concede that the complex belief which they identify as sufficient for grief remains in effect even after the emotion has passed. But Cicero insists that in fact the belief does not remain quite the same, since it ceases to be a *fresh* belief. The mention of freshness in the Stoic definitions of distress thus turns out to play an important theoretical role, protecting the cognitivist account against attacks premised on diminishment. Moreover, it actually establishes the superiority of that account, since freshness, not being solely a matter of time, can also explain those exceptional cases is which grief fails to diminish over a long period.

But if freshness is not just a matter of time, then what do the Stoics mean by it? Apart from what Cicero says here, we have only two pieces of reliable evidence: first, the fact that the word "fresh" *(recens, prosphatos)* occurs only in the definitions for the two emotions concerned with the present (4.14, Stob., *Ecl.* 2.7.10b (90.14–18 W), ps.-Andronicus *On Emotions* 1 *(SVF* 3.391)); and second, a definition in Stobaeus, which says *prosphatos* in the definitions of distress and delight means "such as to produce a movement of irrational contraction or elevation" (Stob., *Ecl.* 2.7.10, 89.2–3 W). The definition, unfortunately, tells us only what we know already: that if a certain complex belief is not "fresh," we will not have those particular feelings we normally identify as distress or delight. It does not tell us what feature, or even what kind of feature, a belief must have to produce such a feeling. The restriction to emotions concerning the present is perhaps more informative. Since beliefs about the present are, as a rule, beliefs about the very recent past, it is tempting to suppose that the feature in question is really a feature of the content of the belief: a fresh belief is just one which includes a reference to some event as recent. On this interpretation, a belief would be sufficient for distress only while it is still a belief that "my child has *just* died," the temporal element being dependent on the assessment of the agent herself and not on the clock or calendar. This yields reasonably good sense. The Stoics would be saying that as time passes, most people will cease to view a given circumstance as recent and will accordingly cease to respond to it as such, even while still believing that circumstance to have been a bad thing for themselves. They would be pointing out, however, that this change is still dependent on the individual: a person of unusual experience or temperament might continue to regard the same event as recent for a much longer period.

Still, if what one means is that someone views an *event* as recent or fresh, it would be somewhat odd to call this a "fresh belief." It is true that the word "fresh" is sometimes applied to the object rather than the belief. In Cicero's account we find this usage at 3.52 (3.55 transferred) and also in 4.39. But the actual definitions consistently assign the term to the belief itself. Probably we should look for some further explanation, and Cicero's language about "greenness" and "drying out" may support one. Already in the Stobaean definition, it should be noted, freshness is explained partly at the material level, since "contraction" and "elevation" are just the material changes in the mind-stuff which we feel as distress and delight (4.15). And beliefs themselves, like everything in the Stoic universe, have a material explanation: they are stretches of mind-stuff bearing a certain somehow meaningful arrangement. It is possible, then, that a belief might be fresh in exactly the same way that a footprint can be fresh—that is, by being very nearly the same arrangement that it was when first formed. In this case, Cicero's language about "greenness" and "drying out" may be illustration rather than metaphor. Compare the illustration used in the early Stoa for an impression *(phantasia)* as a kind of "print" *(tupōsis)* in the soul, like the print of a signet-ring in wax (Sextus, *AM* 7.228 (*SVF* 2.56)).

Even if this material explanation is right, however, we would still want to know what it is that the material explanation accounts for in the belief as the agent herself is aware of it. No doubt this is a point about the perceived saliency of some beliefs within the reasoning process which determines our impulses. That is, Artemisia not only continues to have a certain complex belief about her husband's death, but she also gives that belief the same sort of priority in her reasoning how to act, speak, and feel as most of us give to beliefs about what is temporally very recent.

For remarks on freshness attributed to Posidonius, see Appendix D.

On the Peripatetics see, in addition to the works cited under 3 IIB, Gill 1997, 6–8, Classen 1989, Görler 1989, Moraux 1973, 396–402. Annas 1993, 142–49, is particularly helpful on appeals to nature. The account of freshness given here has most in common with that of Engberg-Pedersen 1990, 194–98, and Nussbaum 2001, ch. 1; so also White 1995, 230. (The different account in Inwood 1985, 146–52, is accepted in Long and Sedley 1987, 1.421.) For the material description of impressions see esp. Sedley 1993, 329–31.

3.71   **Grief comes by nature:** Compare ps.-Plutarch, passage [b] in Appendix A, likewise in connection with Crantor.

your own Crantor: With *vester* Cicero allows his opponents to remind him of his own admiration for Crantor's treatise (Appendix A). As also in 3.22 *(Peripatetici familiares nostri)* and 3.59 *(Antiochus noster)*, the possessive indicates familiarity or esteem, rather than doctrinal alignment. Cicero has indeed named Crantor as a fellow-Academic (3.12), but the Old Academic position which he attributes to him is not one to which he, as a "New" or skeptical Academic, owes any allegiance; it is in fact the very position he is now arguing against. By the same token, "your own" should not be interpreted as a movement on the part of the Peripatetic interlocutors to disown Crantor, whose position is indistinguishable from their own. The disagreement is not between Peripatetics and Academics, but between Stoics and a Peripatetic/Academic coalition.

No more than this: Sophocles fr. 666 Nauck, from an unidentified tragedy.

people experience distress greater than nature requires: The admission is implied by their claims about the "limit"; see further 4.38–42.

3.72   **distress necessarily follows:** Cicero now speaks less carefully than in 3.25. The belief he has just specified is in fact only the first of two necessary conditions. Only in conjunction with one of the additional beliefs that follows does it become sufficient for distress.

they are doing something pleasing to the deceased ... it will be easier to appease the gods: Both are versions of the belief that grief is appropriate, 3.61–64.

how illogical these beliefs are: The fact that we regularly praise those who face death calmly shows that we believe it is not appropriate to feel strong emotion over one's own death. If, therefore, we think it appropriate to grieve over the death of someone else, then we must believe at some level that that other's well-being is more important than our own. But this conflicts with our deepest and most important intuitions about right behavior. For a human's primary orientation is to self, and all our correct judgments about appropriate action are founded on this; see *On Ends* 3.16–23. Thus the belief that grief is appropriate cannot ever be right.

    that saying of lovers: Cicero may have in mind the protestations of love poets; see for instance Catullus 58.3. The mendacity of lovers was proverbial.

3.73   **"when the blow of fortune shifts":** The repetition implies that Sophocles's Oileus, the Peripatetics' example in 3.71, is an instance of blameworthy inconsistency.

    in a different manner than they have enjoined upon others: So Brutus had admonished Cicero to bear his grief for Tullia consistently with his own consolations to others; Cicero was to respond in kind the following year (*Ad Brut.* 1.9). But the advice was standard enough; compare Appendix A, passage [i].

3.74   **their teaching on "moderate amounts":** Just as the Peripatetics claim that emotions are natural but should be limited in intensity (3.22, 4.39–41), so also they say that a properly "moderate" grief will be limited in its duration.

V.   CURES FOR GRIEF

A.   Theory and Method of Consolation (3.75–79)

Descriptions of the task of consolation vary with the schools' positions on the nature of grief. But it is possible to combine a variety of strategies, as I did in my Consolation. As in medicine, success depends not only on the remedy itself but on choosing the best time for its application and on sensitivity to the needs of the patient. Among the remedies available, the most adaptable is that suggested by Chrysippus, though it, like those of other philosophers, is difficult to put into practice.

Cicero now turns, with little in the way of transition, to a discussion of the available means of consolation; that is, to the composition of consolatory speeches or epistles, a familiar task for men of the literate class and a point at which philosophy was expected to demonstrate its practical utility. Reviewing the approaches recommended by the different schools, he finds the method of Chrysippus, which challenges only the belief that grief is appropriate, more workable than those of Cleanthes and Lyco the Peripatetic, both of whom demand a more radical reform of belief. But Cicero's own recommendation is for a flexible approach which will combine the methods of all the schools as seems best suited to the needs of the recipient.

The passage can be helpfully contrasted with those earlier sections of book 3 in which Cicero discusses the proven efficacy of certain standard consolatory arguments and techniques as phenomena requiring explanation in the theoretical accounts of grief (3.28–31, 3.52–61, 3.66). Here, where the emphasis is more practical than theoretical, the views of philosophers are assessed not for their success in dealing with the phenomena of grief but for the extent to which they can work from premises which those in need of consolation are likely to accept. Cicero does not find it unreasonable that philosophical systems should thus be expected to provide some arguments which will seem valid to non-philosophers, even to those who, in Stoic terms at least, are seriously mistaken on matters directly relevant to the problem at hand. For this expectation follows naturally from the analogy between philosophy and medicine which he introduced in the preface to book 3 and continues to employ. To count as a medical science, philosophy must offer some remedies which are usable by the sick, and the discovery of such remedies is as much proper to the science as is the understanding of disease.

As the Epicurean and Cyrenaic approaches have already been discussed at some length, Cicero devotes most of his attention here to the argumentative strategies recommended by two different Stoic authors and by Lyco for the Peripatetics. The method he attributes to Cleanthes concentrates on eliminating the mourner's belief that the bereavement is an evil for him. The Peripatetic method is very similar: it does not deny that the bereavement is an evil, but it argues that it is not a serious evil. The method recommended by Chrysippus compares favorably with these. Chrysippus appears to have pointed out that because both of the two belief-components identified in 3.24–25 are necessary, it should, in theory, be possible to eliminate distress by removing only the second, that is, the belief about appropriateness. The Stoic thus has the option of leaving the deep-seated value unchallenged in time of grief. (The point is explained in more detail in 4.59–62.) Cicero endorses the Chrysippan approach both here and in book 4 as the only one which combines a sound theoretical basis with some possibility of gaining acceptance from the bereaved person. Nonetheless, he prefers his own eclectic approach, arguing that even on the Chrysippan plan one will still be faced with the difficult task of convincing the mourner that his grief is dependent on his own belief that grief is appropriate.

The anecdote about Alcibiades brings out another point about the Chrysippan approach, one which Cicero (and no doubt Chrysippus himself) regards as an advantage. Suppose one seeks to console a person who is distressed over his own moral failings. In this case neither the Peripatetic plan nor the Cleanthean is of any use, since these philosophers will hardly wish to argue that the object in question is not a real and serious evil. Chrysippus, however, can offer a solution based on the two-component analysis. A comparison with the imperfect philosophers of 3.68–70 shows that Alcibiades' sorrow is dependent not only on his perfectly correct belief that his moral failings are bad for him, but also on a further belief that when presented with such an evil it is appropriate for him to be distressed. The philosopher might attempt to remove this second belief, persuading his Alcibiades that distress can never be an appropriate response to circumstances. (For this claim see also 4.61, 4.67). The practical utility of this analysis is minimal, to be sure: few of us are concerned to dissuade others from feeling compunction over their own faults. The motivation for proposing such an example must be interest in exploring the merits of the two-component theory itself.

A brief section on timing at 3.76 recalls a medical metaphor known also from consolation literature: it is of no avail to "treat the disease," i.e. address the mourner, in the period immediately following the bereavement (Appendix A, passage [a]). Cicero's remark in the previous sentence, about the "swelling" in his own mind, touches on the same point. Compare 4.63, where Cicero admits that his own *Consolatio* violated a Chrysippan injunction to refrain from treating the mind's swelling while still fresh. Fragments from *On Emotions* ([m] and [f] in Appendix C) confirm that Chrysippus pointed out as an advantage of his own consolatory approach that it does not waste time trying to refute the belief that preoccupies the mind of the mourner during the "inflammation" *(phlegmonē)*; that is, while the belief which constitutes grief is still very "fresh" (see comm. 3, IVᴅ (on 3.71–75), section 2). Cicero's word "swelling" *(tumor)*, a rough equivalent for *phlegmonē*, is not to be taken literally, since grief is in psychophysical terms not an expansion but a contraction of the mind-material (4.15).

Useful discussions of the theoretical bases of Stoic consolation include Wilson 1997, Donini 1995, White 1995; earlier Hadot 1969, 44–46. White's article also comments in some detail on the Alcibiades anecdote, for which see also Brennan 1998, 51. See also the works cited under 3 IVᴀ (on 3.52–61).

3.76   **Cleanthes:** His views on consolation are otherwise unattested; however, an emphasis on correcting the mourner's values fits well with his treatment of error in *Hymn to Zeus* 22–31.

   there are yet others: Since this is the view attributed to the Cyrenaics at 3.28 and 3.52, Pohlenz and some other editors assume that a reference to the Cyrenaics or to Aristippus must have dropped out of the text at this point. But the expedient is not only Cyrenaic; see 3.55.

And the list goes on: The manuscripts have *nihil mali,* "and no evil at all," which makes little sense at this point. The translation given here renders Giusta's conjecture *nihil non alii,* more literally "and others also have views."

it is important to choose the right moment: In addition to the passages from ps.-Plutarch and Chrysippus cited above, compare Seneca, *Consolation to Helvia* 1.2, *On Anger* 3.39.2, Pliny the Younger, *Letters* 5.16.11.

Aeschylus's play: *Prometheus Bound* 379–82; the first speaker is Oceanus.

3.77   **pointless mourning:** The pointlessness of grief was a commonplace of consolation; see for instance Appendix A, passages [a] and [h], and compare 3.66.

Alcibiades: The anecdote may have its origin in Plato, *Symposium* 215e–216c.

3.78   **Lyco's method:** Lyco was head of the Peripatetic school in Athens in the mid third century (D.L. 5.65–68). *On Ends* 5.13 makes him "rich in eloquence but somewhat impoverished in actual substance." His recommendation is Peripatetic as in 3.76, belittling misfortune without denying it is bad. For the division of goods and evils into those of the body, mind, and fortune, see on 4.62, p. 174.

3.79   **the same** *status:* The *status* (Gr. *stasis*) is that which is identified as the point of contention in a forensic argument. There were several different kinds; see *Topics* 93–94; Quintilian, *Instruction of the Orator* 3.6.

B.   Conclusion: Let Us Do Everything We Can (3.80–84)

But I digress. Our original question is clearly to be answered in the negative: the wise person cannot possibly be subject to distress, since distress cannot arise except through beliefs which the wise person will never hold. My chief concern here has been with grief at bereavement. This is not the only form of distress, but there is no need to deal with each form individually. Simply eliminate the notion that it is appropriate to be distressed by untoward events, and distress, properly so called, will cease, though lesser vestiges may remain.

The conclusion insists that the thesis proposed in 3.7 has been successfully proven false. Once it has been established that we do not grieve unless committed to certain beliefs about present circumstances, the rest is easy. For not only do the Stoics deny that the wise person can regard any present circumstances as an evil, but even the Peripatetics will not want their wise person to believe that any present evil is a serious one. The primary difference between the two ethical systems can thus be set aside.

With the words "that one type of distress" (3.81), Cicero signals a shift in his usage of *aegritudo*. Hitherto, it has referred primarily to grief as occasioned by bereavement, singled out as the most important of a class of emotions directed at present evils. Beginning with book 4, "distress" assumes a more colorless and theoretical role as the genus-emotion itself. Distress in this broader sense has not been treated exhaustively here, since there are many other species, which Cicero proceeds to enumerate. Some of these will be discussed in more detail in book 4, although none will be given the kind of attention that has been devoted to grief at bereavement. Those who wish can easily extend the paradigm to cover any of the other species.

In restating his case for the last time, Cicero makes a concession which at first seems puzzling. Even though the wise person is not subject to distress, she may yet experience an occasional "biting" or "slight contraction" *(morsus tamen et contractiuncula)* which does not require "voluntary belief" and may be called "natural." Within its context here, this looks like an allowance tailored to the Peripatetic position on value which Cicero has just mentioned, a natural but minuscule emotion corresponding to the miniscule significance of external goods. And this may in fact be the role that Cicero means it to fill. Parallels in other Stoic texts suggest, however, that the feeling of which he speaks is also integral to the Stoic theory, where it serves to clarify the Stoic point about the defining role of assent.

"Biting" and "contraction" ordinarily name the psychophysical "effects" associated with distress proper (see comm. 4, IIв (on 4.14–22), section 1, and, for "biting," on 3.83). The Stoic position is that these and other psychophysical manifestations of emotion are not blameworthy in themselves. They count as wrong actions only when they come about through assent to a particular kind of falsehood. Precisely the same psychophysical effects may occur in the wise person (and thus be counted as natural), provided they are generated without such mistaken assents. The well-reasoned affects or "consistencies" *(eupatheiai)*, to be discussed in 4.12–15, provide one instance of this: though indistinguishable from emotions at the psychophysical level, they come about through assent to true impressions only. But several texts indicate that very slight and short-lived versions of any of the effects may also come about even without assent, i.e., not in the form of impulses but as part of that prior mental event which is an impression only. Before I can come to believe that something I consider good or bad is present or in prospect, it must first cross my mind that this is so; and even this impression will manifest itself in some kind of feeling. Such phenomena as startling, tears, sexual arousal, or changes in complexion may for this reason be observed even in the absence of assent. Moreover, since these "pre-emotions" *(propatheiai)* or slight versions of the effects may occur as well with impressions which are about to be rejected as with those which are about to be endorsed, there is no reason why the wise person should not experience them even in response to present evils.

The most informative texts on the pre-emotion come from later authors, especially from Seneca (*On Anger* 2.1–4; *Ep.* 11, 57.3–5, 71.29, 74.31–2), Epictetus (fr. 9 = Aulus Gellius 19.1.15–20), and Origen (*Commentary on Psalms* 4.5). It is significant, however, that the concept is known also to the Jewish commentator Philo of Alexandria (early 1st century c.e.) who at *Questions on Genesis* 4.73 describes a preliminary to grief in much the same way as Epictetus describes the preliminary to fear, and who also knows the term *propatheia* (*Questions on Genesis* 1.79). As Philo cannot have derived his information from either Cicero or Seneca, we must suppose that he found it in earlier Stoic writings. A striking parallel to Cicero's remark here can be discerned in *Questions on Genesis* 2.57, which gives an allegorical interpretation of *Genesis* 9.3:

> The passions resemble unclean reptiles, while joy resembles clean reptiles. For alongside sensual pleasures there is the passion of joy. And alongside the desire for sensual pleasure there is reflection. And alongside grief there is remorse and compunction [literally "biting and contraction"]. And alongside desire [*pothos*, in error for *phobos*, "fear"] there is caution.

Despite the awkwardness occasioned by repeated translation (the full text of the *Questions on Genesis* is preserved only in Armenian), it is clear that Philo is here drawing on a source which listed the three well-reasoned affects in correspondence with the four genus-emotions (see comm. 4, IIa (on 4.10–14), section 2). As there is no *eupatheia* which corresponds to distress, Philo or his source has substituted "biting and contraction" as the only "clean" affect which can be associated with present evils. Compare also Plutarch, *On Moral Virtue* 449a, and Seneca, *Consolation to Marcia* 7.1, *Ep.* 99.15–16.

See further Graver 1999, Inwood 1993, Abel 1983. The translation of Philo quoted above is that of Marcus 1953; for the *propatheia* fragment, see Petit 1978, 83. Sorabji 2000 reviews the posthistory of the pre-emotion concept.

3.80   **invent additional beliefs:** In this and the previous sentence Cicero lists again the two belief-components necessary for emotion. The "additional beliefs" mentioned simply rename the second of these components (*nec* adding an elaboration, see *OLD* s.v. *neque* 4b). But Cicero's phrase *opinione adfingat adsumatque* may be a Latin rendering of *prosepidoxazein,* a term of art for the addition of (usually false) interpretation to raw sense-data. Compare Aulus Gellius 19.1.19 (Epictetus fr. 9.18).

the shameful: This category technically includes all actions and states which are not honorable *(honestum, kalon)* in the strict sense of the word. The question Cicero here declines to investigate is exactly the inquiry of book 5: whether there are any genuine goods and evils apart from those identified in the Stoics' stringent account of value.

3.81 **certain remarks which it is customary to make:** Cicero has already given a sample of arguments concerning poverty and failure to gain office at 3.56–57. An example of a one-book treatise concerning the loss of homeland is that of Clitomachus; see on 3.54 and, for the disputation format used in such works, comm. 3, IVA (on 3.52–61) and p. xv.

3.83 **will still feel a bite, still be contracted a little:** In addition to the Stoic parallels mentioned above, compare 3.61 "stings them very lightly" and 3.13 "there will perhaps be something left over." "Biting" *(morsus, dēxis* or *dēgmos)* was well established in ordinary usage for the feeling component of grief: see *Att.* 12.18.1, 13.12.1, and compare the last line of passage [g] in Appendix D. For the use of this term in the early Stoa see Galen, *PHP* 4.3.2.

the roots of distress: Cicero is inconsistent in his use of this image. Here, it refers to those emotions which are related to distress as species to genus. In 3.13, however, the root-fibers are the vestigial feelings which remain even in the wise, while in 4.57 and 4.83 error is the root, i.e. the cause, of emotions in general.

if "free time" it can be called: A reference to the current political situation, as also at *Tusc.* 5.121.

Envy ... rivalry, jealousy, ... : See 4.16, where the same fourteen species of distress are listed. The ordering of the list here differs slightly, probably only for the sake of euphony.

3.84 **the terms ... all mean the same:** Four of the terms *(maeror, dolor, molestia,* and *luctus)* are in fact used interchangeably in Cicero's own account, except at 4.16–18.

BOOK 4

ON EMOTION

PREFACE: THE HISTORY OF PHILOSOPHY AT ROME (4.1–7)

Although philosophy was not invented at Rome, it was adopted by the Romans from a very early period in their history. There is good reason to think that Pythagorean thought, at least, was influential in the early Republic. However, philosophy in the tradition of Plato, Aristotle, and the Stoics has not, for the most part, been recorded in writing at Rome; some Epicurean writings have appeared, but these, though popular, are simplistic and poorly reasoned. My own habit is not to adhere fixedly to any one school but to seek the most plausible answer to each question.

After offering, again, the customary dedication, Cicero appeals to Roman history as a means of justifying his own endeavor. In choosing to write on philosophical topics he is not by any means importing new ideas, for the upper classes have long been familiar with mainstream philosophical thought. Nonetheless, his achievement is significant in that it sets a new standard in philosophical writing in Latin. The popularity of the Epicurean Amafinius demonstrates that Romans are eager to read philosophy in their own language. It is as a matter of patriotic duty, then, that Cicero now undertakes to provide them with more sophisticated and edifying material.

To support his claim that the Romans of the early Republic practiced philosophy, Cicero offers four arguments: (1) The cultural dominance of Greek cities on the Italian peninsula during the early Republic, and the importance of philosophy (represented by Pythagoreanism) in those cities, made it possible for early Romans to have learned Greek philosophy; (2) The fact that Numa Pompilius was believed from an early date to have been a Pythagorean shows that those who held this belief were familiar with Pythagoreanism as promoting justice and self-control; (3) Records (viz. Cato's *Origins* and the Twelve Tables) indicate that early Romans made use of music and poetic meters, both of which were prominent features of Pythagorean philosophy (and, presumably, might be thought to have spread together with it); (4) That Greek cities chose philosophers to serve in the embassy of 155 B.C.E. shows that they believed Roman statesmen to have an interest in philosophy. The antiquarian flavor of the preface is in keeping with contemporary interests: Varro, Atticus, and Cornelius Nepos had all written on the comparative chronology of events in Rome and in the Greek world, and another of Cicero's scholarly friends, the religious historian P. Nigidius Figulus, was especially interested in Pythagoreanism.

Cicero remarks in 4.6 that the Stoic teaching is the same as the Peripatetic, "though they say things differently." The claim is strongly reminiscent of statements he elsewhere attributes to Antiochus of Ascalon, e.g. at *ND* 1.16, *On Laws* 1.54. In the present context, where the major virtue traditions are mentioned together as against the hedonist ethics of Epicurus, the differences between Stoics and Peripatetics are indeed inconsequential, and it is perhaps not surprising to find Cicero minimizing them on his own account. Nonetheless, the remark sits oddly with his effort in this and the previous book to show up an important difference between the two schools. It may be that Cicero drew the preface to Book 4 from the notebook of prefaces mentioned in *Att.* 16.6.4: written separately, these will have addressed the broad objectives of the philosophical project as a whole, rather than the aims of specific books.

Rawson 1985 provides detailed information on antiquarianism and the history of philosophy in Italy, including Pythagoreanism. More specifically to the reception of philosophy at Rome see Barnes 1997b, Gill 1997, Long 1995, Griffin 1995 and 1989. For the apparent syncretism of 4.6 see Barnes 1989, 78–81; on the philosophical prefaces, Ruch 1958.

4.1   **these present studies:** Philosophy, as in 3.1. Instead of this phrase, *his studiis,* which is the reading of all the major manuscripts, Pohlenz and other modern editors print *iis studiis,* "those studies." This makes all of 4.1–4 an admiring comment on a variety of studies imported from Greece, poetry and oratory as well as philosophy. But the emendation cannot be right: it is clear from the beginning of 4.2 that philosophy is indeed the principal theme, while the mention of other fields at 4.5 is merely incidental. The reference here is confirmed again by the repetition of the verb "sought out" *(expetita)* in 4.2, where its object can only be *studia doctrinae* ("the study of philosophy," as at 4.5).

after considerable delay: Romans dated the founding of their city to 753, but Cicero does not mean to claim that philosophy was studied in the city from that date forward but only from the founding of the Republic in 509.

the class-divisions: Literally "the distinction between cavalry and footsoldiers." Social rank at Rome was in name, and initially in fact, based on property qualification for military service.

4.2 **Pythagoras . . . was in Italy:** Cicero's source for his life was Heraclides Ponticus of the fourth-century Academy (*Tusc.* 5.8–10).

Lucius Brutus: The revolutionary leader; see on 3.27.

4.3 **King Numa:** Rome's semi-legendary second king. Cicero in *On the Republic* 2.28–29 dates the arrival of Pythagoras to 529, some 140 years after Numa's death. The story that Numa was a pupil of Pythagoras is known also to Livy (1.18), who likewise rejects it.

Cato, the most reliable of sources: M. Porcius Cato "the Censor." His *Origins* was the first historical work written in Latin. Cicero cites this item from it also at *Tusc.* 1.3.

4.4 **the poem of Appius Caecus:** Appius Claudius Caecus, censor in 312. On what grounds Cicero finds his poem "Pythagorean" we do not know, since only a few maxims survive from it.

Panaetius . . . in a letter to Quintus Tubero: Panaetius, who identified himself as a Stoic philosopher, was resident in Rome intermittently from the 140s. The work mentioned here is a consolatory epistle; see *Acad. Pr.* 2.135, *On Ends* 4.23.

4.5 **the time of Laelius and Scipio:** Gaius Laelius (consul 140) was a close associate of P. Cornelius Scipio Aemilianus (consul 147, 134) and assisted him in prosecuting Tiberius Gracchus (see on 3.48). He appears as a speaker in Cicero's works *On the Republic* and *On Friendship*.

a Stoic, Diogenes, and an Academic, Carneades: A "delegation of philosophers" to Rome in 155 is mentioned in numerous sources, most of which name, in addition to Carneades and Diogenes of Babylon, a third philosopher, the Peripatetic Critolaus. Cicero argues here that the choice of philosophers for the embassy evidences an awareness on the part of the Athenians that Roman statesmen had some knowledge of the subject. The implied compliment would then be conducive to the diplomatic purpose of the mission.

4.6 **Gaius Amafinius came forward with his appeal:** Amafinius is mentioned several times as a proponent of Epicureanism writing in Latin (*Fam.* 15.19.2, *Acad.* 1.5). The account here (which is the fullest we have) does not give any clear indication when it was that his writings came into circulation.

4.7   **easily mastered:** Or "memorized" *(ediscantur)*. Epicureans were encouraged to memorize as much of their founder's teachings as possible and were provided with epitomes to facilitate this (D.L. 10.12, *Ep. Hdt.* 36).

they are crudely formulated: The Epicureans in Italy are criticized at *Tusc.* 1.6 and 2.7 for sectarianism and clumsiness of expression. In *Acad.* 1.5 and *On Ends* 3.40, the complaint is that their system of thought is simplistic and neglects classification and definition.

I will not be tied to the tenets of any single school: See comm. 3, Ic (on 3.12–13). As at 3.51, Cicero contrasts Epicurean dogmatism with his own uncommitted stance.

PART I: THE QUESTION TO BE ADDRESSED

A.   Does the Wise Person Experience Any Emotions at All? (4.7–9)

So it went on our fourth day of conversation at Tusculum, where the topic was this: Now that we have agreed that the wise person is not subject to distress, will we say the same about the other emotions?

The format of the discussion is as in book 3; see 3, IA. Initially stated in a slightly different form from that of book 3, the thesis is quickly reformulated to establish the parallelism between the two books.

The argument concerning the emotions in general commits Cicero and the philosophers he treats to the assumption that all emotions can be subjected to the same analysis. This assumption has been questioned, not unreasonably, by some modern theorists: even if, say, fear and love can be studied together, it is not obvious that conclusions reached in that study can be extended to curiosity or depression. The ancient assumption, however, is not that all the experiences anyone might choose to call emotion are essentially alike, but that certain central cases can usefully be analyzed as a class. When Cicero writes "every emotion," then, he is referring to those emotions which are regularly regarded as problematic in ancient ethics, i.e., fear, desire, love, anger, and grief, together with any others which are similar enough to these to be subsumed under the same analysis.

4.8   **Two emotions are left:** The other two of the four genus-emotions, mentioned already in 3.24.

B.   The Procedure to Be Followed Here (4.9–10)

The first part of our discussion will proceed in the dialectical or Stoic manner; that is, with careful attention to definitions and classifications, rather than in the more rhetorical mode which the Peripatetics use.

More sharply than in book 3, Cicero contrasts two modes of presentation: a "dialectical" mode which he associates especially with the Stoics, and a "rhetorical" mode which he associates with the Peripatics but which will here be used to argue against their views. The nautical imagery warns the reader that the section immediately following will be unusually difficult. And warning is needed, for 4.11–33 will be a meticuously technical barrage of definitions unrelieved by any of the usual Ciceronian ornaments. It is in fact very similar in style and content to the handbook material that survives in Stobaeus and Diogenes Laertius.

A similar contrast between Stoic and Peripatetic methods is drawn in *On Ends* 4.5–7. There, as here, the Peripatetics are commended for excellence in rhetoric, while the Stoics are preeminent in linguistic and logical precision. In that passage, however, the speaker's approval is given entirely to the Peripatetics, on the grounds that while Stoics choose important themes and treat them plausibly, they offer almost nothing in the way of therapeutic discourse ("consolations, exhortations, warnings, and advice," *On Ends* 4.6). See pp. xxvii–xxix.

There is some historical significance to Cicero's comment on the Peripatetics' lack of interest in definition and classification. We know from other sources that a definition of emotion was developed at some time during the first century B.C.E. by Andronicus of Rhodes, a key figure in the history of Aristotelianism. But Cicero never mentions Andronicus and names among Peripatetics chiefly Cratippus (see on 3.22) and the earlier Staseas of Naples (intro., note 22). In many contexts, his preference can easily be explained by his preoccupation with what Peripatetic thought can contribute to the training of young orators. In the present passage, however, it is safe to assume that Cicero would have spoken differently had he been aware of the Andronican definition. Either Andronicus's work was not available to him because of date (accounts of the chronology vary considerably), or he has on this occasion been unusually careless in researching his topic.

In view of the issues that will arise over the Stoic definition, it is helpful to see how Andronicus and his pupil Boethus formulated their definition. For these Peripatetics, an emotion is

> an irrational movement of the mind due to a supposition concerning what is bad or good, where "irrational" means not "opposed to reason" as the Stoics have it, but a movement of the irrational part of the mind. (Aspasius, *On the Nicomachean Ethics* 44.21–24 Heylbut)

This differs from the Stoic definition as to the kind of mental event that is required but resembles it in naming an evaluative belief as an important cause (though not necessarily the only cause) of that event. Boethus's definition, which follows immediately in Aspasius, adds, after "mind," the words "having a certain magnitude"; this may refer to the contemporary discussion concerning pre-emotions, for which see comm. 3, VB (on 3.80–84).

On Andronicus and the Peripatetic definition, see Barnes 1997b, esp. 21–24; Dillon 1993, 193–94; Gottschalk 1987, 1094–97, 1114–16; Moraux 1973, 45–58, 176–78, 305–8.

4.9　**leave out the thorny bits:** This contradicts *On Ends* 4.5, which credits the early Peripatos and Academy with "apt and polished" work in this area. For the thorn metaphor see comm. 3, IIA (on 3.13–21).

PART II.　STOIC TERMINOLOGY EXPLORED

A.　Rational and Irrational Affect (4.10–14)

Philosophy since its inception has distinguished between the rational and the irrational mind; emotions belong to the latter. The Stoics define emotions as "excessive impulses" and divide them into four classes (distress, fear, gladness, desire) according to whether their objects are perceived as good or bad and as present or prospective. They theorize that the rational mind is subject to movements analogous to emotion in three of the four possible cases, and they reserve special terminology for those movements.

In laying out the Stoic case against the emotions in general, Cicero seeks first to establish that their theory does not exclude every affective response from the best human life, but only emotions as irrational movements— that is to say, emotions as we know them. A normatively rational human may still, in Stoic theory, be subject to "consistencies" or well-reasoned affects *(eupatheiai)*. These have the same psychophysical description as the emotions (as elevations, reachings, or withdrawings; see comm. 4, IIв (on 4.14–22), section 1) and come about through impression and assent in a manner analogous to emotions. The wise person's susceptibility to *eupatheiai* is an important point in the theory, for it means that a capacity for affective response is indeed part of human nature, even though the emotions we experience in our current state of error are not.

1.   The Twofold Division of Mind

For the purpose of exposition, Cicero prefaces the distinction between rational and irrational forms of affect with an even more basic distinction between rational and irrational "parts" *(partes)* of the human mind. This more basic distinction, he says, is one employed of old by Plato and Pythagoras. Invoking the authority of these philosophic forebears gives Cicero a rhetorical advantage in his debate with the Peripatetics, since it puts the Stoics in the philosophic mainstream. From a philosophic standpoint, however, the comparison with older psychologies is clumsily made and, if pressed, threatens the integrity of the account.

The words "reason" *(ratio, logos)* and "rational" are regularly employed in two senses: a descriptive sense, in which to be rational is to be capable of taking in, comparing, asserting, and acting upon information in the form of propositions; and a normative sense, in which to be rational is to do all these same things correctly, consistently with oneself and with universal right reason. What is needed in order for the distinction between *pathē* and *eupatheiai* to make sense is for Cicero in 4.10 to distinguish between two sorts or conditions of mind, one rational in the full normative sense, the other irrational in that sense though still rational in the weaker descriptive sense. That is, he needs to distinguish the fully rational minds of sages from the incompletely rational minds of ordinary adult humans: the former will be subject only to well-reasoned affect, the latter to emotion. This is perhaps a possible reading of his expressions in 4.10, if we assume that *partes* means "classes" or "types" (the meaning it carries just below in 4.11; cf. *partiri* 4.9 and *partitio* 4.11) and that "does not partake of reason" means "is not rational in the normative sense." The sentence will then be in conformity with Stoic thought, which, as Cicero himself makes clear in 4.22, treats emotions as a rebellion against *right* reason for which the (descriptively) rational mind is responsible as a whole.

The manner of expression, however, suggests as primary a different interpretation, according to which *partes* means "parts," i.e., segments or opposed sources of motivation within each individual mind, and "rational" and "irrational" mean respectively "rational in the descriptive sense" and "not rational at all." It is this second distinction which is most easily attributed to Pythagoras and Plato (see below on 4.10), and we must believe Cicero has it in mind, since the language used here is very similar to that used in *Tusc.* 2.47 to explain a division of mind on exactly these lines. If this is what is meant, however, then Cicero has gained the connection with Pythagoras and Plato only by giving up the distinction he needs for his argument. Moreover, this second version of the rational/irrational distinction, if pressed, will be a bad rhetorical error, since it will be open to the Peripatetic opponents to argue, as do later Platonists, that the non-rational "part" which is responsible for emotions is an essential component of the human mind and thus not subject to elimination (Galen *PHP*, books 4–5; Plutarch, *On Moral Virtue* 441c–443d; Alcinous, *Handbook of Platonism* 32.1). It is to his credit as an expositor of Stoic views that Cicero makes no application of the division posited here except insofar as it is needed to distinguish well-reasoned affect from ordinary emotions.

2.   Well-reasoned Affect

Another possible confusion, though a less serious one, is created by Cicero's use of the word "consistency" (*constantia*) to render *eupatheia.* "Consistency" in 4.10 is, as usual, the Latin equivalent for *homologia*, that stable mental condition in which a person's beliefs and actions are in agreement with one another and with right reason; that is, virtue or wisdom itself. In 4.12, however, a "consistency" is a movement, a response by one in a state of wisdom to some particular impression concerning what is good or evil for himself. As Cicero is certainly aware that he is using a single Latin word for two different Greek terms, we must assume the equivocation is deliberate. He perhaps feels that an exact Latin translation for *eupatheia* would create even more confusion ("good feeling" = *bona perturbatio?*) and so opts to bring out the positive meaning of the prefix *eu-* by using a term which also refers to the Stoic *summum bonum*.

That both "consistencies" and emotions require rationality in the descriptive sense is made clear by the specification of emotions in terms of beliefs in 4.11–12. The requisite belief-types have already been laid out in 3.24–25; they are repeated now in order to contrast them with the belief-types involved in well-reasoned affect, as in figure 2.

The difference between the beliefs required for an emotion and for a consistency is again expressed by the tricky word "rational": the wise person

THE GENUS-EMOTIONS

	PRESENT	IN PROSPECT
GOOD	**DELIGHT** (ELEVATION)	**DESIRE** (REACHING)
EVIL	**DISTRESS** (CONTRACTION)	**FEAR** (WITHDRAWING)

THE (GENUS-)CONSISTENCIES

	PRESENT	IN PROSPECT
GOOD	**JOY** (ELEVATION)	**VOLITION** (REACHING)
EVIL	——	**CAUTION** (WITHDRAWING)

FIGURE 2

believes in a *rational* way that a good is present or impending, or that an evil is impending, and on that basis experiences joy, volition, or caution. This must be the normative sense of "rational": the wise person believes, for instance, that a good is present just when that proposition is in fact true. An important corollary is that the consistencies are directed only at those objects or states of affairs which are either genuinely good in Stoicism—"goods which are real and are the mind's own," as Seneca says (*Ep.* 59.2)—or, in the case of caution, genuinely bad. Thus the wise person's "joy" must be an elevation of mind upon the correct supposition that virtue (or a virtuous action or condition) is at hand, "caution" must be a shrinking back from the prospect of losing virtue, and so forth. (For a difficulty concerning prospective evils see on 4.66 **confidence.**) This interpretation is confirmed by the absence of any consistency directed at present evils, since genuine evils (i.e., moral failings in the self) are excluded by definition from the best human life. To such commonly supposed evils as bereavement or poverty, as to all indifferents, the wise person will have no response except for the short-lived and morally insignificant "pre-emotion" which is produced without assent (see comm. 3, VB (on 3.80–84)).

Since the consistencies as laid out here correspond to the genus-emotions, we might have expected to find also a list of species-consistencies to correspond to the species-emotions of 4.16–21. Such lists are found in some of our Greek sources, especially Diogenes Laertius (7.116) and ps.-Andronicus (*On Emotions* 6 = *SVF* 3.432), both of whom list as species of joy "enjoyment" (*terpsis*), "cheerfulness" (*euphrosunē*), and "good spirits" (*euthumia*); as species of volition "good intent" (*eunoia*), "goodwill" (*eumeneia*), "welcoming" (*aspasmos*), and "affection" (*agapēsis*); and as species of caution "modesty" (*aidōs*) and "reverence" (*hagneia*). There may have been others as well: Plutarch mentions "eagerness" (*prothumia*, *On Moral Virtue* 449a), and Stobaeus "confidence" (*tharros*; see on 4.66). Some interpreters believe erotic love was for Zeno a species of volition; see comm. 4, IVB (on 4.62–79).

On "parts" in Platonic and Stoic psychology see Annas 1999, 117–36; Gill 1998; Price 1995; Inwood 1993; Frede 1986. More specific to Middle Platonism is the detailed study by Vander Waerdt 1985, which also reviews the late-Pythagorean material; also Dillon's edition of Alcinous (Dillon 1993), 149–50, and Dillon 1983. On well-reasoned affect, see Brennan 1998, 31–35, 54–57; Inwood 1985, 173–75; Striker 1991, 68–73.

4.10   **rather than "sicknesses":** See comm. 3, IA (on 3.7–8).

by Pythagoras and later by Plato: The linking of Pythagoras with Plato in this connection appears to have been standard in the Hellenistic Academy; compare Galen *PHP* 4.7.39, 5.6.43 (attributing it to Posidonius), Aetius 4.4 (Diels pp. 389–90); Iamblichus in Stob. 1.49.34 (369.9–11 W). The bipartition of mind is similar to that of Plato in *Republic* 10.603d–604e. Cicero is also familiar with Plato's threefold partition (*Tusc.* 1.20, referring to *Timaeus* 69c–72d), but *three* mind-parts would hardly serve his purpose here.

tranquillity: *Tranquillitas*, the regular word in Latin for the unruffled calm of bodies of water in still weather, equivalent to *galēnē* in Greek. The imagery, made explicit at 4.57, 5.16, is as old as Plato (*Phaedo* 84a) and Democritus (Cicero, *On Ends* 5.23; D.L. 9.45). As a description of the highest good it is usually Epicurean rather than Stoic, but both Cicero and Seneca find it fully compatible with Stoic thought on the emotions.

4.11   **"a movement of mind contrary to nature and turned away from right reason":** The standard Stoic definition, as at D.L. 7.110, Stob., *Ecl.* 2.7.10 (88.8–10 W).

a too-vigorous impulse: "Too vigorous" (*vehementior*) renders *pleon-azousa,* "excessive"; elsewhere he sometimes has simply "vigorous."

the things we fear ... are the very things that bring distress: The sameness of object is basic to the fourfold classification of genera; see comm. 3, IIB (on 3.22–27), section 2, and compare also Epictetus, *Discourses* 4.1.84.

4.12   By nature: The belief that it is appropriate in some circumstances to elevate, reach out, or withdraw need not be false. The difficulty over it is that ordinary agents cannot properly identify the correct circumstances. Cf. 4.67, and see comm. 4, IVA (on 4.58–62).

unbridled longing: "Unbridled," which Cicero uses of desire also at 3.11 and 4.15, makes the same point as "vigorous" or "excessive" in the definition of emotion in general. See the discussion of these terms, including the metaphor of horsemanship, at comm. 4, IIB (on 4.14–22), section 2.

B.   The Definition and Classification of Emotions (4.14–22)

Definitions for each of the four generic emotions seek to make it clear that emotions proper are both erroneous and voluntary; their emphasis on judgment, however, does not fail to take note of the way an emotion feels to the one who experiences it. Each of the generic emotions subsumes a number of specific emotions, and the Stoics have definitions for these as well. But in all emotions there is a loss of control, when the mind rebels against right reason.

Cicero has now to show that the broad Stoic claims of 4.11–14 can give a recognizable account of emotions as we know them, and that the fourfold classification scheme can be made fine-grained enough to account for the variety and complexity of our emotional lives. Accordingly, the first and last parts of this section turn to examine more closely the general definition of emotion, while the long middle part lays out a classification of thirty-two different species-emotions with definitions for each.

The treatment of the general definition passes quickly over the role of judgment, the related question of voluntariness, and the inclusion of the term "fresh," all of which have been treated already in the analysis of grief, 3.24–26 and 3.64–75. Note that the definitions given here are formulated in such a way as to be consistent with that analysis: each mentions two beliefs, the first that when certain conditions obtain it is right or appropriate to feel a certain way, the second that such circumstances (namely the presence or prospect of supposed goods or evils) do in fact obtain. It is the logical connection between these two beliefs that generates the emotion. To this now-familiar causal history the present section adds two further points: in 4.15, that each genus-emotion is associated with a psychophysical "effect"; and later, in 4.22, that the experience of emotion involves a loss of control.

1.   The Psychophysical "Effects"

What Cicero calls the "effects" of the emotions (*illa ... quae efficiuntur perturbationibus*) are not additional mental events—not results, as it were— but the same impulses as are identified in the definitions, now considered as psychophysical events. A rich variety of terms was employed in such descriptions: in addition to "elevation," "contraction," "reaching," and "withdrawing," both Zeno and Chrysippus also used the terms "outpouring," "lowering," and "biting." See further on 4.14–15. The figurative language of 4.13–14 and 4.66–67, as well as 4.14–15, indicates that Cicero, too, is familiar with all these terms. Except for "biting," which was well established in ordinary usage (see on 3.83), all the terms specify changes in the shape or position of some material substance, viz., the mind-material or *pneuma*, though neither Zeno nor Chrysippus is likely to have been much concerned with the precise nature of those changes. Compare the role that might be played in a modern account by talk about chemical or electrical changes in the brain. Such changes are what happens when one has a certain emotion and seem to us to explain certain sensations we may have such as pleasure or agitation. For these reasons, we may be inclined to say that emotions *are* chemical or electrical changes. But such changes do not explain the emotion in the way it is explained when I say, for instance, that I am delighted that my guests have arrived.

It is important to note that while each instance of a given emotion is also an instance of the corresponding effect, not every instance of that effect is also an emotion. A "reaching," for example, might be either "well reasoned" or "ill reasoned"; only in the latter case is the reaching a desire. For what identifies a mental event as an emotion is not the effect-type it instantiates, but a certain characteristic reasoning process. A movement of the same psychophysical type might come about through a different reasoning process, using true premises rather than false ones; in that case, the movement would be a well-reasoned affect, rather than an emotion. Thus the wise person's analogues for the emotions could involve effects (or, as we might say, *feelings*) very similar to what ordinary persons experience in delight, desire, and fear. In addition, both wise and non-wise persons may experience short-lived versions of the effects even without assent. For these morally insignificant "pre-emotions" see comm. 3, VB (on 3.80–84).

2.   Loss of Control

The last paragraph of this section (4.22) explains what is meant by saying that the emotions are "turned away from reason" or "disobedient to reason." Despite the awkward language of twofold division at 4.10, Cicero is now quite clear that the rebellion against reason is not a rebellion of a lower, non-reasoning part of the mind against a reasoning part, but a rebellion in the reasoning mind as a whole against right, i.e., normative, reason. Compare *Acad.* 1.38–39, which attributes to Zeno a denial of bipartition in connection with the claim that loss of control is the "mother" of the emotions. Plutarch explains the Stoic position in more detail in *On Moral Virtue* 446f–447a and especially in 441cd:

> They [Zeno, Chrysippus, and other Stoics] hold that the emotional [part or power] is not distinguished from the rational by some difference in its nature, but that it is the same part of the mind—I mean that which they call the intellect or directive faculty. During emotions and [other] changes in accordance with a condition or state *(diathesis)*, this directive faculty is turned and changed throughout its whole, becoming vice and virtue. And it has nothing irrational in itself, but is called "irrational" when it is carried away by the excessiveness of the impulse toward some ill-suited object contrary to reason's choosing. For emotion, they say, is wicked and uncontrolled reason which gains additional vehemence and strength through a bad and erroneous judgment.

Since both Plutarch and Cicero say clearly that in emotion the mind functions "as a whole," we may well wonder how it is that Cicero also speaks of the "dictates" of reason and of the restraint which reason exercises over the impulses. The only possible answer is that "reason" carries its normative rather than its descriptive sense throughout the paragraph, so that the restraint which reason exercises is merely the maintenance of order and consistency among all the mind's activities, its "impulses" and "judgments." The absence of such restraint may also be described as a deficiency in temperance or self-control *(sōphrosunē)*, since self-control is the virtue especially concerned with regulating the impulses (see 3.17, with comm. 3, IIA (on 3.13–21), section 2). Again, no conflict between reason and impulse is implied: the impulses of the wise person are in fact stable and consistent, and this is what we mean when we say that he or she is temperate.

In addition to this explicit point about the relation between emotions and normative or right reason, Cicero's language about "turning away,"

disobedience, and rebellion suggests that he is familiar with a further theoretical point which was sometimes expressed in these terms. A series of
discussions in Chrysippus (Appendix C, passages [c]–[e], [l]) refers such
language in Zeno's definitions to the sense which most people have that
they are sometimes "carried away" by strong emotion against their own
better judgment. Chrysippus insists that the Stoics' causal analysis can account for this phenomenon without invoking a division of the mind into
rational and irrational parts. An excessive (or vigorous) impulse, he argues,
is one which overrides subsequent impulses to the contrary, as when an impulse to run, by creating forward momentum, overrides a subsequent impulse to stop. No cause other than the vigorousness of the first impulse
need be invoked to explain the failure of the body to obey the second. Similarly, we often cannot prevent ourselves from feeling and acting upon
some emotion, even when we consciously judge that it would be better not
to do so: this "disobedience," however, does not show that the emotion is
any less rational and voluntary than the impulse which seeks to prevent it:
the emotion-impulse simply precedes the "stopping" impulse in time and,
being a *vigorous* impulse, overrides it. Only in this sense is the emotion contrary to one's own reason in the descriptive as well as the normative sense.

Some Stoic texts express the same point also by analogy with a horse
which "throws off the reins," disobeying the driver's command to stop
(Galen, *PHP* 4.2.27, 4.5.18; Stob., *Ecl.* 2.7.10a (89.8–9 W). This second and
(for Stoic purposes) somewhat less apt comparison may be understood as
a reinterpretation of Plato's charioteer analogy in *Phaedrus* 253c–254e; it, too,
may be Chrysippan. Compare Cicero's references to "unbridled" desire at
3.11, 4.12, 4.15, and Seneca's use of the same image in *On Anger* 1.7.3. Posidonius presses the point; see Appendix D, passage [c].

3.   The Species-emotions

The list of species-emotions need not be exhaustive: what is important
is only that it should show how some suitably large number of emotion-
terms in common use may be convincingly ranged under the four genera
defined by Stoic theory. The emphasis on distress, which is even more
marked here than in Greek versions of the list, perhaps reflects the importance of grief and suffering in the literary tradition as well as Cicero's own
interest in the subject. Compare his claim at 3.27 that distress is the worst
of the emotions and the one most in need of philosophical attention.

The species-definitions consistently include the genus-term. (Some
species of desire list anger as their genus; see 4.21.) To the genus-term is

added either a more particular description of the object, as when pity is said to be "distress at the misery of another who is suffering unjustly," or some further description of the movement itself (the feeling): anxiety, for instance, is "oppressive distress." Compare Stob., *Ecl.* 2.7.10d (92.18–20 W). Either method is satisfactory for Stoic purposes. An apparent anomaly at the end of the list (4.21, the second account of need) turns out not to be a species-definition at all, but a further point about emotions generally: that they are directed not at things (e.g., money) but at what is predicated of things (e.g., "to have money"). See further on 4.21.

Such lists were also collected by rhetorical theorists and may have entered the philosophical tradition from that source. Certainly there are some striking correspondences of detail with Aristotle's list of species in *Rhet.* 2.1–11, especially as concerns envy, rivalry, and pity (see on 4.17, 18). But even if Cicero had read the *Rhetoric* (and the knowledge of it which he shows in *On the Orator* 2.206–15 is vague at best), he need not have drawn these items directly from that source. Aristotle's definitions are themselves drawn from earlier discussions which may have survived independently.

Moreover, the material appears to have been reshaped by an author with Stoic commitments prior to its inclusion here. Pity, for instance, comes under the same condemnation as the other emotions, even though the definition given for it is hardly different from that given by Aristotle, who regards it with favor (*Rhet.* 2.8). The trio envy, rivalry, and jealousy corresponds in part to Aristotle's treatment of indignation (*nemesis*), envy, and rivalry in *Rhet.* 2.9–11. For Aristotle, however, both indignation and rivalry are good emotions, such as are felt by good persons: indignation is distress at undeserved good fortune in others, rivalry distress which motivates us to obtain the goods others have. The Stoic list dispenses with indignation, reinterprets rivalry as a bad emotion, and introduces jealousy as yet a further bad emotion. This leaves the Stoics with three bad emotions concerned with good fortune in others, seemingly a superfluity. Yet all three are carefully distinguished: envy is when I am distressed at another's good fortune without reference to my own condition; rivalry is when I am distressed that another has obtained what I wanted for myself but did not get; jealousy is when I am distressed that another has obtained what I wanted even though I also have obtained it. See also 4.46.

Nearly half of Cicero's list corresponds exactly with other versions of the Stoic list preserved in our principal Greek sources (see table 1). But his list also exhibits significant differences from theirs. A number of the terms and definitions which he includes are lacking in all three of the Greek lists, while some items not found here are included in all of them, sometimes un-

TABLE 1.   THE SPECIES-EMOTIONS

CICERO'S TERM	GREEK TERM
envying *(invidentia)*	*phthonos*[a,b,c]
rivalry *(aemulatio)*	*zēlos*[a,b,c]
jealousy *(obtrectatio)*	*zēlotypia*[a,b,c]
pity *(misericordia)*	*eleos*[a,b,c]
anxiety *(angor)*	*achthos*[a,b,c]
grief *(luctus)*	*penthos*[a,b,c]
weariness *(aerumna)*	*odunē*[a]
worry *(sollicitudo)*	*ania*[b,c]
indolence *(pigritia)*	*oknos*[a,b,c]
spite *(malivolentia)*	*epichairekakia*[a,b,c]
enchantment *(delectatio)*	*kēlēsis*[a,c]
anger *(ira)*	*orgē*[a,b,c]
heatedness *(excandescentia)*	*thumos*[a,b,c]
hatred *(odium)*	*mēnis*[b,c]
rancor *(inimicitia)*	*kotos*[b,c]
need *(indigentia)*	*spanis*[c]

Note: Species listed here correspond closely both in term and definition to material in one or more of the later Greek lists. In addition, shame *(pudor)*, for which Cicero's definition is lacking, corresponds to *aischunē*; see on 4.19.

a.   Diogenes Laertius 7.111–114.

b.   Stob., Ecl. 2.7.10b–c (90.19–92.17 W).

c.   ps-Andronicus, *On Emotions* 2–5.

der identical, and peculiar, definitions. For instance, all three Greek lists include consternation *(ekplēxis)*, defined as "fear of an unfamiliar impression"; confusion *(thorubos)*, defined as "fear which hastens with the voice"; and erotic love *(erōs)*, defined as "an effort to form a friendship, through perceived beauty." The close resemblance among the Greek sources does not, however, invalidate Cicero's evidence. While it is possible that Cicero has quietly altered some items in his Stoic source to adapt them to the Latin vocabulary of emotion, he is not at all likely to have credited the Stoics with a list half of his own invention. We should infer, rather, that he is drawing in part on a compilation not used by the later Greeks, perhaps that of Sphaerus, who is later mentioned for his skill in definition (4.53). Alternatively, all three Greek sources may make use of handbook material not known to Cicero.

Although erotic love is treated as an emotion in 4.68–76, it not included
among the definitions here. For the status of love in Stoic accounts, see
comm. 4, IVB (on 4.62–79). It is worth noting, also, that all three Greek
sources include as species-emotions several items of the kind Cicero lists as
"sicknesses" in 4.23–26; in this, at least, it is he who adheres the more closely
to the theoretical bases of his account. See further comm. 4, IIc (on
4.23–33), section 1.

On the psychophysical effects see Sedley 1993, 329. The point about excessiveness and loss of
control has been much discussed; important recent treatments include Gill 1998, 114–23; Inwood
1997 and 1985, 155–73; Engberg-Pedersen 1990, 182–99. Inwood 1985, 60–66, is helpful on predicates as the objects of impulses. On the definitions in Aristotle's *Rhetoric* see especially Striker
1996b. Barnes 1997b, 50–54, establishes that the *Rhetoric* was available in Rome; for arguments for
and against first-hand knowledge on the part of Cicero, see Wisse 1989, 105–63; Fortenbaugh
1989; Long 1995, 52–58. Ps.-Andronicus and the later species-list tradition are treated in Glibert-
Thirry 1977.

4.14–15   **lower and contract . . . biting pain . . . outpouring of hilarity:** Cicero works into his account a number of terms known to us from other
Stoic sources as terms for the effects. His "elevation," "contraction,"
and "reaching" are equivalent to Gr. *eparsis, sustolē,* and *orexis* respectively, his "lowering" to *tapeinōsis*, "biting" to *dēxis* or *dēgmos*, and "outpouring" to *diachusis*. For Zeno's and Chrysippus's use of all these terms
see Appendix C, passage [b], with Galen, *PHP* 4.3.2, 5.1.4, and compare
also Plutarch, *On Moral Virtue* 449a.

4.15   **"opining" . . . a weak assent:** For the importance of this definition see
comm. 3, IIB (on 3.22–27), section 1. Note that a "weak" assent is not
one that, as it were, lacks conviction; rather, it is assent given from an
epistemically weak state, which is just the state of the non-sage
(Plutarch *On Stoic Self-contradictions* 1057b; Stob., *Ecl.* 2.7.11m (III.18–112.5
W). Cicero's word "opining" (*opinatio*, his own coinage) here serves to
pick out the verbal notion in *opinio*, as does *doxazein* in the Stobaean
definition (*Ecl.* 2.7.10b (90.8 W)). Elsewhere (e.g., 4.26) *opinio* and *opinatio* are interchangeable.

4.16   **the less familiar word:** That is, *invidentia* "envying" rather than *invidia*
"envy"; see on 3.20.

pleasure: Cicero now reverts to *voluptas*, rather than *laetitia*, as a translation for *hēdonē*.

that kind of spite which rejoices in another's ills: The paren-
thesis explains that *malivolentia* ("spite") is Cicero's translation for
epichairekakia, "rejoicing at ills."

4.17   **if Agamemnon is aggrieved:** Since Hector's victory means Agamemnon's own defeat, one would expect the latter to be distressed at it, but one would not use the word "envy" for that sort of distress.

   Rivalry is used in two senses: So also the account in Stobaeus notes that rivalry can be used in senses other than the one picked out by the Stoic definition, including "imitation on grounds of superiority."

4.18   **Pity:** For the Stoic position on pity see also 3.21, 4.32, 4.56, and compare Seneca, *On Clemency* 2.4.4–2.6.4.

   no one is moved to pity by the punishment of a parricide: Compare Aristotle, *Rhet.* 2.9.4: "no good person is distressed by the punishment of parricides or murderers."

   the untimely death: For *acerbus* with the meaning "untimely" see on 3.29.

   distress that is inclined to weep … accompanied by sobbing: The list in ps.-Andronicus similarly includes *klausis* "crying" and *goos* "lamenting."

   toilsome distress: The definition given in Stobaeus and ps.-Andronicus is "distress which gets in and settles."

   distress accompanied by thinking: The definition given by Diogenes Laertius is "distress with thinking that lasts and increases."

   fear of impending work: The definition given in the Greek sources for *oknos*, which stands first in its genus in all the lists, is "fear of impending activity"; *oknos* regularly means "reluctance." Cicero apparently understands "activity" *(energeia)* to mean "work" and translates accordingly.

4.19   **Hence shame is accompanied by blushing:** A definition for shame has dropped out of the text between those for indolence and terror. All three of our Greek sources offer "fear of disgrace." But Cicero's definition may have included some mention of the blood (as Pohlenz suggests), since he seems to say that the species-definitions provide an explanation for the contrary physiological manifestations of shame and terror.

   then panic drove all wisdom from my breast: From Ennius's *Alcmeon*, fr. 14 Jocelyn, and see Jocelyn, 190–91; Cicero quotes at greater length in *On the Orator* 3.218. Alcmeon (or Alcmaeon) serves as an example of frenzied insanity in 3.11.

4.20   **Enchantment:** Like its Greek equivalent *kēlēsis*, Cicero's term *delectatio* may refer to an enticement by magic arts as well as to ordinary enjoyment of music and the like. *Kēlēsis* does not appear in Stobaeus's list; however, both Stobaeus and ps.-Andronicus list *goēteia* ("bewitchment") as a species of delight.

4.21   *thumōsis:* The parallel texts all use the term *thumos.* Cicero's rendering *excandescentia* suggests that he links *thumos* with *thumiaō,* "burn." Compare Chrysippus's observation that anger *(thumos)* comes about when "the heart flares up *(anathumiōmenou)* and pushes outward against someone and blows into the face and hands" (Galen *PHP* 3.1.25). See also Nemesius, *Nature of the Human* 21 *(SVF* 3.416), and see on 4.78.

   inveterate anger . . . anger biding its time for revenge: The lack of correspondence with Diogenes Laertius (see table 1) is perhaps due to a copyist's error: our text of Diogenes lacks any definition for rancor but defines hatred as "inveterate anger, *rancorous and* biding its time for revenge."

   Soreness of heart: Mention of the heart *(cor)* in the definition serves to explain Cicero's choice of *discordia,* literally perhaps "apartness in heart." In ordinary usage the word normally refers to a social situation, "quarrel, enmity."

   desire which cannot be satisfied: The item does not appear in the Stobaean list. The definition given by Diogenes Laertius is "desire hindered and blocked from its object, stretched and hollow in its attraction."

   They also draw this distinction: The distinction between desire and need cannot be reconciled with the definition just given of need as a species of desire. Desire here merely serves as an example of an emotion-impulse, the point being that as impulses, emotions are directed at (have as their objects) predicates concerning certain things, rather than at the things themselves. Hence need, in this second account, is not an emotion at all but only an example of what emotions are not. Compare the statement of Stobaeus, at a corresponding point in his discussion, that "impulses are directed at the predicates contained in propositions" *(Ecl.* 2.7.9b (88.4–5 W)).

4.22   **loss of control:** Cicero's term is *intemperantia.* The Greek equivalent is *akolasia,* which appears in Stoic texts in several different contexts. Closest to its importance here is the reference to "uncontrolled reason" *(akolastos logos)* in Plutarch, *On Moral Virtue* 441d, quoted above, p. 141. In other passages it appears as the cardinal fault opposed to self-control or temperance (Stob., *Ecl.* 2.7.5a (57.20–22 W)) and as a "sickness" (D.L. 7.111); the last is what Cicero calls stubbornness *(pervicacia)* in 4.26.

   rebellion: The Greek is perhaps *akatastasia,* "unsettled condition," as in Appendix C, passage [j]. Cicero's figurative language brings out the political connotations of the Greek term; compare "disturbance and riot" later in the paragraph.

   in the mind as a whole against right reason: As "mind" and "right reason" are not synonymous, the manuscript reading *a tota mente a recta ratione* requires taking the preposition *a* in two different senses, first "by" and then "against." Pohlenz's omission of the first *a* gives a smoother syntax: *tota mente* without preposition is local ablative, "in" or "throughout" the mind as a whole. See also the parallels cited by Lundström 1986, 109–10.

impulses: The same term, *adpetitio*, is elsewhere used to render *orexis* ("reaching"; 3.24, 4.12, etc.), while *hormē* ("impulse") is rendered by *adpetitus*. But self-control does not regulate only desires, but distress, fear, and other emotions as well. Compare 3.17 and note.

C.   The Character of Individuals (4.23–33)

The Stoics draw an elaborate comparison between the mind and the body. Lasting states which have their origin in the unchecked occurrence of particular emotions are called by them "sicknesses"; these are defined as erroneous beliefs about the value of certain objects and are closely related to "infirmities" and "aversions." An individual who is prone to a certain failing is said to have a "proclivity," while a proneness to what is good is a "facility." There are also traits of character, both negative and positive. But the body–mind analogy has definite limitations.

Cicero has now to show that a strictly cognitive analysis of emotion can also account for variations in character: that is, that it can explain why different individuals have different kinds or levels of emotion in similar situations, and to what extent such differences can and should be eliminated. The problem is addressed through an analogy with bodily health: just as bodies may be imperfect through disease, through weakness, through mere susceptibility to disease, or through unsightly but not debilitating defects, so also the mind may fall short of the moral and epistemic ideal in several different ways which have different kinds of ethical significance. Even the virtuous or "healthy" state of mind has some room for individual variation.

Evidence suggests that the early Stoa worked energetically on the problem, and indeed the matter required some energy, for making the analysis work in cognitive terms requires a careful layering of psychological concepts. In Stoic theory we do not experience emotions at all unless in a state of fault, or vice. But vice, like virtue, is a state which does not admit of differentiation: everyone who is not virtuous is equally not virtuous, just as everyone who is underwater is equally underwater, even though some are nearer to the surface than others (*On Ends* 3.48; Plutarch, *On Common Notions* 1063ab; see further on 4.29 **condition or state**). To give a more richly varied description of character, then, the account must have reference to something other than consistency or lack thereof within the belief-set. It will have to work with differences in personal history, or with differences in structure among incoherent sets—for instance in the degree to which one or another error has become entrenched in the mind—or perhaps with other characteristics of the mind which are not beliefs at all. Cicero is not prepared to provide such a complicated discussion here. Careful of his readers' patience, he contents himself with a brief sketch showing what lines the analysis should take. Where a particular distinction is difficult to uphold, he declines to make the effort, offering both terms but emphasizing what they have in common, and indicating that the treatment in his source was more elaborate. This happens not only with sicknesses and infirmities, which he treats as interchangeable in 4.23–26, but also with proclivities and sicknesses in 4.28.

Nonetheless, there are three important distinctions which Cicero does uphold:

(1) Movements, including primarily bouts of emotion but also impulses in general, are distinguished from the states one must be in to be subject to them, most importantly from the states called "sicknesses,"

(2) A proclivity to experience some particular kind of emotion is distinguished from the emotion itself; alternatively, a proclivity to acquire some particular sickness is distinguished from the sickness itself.

(3) Those bad or good states which count either as sicknesses or as virtues in the fullest sense of the word are distinguished from other bad and good states which do not.

These three distinctions are enough to give a loose general notion of how the Stoics set about defining and explaining several kinds of character-traits without having to resort to those broader and less flexible categories which make all individuals either virtuous or not-virtuous without differentiation. However, the account as it stands here presents several fairly serious difficulties, the most noticeable being a tendency for (2) to collapse into (1). It is an open question whether the difficulties result from Cicero's simplified presentation, from his combining two or more earlier versions of the analysis into one, or from tensions within an earlier account.

Of the other surviving accounts of this portion of Stoic psychology, the most informative overall is that in Stobaeus, which not only includes all the points covered by Cicero but also preserves traces of an even more complex scheme distinguishing among states, movements, conditions, kinds of knowledge, crafts *(technai)*, and specialties *(epitēdeumata)*. Diogenes Laertius reports more briefly concerning the sicknesses and proclivities, and single points are mentioned in other authors, especially Seneca and Galen.

1.   Sicknesses and Infirmities: States vs. Movements

A "sickness" is said to consist in a "deeply attached and rooted" belief in the goodness of some object which is not, in fact, good. How such evaluative beliefs predispose agents to emotion is clear from the general analysis of emotion; see comm. 3, IIB (on 3.22–27), section 1. In order to desire money, for instance, a person needs not only to be aware of some prospect of acquiring it, but also to possess two prior beliefs, (a) that "acquiring money is a good thing for me," and (b) that "when a good thing is in prospect, it is appropriate for me to pursue it." While any non-sage might believe (a) in some degree, the greedy person has an unusually strong commitment to it and is thus especially likely to experience a desire to acquire money when there is a prospect of doing so, or gladness over money actually acquired. Greed can thus be treated as a capacity of a more particular and individual kind than the general capacity for weak assent which is required to experience any emotion at all.

Similar accounts can be given for any object-type, with positive evaluations called sicknesses (or, without distinction, "infirmities") and negative evaluations called "aversions." Hence the Greek names listed for sicknesses and aversions are nearly all derived from the words for specific object-types, e.g. *philarguria* "fondness for money" or *misogunia* "hatred for women." Cicero's translations (table 2) do not always make this clear.

TABLE 2.   SICKNESSES, AVERSIONS, PROCLIVITIES

CICERO'S TERM	GREEK TERM(S)
Sicknesses	
greed *(avaritia)*	*philarguria*[a,b,f]
	philoploutia[b]
desire for glory *(gloriae cupiditas)*	*philodoxia*[a,b,f]
	philotimia[c]
	doxomania[e]
liking for women *(mulierositas)*	*philogunia*[b,e]
	gunaikomania[d,e]

TABLE 2. *continued*

Cicero's term	Greek term(s)
	lagneia[c]
stubbornness *(pervicacia)*	*akolasia*[a]
gluttony *(ligurritio)*	*opsomania*[e]
	gastrimargia[c]
fondness for wine *(vinulentia)*	*philoinia*[be]
	methē[a]
	oinophlugia[c]
covetousness *(cuppedia)*	*philochrēmatia*[c]
——	*philēdonia* ("fondness for pleasure")[abcf]
——	*philozōia* ("fondness for life")[c]
——	*ornithomania* ("fondness for birds")[de]
——	*ortugomania* ("fondness for quail")[e]
——	*philosōmatia* ("fondness for the body")[c]

Aversions

hatred of women *(mulierum odium)*	*misogunia*[b]
hatred of humanity *(generis humani odium)*	*misanthrōpia*[b]
hostility to guests *(inhospitalitas)*	——
——	*misoinia* ("hatred of wine")[b]

Proclivities

anxiety *(anxietas)*	——
irascibility *(iracundia)*	*orgilotēs*[b]
(to be) envious *(invidi)*	*phthoneria* ("enviousness")[ab]
(to be) spiteful *(malivoli)*	*erides* ("quarrelsomeness")[a]
(to be) desirous *(libidinosi)*	——
(to be) timid *(timidi)*	*deilia* ("cowardice")[f]
(to be) pitying *(misericordes)*	*eleēmosunē* ("tendency to pity")[a]
——	*epilupia* ("tendency to grief")[b]
——	*akrocholia* ("tendency to wrath")[b]

Note: A dash indicates the lack of an equivalent term.

a. D.L. 7.111, 7.115.

b. Stob., *Ecl.* 2.7.10b, c, e (91.3–4, 19–20, 93.1–14 W).

c. ps.-Andronicus, *On Emotions* 4 (*SVF* 3.397).

d. Chrysippus in Galen (Appendix C, passage [i]).

e. Athenaeus *Dinner-Sophists* 11.464d (*SVF* 3.667).

f. Plutarch, *On Stoic self-contradictions* 1050c.

Sicknesses come into being through repeated experience of the positive emotions (i.e., desire and gladness) toward some particular object, the repetition causing the belief in the value of that object to become "deeply attached and rooted." The genesis of the aversions is analogous, through the negative emotion of fear (see further on 4.23, and the Epictetus passage cited on 4.24). Cicero explains these claims only through a series of anatomical metaphors, but an interpretation in terms of belief is ready to hand. Anyone who is not a sage may, on occasion, assent to the propositions required for a single movement or "bout" of emotion, but when an agent has, on several different occasions, assented to the same evaluation of some particular object-type, he begins to form a more extensive system of beliefs linking that positive or negative evaluation to numerous other opinions he happens to hold. When thus entrenched in a system, the false value will be especially likely to come into play as he processes further impressions and will thus predispose him to experience further emotions in relation to that object-type. It will also be increasingly difficult to eliminate, since doing so would require the elimination of increasingly large numbers of interconnected beliefs.

The passage at 4.26 steadfastly refuses to distinguish infirmities from sicknesses, even giving to "infirmity" alone the definition which all other sources assign to sickness. Nonetheless, Cicero must be familiar with a Stoic account which does distinguish the two, since he gives the infirmities their own contraries and in 4.28 their own definition, "a sickness accompanied by weakness," the same definition we have in Stobaeus and elsewhere. "Weakness" is undoubtedly the essential point: the Greek equivalent *arrōstēma* means simply "lack of strength." Compare the frequent mention of "weakness" in discussions of assent and opinion, where it refers to the failure of non-sages in general to establish tight logical relations among beliefs they hold (comm. 3, IIA (on 3.13–21), section 1; 4.15; and see Appendix C, passage [k]). The point of giving a separate definition to "infirmity" will be to emphasize that while deeply entrenched erroneous values always set up long-lasting patterns of improper assent, there are some individuals whose minds are so lacking in tension that they are unlikely ever to adopt more true and coherent beliefs. In these cases vice will be either incorrigible or nearly so.

In identifying the emotions as movements rather than conditions (4.30), Cicero makes clear a distinction which tends to become obscured in Stoic texts. We have already noted how in 3.7 and 3.23 Cicero himself sometimes makes *pathos* mean both "emotion" and "sickness," glossing over the fact that emotions ought properly to be the movements to which we are disposed by the conditions called "sicknesses" (see comm. 3, IA (on 3.7–8)). The same double usage can be found in Chrysippus, notably in passage [j] of Appendix C. Galen, writing on medical terminology, explains the usage:

> When the change comes to be a condition *(diathesis)* that lasts, it is termed a "sickness" *(nosēma)*, that is, a condition contrary to nature. But we sometimes refer to a condition of this kind as a *pathos*, misusing the term. *(On the Places Affected* 1.3 *(SVF* 3.429, Kühn 8.32))

No doubt this is the reason why some of the later sources list among the species-emotions the items here identified as sicknesses. Diogenes Laertius attributes to Chrysippus definitions for greed, drunkenness, and stubbornness analogous to the usual definitions for sicknesses but calls all three *pathē* rather than *nosēmata* (7.111 = Appendix C, passage [h]).

2.   Proclivities

The traits listed here as proclivities differ from the sicknesses and aversions in that they take their names directly from various emotions rather than from the objects at which the emotions may be directed. The same is true in the Greek sources, where "sicknesses" have names like "love of glory" *(philodoxia)* and "love of money" *(philochrēmatia)* but proclivities names like "enviousness" *(phthoneria)* and "quarrelsomeness" *(erides)*. This difference in terminology suggests that some early accounts did indeed make a theoretical distinction between proclivities and sicknesses, despite Cicero's blurring of those categories in 4.28. What might have been the basis for the distinction?

One possibility is that proclivities predispose us to experience a particular emotion in an unusually wide variety of situations, in contrast to sicknesses and aversions, which predispose us to a variety of positive or negative emotions in connection with some particular object. On this interpretation, the proclivity might be related to the second of the two belief-components identified in 3.24–25 in the same way that the sicknesses and aversions are related to the first, or evaluative, component. That is, persons who have a proclivity are ones who have an unusually strong or persistent commitment to some specific version of the belief that "in certain situations it is appropriate for me to have *this* feeling." For instance, they might believe that anger is appropriate in an unusually wide variety of situations. This interpretation requires us to understand what are called proclivities "toward illness" as disposing us not to the conditions just called sicknesses, but to the relevant emotional movements themselves. This would be the same "misuse" of *pathos* as we have noted in the previous section and on 3.7. The switch in meaning from one paragraph of Cicero's account to the next would be disturbingly abrupt, but such flaws are perhaps to be expected in a condensed account.

Alternatively, we might suppose that the illnesses to which proclivities dispose us are indeed the sicknesses of Stoic theory. In this case we will be dealing with a tendency toward a particular emotion at two removes from the emotion itself: one would first be disposed to accept the relevant false value, then further disposed by that value to experience the emotional movement. This is the understanding of Seneca in *Ep.* 94.13 (see on 4.28) and may be implied also in Cicero's statement that proclivities may as well be called infirmities, *provided it is understood* that this means "a proclivity to become infirm." On this interpretation, proclivities will not necessarily consist in false belief; they may be traits of a different order, as are "weakness" or "slow-wittedness" (see on 4.32). In this case they may be innate. Compare *On Fate* 8, which makes Chrysippus compare the proclivities to "natural" likings for sweet or bitter tastes. See further 4.80, with the anecdote about Socrates and the physiognomist Zopyrus.

Cicero points out in 4.31 that inasmuch as the Stoic theory makes mental "health" or virtue a stable condition no longer susceptible to disease, it loses the analogy with bodily health. A similar but more fully developed objection is attested for Posidonius, reviewing the position of Chrysippus (Appendix D, passage [d]).

3.   Mere Faults and Non-intellectual Virtues

In both good and bad qualities Cicero identifies certain traits of character which belong to the same broad categories as the intellectual or knowledge-virtues on the one hand, and the sicknesses and cardinal faults on the other, but which do not satisfy the precise definitions Stoics give for those concepts. His account of these traits is obscure at several points, especially as concerns the different uses of the word "fault" (or "vice," *vitium*). Nonetheless, it gives us some basis for thinking that the Stoics did attempt to provide an analysis of positive and negative traits in terms more flexible than the undifferentiated "virtue" and "vice."

Faultiness (*vitiositas*) is a general term for all incoherence in belief. Sicknesses and infirmities are particular forms of fault, but one may be inconsistent with oneself (and thus equally "faulty") without having become entrenched in any of the particular misevaluations described in 4.26. There might be myriad inconcinnities of belief which are less deeply rooted, or less likely to result in inappropriate responses, than are the sicknesses themselves. It is thus that such *mere* faults are compared to minor imperfections of body, unsightly defects of shape or proportion which do not affect one's actual health. They may still be present, for instance, in advanced progressors who have rid themselves of the more dangerous forms of error.

Later in 4.32 Cicero mentions, as a separate concept, the "extreme faults which are the contraries of the virtues." These can only be the cardinal faults of intemperance, injustice, imprudence, and cowardice (D.L. 7.92). While Stoic texts tend to treat vice in general as an undifferentiated state, coextensive with the absence of virtue, this passage gives the cardinal faults a more limited extent, since it makes them actually less difficult to eradicate than are the sicknesses. We are perhaps to think of them as specific and glaring forms of error: injustice as the particular belief that one's own interests must always prevail over those of others, intemperance as the belief that one's own desires are always to be indulged, and so on. Compare Seneca, *On Benefits* 4.27, which insists that even though Stoic theory does make faults undifferentiated and interentailing overall, it also allows for some faults, including injustice and cowardice, to be present in especially "active" versions in some individuals. Such faults might consist in certain especially dangerous errors of judgment, as above. An individual conventionally regarded as virtuous may not hold these particular erroneous views; indeed, insofar as his actions are appropriate, his beliefs are likely to have been correct. Yet a life filled with appropriate actions may still fall short of the ideal. The virtuous person knows for certain that his actions are appropriate; the ordinary person merely believes this, retaining the capacity for error even where no wrong was actually committed. On this stricter understanding, even Aristides "the Just" cannot be absolved of injustice, and even Achilles was a coward.

The virtues most often discussed in Stoic ethics are intellectual virtues; that is, they are forms of knowledge *(epistēmai)*. But a number of sources also mention an additional class of virtues which are named by analogy with various kinds of excellence in the body. Chrysippus, for instance, discusses mental "strength," "good tension," "health," and "beauty" (Appendix C, passages [j] and [k]). The account in Stobaeus, which is very similar to Cicero's, points out that such virtues "do not consist in theorems" and are not crafts *(technai)* but "follow upon" the knowledge-virtues *(Ecl.* 2.7.5b4 (62.17–20 W)). Diogenes Laertius, following Hecaton of Rhodes, adds that the non-intellectual virtues "do not involve assents" and compares the relation between health and temperance to that between the strength of an arch and the arch itself (7.90–91). Presumably this means that as the strength of the arch comes into being when the arch is made yet is not identical with the arch, so health is always present in those who are temperate yet is not the same as temperance.

Cicero indicates that there were alternative views as to the nature of these virtues. The account which makes them merely the same thing as temperance, courage, and so forth may be an older view: remarks of this kind are attested for Cleanthes (Plutarch, *On Stoic Self-contradictions* 1034d) and Ariston of Chios (Plutarch, *On Moral Virtue* 440f), both pupils of Zeno. But all the surviving accounts make it clear that even if they are not forms of knowledge, these virtues still belong to the mind and can be described in cognitive terms. "Health," for instance, is a "correct mixture" among the beliefs, "beauty" a "due proportion" in reasoning, and so on. See further on 4.30.

What role the non-intellectual virtues play in the system is unclear. They are not well suited to provide a theoretical basis for differences of character among wise persons, and in any case that task falls to the "specialties" *(epitēdeumata)* also mentioned by Stobaeus, areas of interest and experience such as "love of music" (*Ecl.* 2.7.5b11 (67.5–12 W)). Perhaps they are nothing more than exuberant elaboration upon the body–mind analogy.

Stobaeus's account observes that such virtues come about "through practice *(askēsis),*" though it seems likely enough that a wise and virtuous person would possess them even without additional practice. Stobaeus also puts into this category both "power" and "great-spiritedness" (*Ecl.* 2.7.5b (58.13–14 W)). As Cicero has mentioned the latter already as a quality acquired through one of the traditional forms of *askēsis* (see on 3.15, 3.30), we might have expected some mention of it here. Stobaeus also has a class of "bad qualities which are not forms of ignorance and not lacks of skill"; these qualities, which include small-mindedness, lack of power, and weakness, are clearly related to cognitive vices in the same way as the non-intellectual virtues are related to the knowledge-virtues.

For a slightly different account of sicknesses, infirmities, and proclivities, see Brennan 1998, 39–44. On the structure of the Stobaean account see Long and Sedley 1987, 1.376–77; Long 1983. Rabel 1981 usefully compares the sicknesses with material in Aristotle. Sedley 1993, on the *On Fate* passage, discusses environmental influences.

4.23   **a wrongful aversion:** Cicero's term *offensio,* like *proskopē* to which it
corresponds in Stob., *Ecl.* 2.7.10e (93.10 W), may be either literal, in the
sense of a "collision," or metaphoric, in the sense of "affront." Hence
the contraries to sicknesses/infirmities may be described as "involving
aversions" or "arising from aversions" but are also simply termed
"aversions."

   Next come infirmities: Cicero appears to say that infirmities are acquired *after* sicknesses This is inconsistent with his treatment of infirmities as essentially the same thing as sicknesses (4.26) but accords well
with the definition of infirmities as sicknesses together with weakness
(4.28).

4.24   **When a person has conceived a desire for money:** This account of
the genesis of infirmities is extremely close to Epictetus, *Discourses*
2.18.8–10. Epictetus's slightly fuller version explains that if reason is not
"applied," the directive faculty remains in the changed condition, so
that upon subsequent occurrences of the relevant impression it experiences desire more quickly, finally after repeated episodes developing
"scar tissue" which fixes the pattern of response.

   cannot be removed: This contradicts what we are told in 4.32,
which clearly implies that while sicknesses are sometimes very difficult
to remove, it is not theoretically impossible to eradicate them.

4.25   **desire for glory:** Desire for glory, also called "ambition" (4.26), is
the "sickness" that served as an example in the preface to book 3; see on
3.3–4. Cicero regularly pairs it with greed: 3.73, 4.79.

   and the other sicknesses and infirmities: The redundancy is due
to inadvertence, Cicero having lost his train of thought after the paren-
thesis.

   the *Misogyne* of Atilius: *Misogunia* "hatred of women" is one of Stobaeus's examples of an aversion; Cicero makes it into a literary allusion.
Atilius was a comic playwright of the early second century.

   Timon, who is called "the Misanthrope": Timon is already a type-
example of misanthropy in the plays of Aristophanes (*Birds* 1549, *Lysis-
trata* 805–20) and Phrynicus (fr. 19 Kassel-Austin).

4.26   **They define an infirmity:** As the definition is well attested elsewhere
for sickness (Stob., *Ecl.* 2.7.10e (93.6–9 W); D.L. 7.115; Seneca, *Ep.* 75.11),
Cicero must now be using the two terms interchangeably. This is confirmed by the examples given in the next paragraph, which are of exactly
the same kind as the "sicknesses" listed above and in several cases merely
repeat them.

4.27   **Hippolytus:** In Euripides' play his intense aversion sets in motion the events leading to his gruesome death.

Irascibility is different from anger: *Iracundia* (here "irascibility") is formed from the adjective *iracundus* ("prone to anger, irascible"). However, normal Latin usage did not always maintain a distinction between *iracundia* and *ira*, and the two are used interchangeably even elsewhere in this book, e.g. throughout 4.43–50. In Cicero's earlier *On the Orator* (e.g., at 1.220), *iracundia* is the preferred term.

also in many of the faults: It is not clear what Cicero can mean by "faults" in this context. If, however, a proclivity is toward an emotional movement rather than toward a condition, then there might be room for proclivities toward other sorts of movements as well, e.g., toward unjust actions. This at least is the import of the parallel text in Stobaeus (*Ecl.* 2.7.10e (93.4–6 W)), which mentions at this point proclivities to stealing, adultery, and violence, likewise without offering single terms for them.

4.28   **a proclivity to become infirm:** Compare Seneca, *Ep.* 94.13: "Either there is in the mind a fault contracted from false opinions, or, even if it is not occupied by false opinions, it is prone (*proclivis*) to them and quickly corrupted by a presentation to which it should not assent. Therefore we ought either to cure the sick mind and free it from faults. or to forestall the one which is indeed free of them but is prone to the worse."

the former term: i.e., "facility," since "proclivity" is to be reserved for vicious tendencies. *Proclivitas* means literally "a downward slope."

a sickness accompanied by weakness: The same definition is found in Stob., *Ecl.* 2.7.10e (93.11–13 W), and D.L. 7.115.

4.29   **"faultiness":** *Vitiositas,* a rather awkward abstract noun coined by Cicero from *vitium,* "fault." Like *vitium,* it is frequently translated "vice." See 4.34 and note.

condition or state: Both terms, *habitus* and *adfectio,* are among Cicero's usual renderings for *hexis.* Some of our sources for Stoicism draw more careful distinctions among various kinds of states, viz. *schesis* (status), *hexis* (condition), and *diathesis* (undifferentiated state, but elsewhere = *hexis*). See Simplicius, *On Aristotle's Categories* 237.25–238.20 Kalbfleisch (*SVF* 2.393), and compare Stob., *Ecl.* 2.7.5f, 5k (70.21–71.14, 73.1–12 W); D.L. 7.98.

the other to inconsistency and self-contradiction: i.e., *merely* to inconsistency and self-contradiction.

4.30 **faults are conditions that last, but emotions are in movement:** The distinction is similarly expressed in Seneca, *Ep.* 75.11–12. Stobaeus, too, notes that emotions are not faults (*Ecl.* 2.7.5b (58.17–18 W)): they must rather be "activities *(energeiai)* of fault" (*Ecl.* 2.7.5f (71.12–14 W)).

preferable traits: Corporeal beauty, strength, health, and quickness are classed as "preferred" indifferents *(praecipua)*; see *On Ends* 4.72, D.L. 7.106. The mental traits called by these names are, however, genuine goods.

with all its elements fitting properly together: The elements are the hot, the cold, the dry, and the wet; cf. Appendix C, passage [j]. The physiology is not specifically Stoic.

follows upon it and has no independent aspect: *Subsequi* ("follows upon") renders *epigignesthai*, as in Stob., *Ecl.* 2.7.5b4 (62.17 W) and D.L. 7.90. Compare D.L. 7.94, where joy and good spirits "follow upon" virtue: they occur only in the virtuous, yet they are not the same thing as virtue, nor does the virtuous person experience them at every moment.

another sort of "health": The doubling in the account is probably what is behind the puzzling assertion of D.L. 7.91 that health and the like "are found also in the non-virtuous."

by medication and the care of doctors: The word *purgatio* (here "medication") suggests the use of emetics, laxatives, and the like. Mental illness as we understand it was attributed by Stoics to an imbalance of humors; see comm. 3, IB (on 3.8–11).

4.31 **a nice configuration of the limbs together with a pleasant coloring:** The same definition is given by Philo of Alexandria, *On the Life of Moses* 2.140 (*SVF* 3.392).

a certain toughness and stability: The virtues, like knowledge in general, have "solidness" *(to bebaion)* and, of course, "tension" (Stob., *Ecl.* 2.7.5l (74.1–3 W)).

bodily aversions: When used of the body, Cicero's word "aversion" cannot bear the sense that it has in 4.23–27. What is meant is probably traits in the body which offend others.

they do have similar behavior: Compare Seneca, *On Anger* 1.3.6: "speechless animals lack the emotions of humans, although they have some impulses similar to emotions." Cicero's *simile quiddam faciunt* and Seneca's *similes quosdam inpulsus* are equivalent expressions, both making the point that observed animal behaviors may sometimes resemble emotional behavior in humans without necessarily arising from similar mental states. Stoics deny emotions to non-human animals in the interests of maintaining the necessary connection between emotion and

rationality. The point was contested by Posidonius (Appendix D, passage [f]) as well as by the Peripatetics.

4.32   **natural endowments:** Some persons are born with a particular
aptitude for acquiring virtue. Cicero renders *euphuēs*, the Stoic term
for such persons (Stob., *Ecl.* 2.7.11m (107.14–108.4 W)), as *ingeniosi;*
he assumes, perhaps correctly, that it refers to native intelligence.
So also *On Ends* 5.36. Persons who lack such natural endowments are
"slow-witted."

   For it is not subject to any: The text is not secure. The translation
given here renders Bentley's conjecture *non enim in ulla,* for *non enim multa*
in the manuscripts. But it may be better to assume, with Pohlenz, that
some words have dropped out of the text at this point.

   an initial semblance of humaneness: Failure to grieve might in
some circumstances appear inhumane; see 3.12 (Crantor) and compare
Seneca, *Ep.* 99.15. For pity see on 4.18.

   the faults can be eradicated: These are, again, the extreme or cardinal faults.

4.33   **the reefs of precision:** Literally "scrupulous reefs," *scrupulosus* being
a pun: a *scrupus* is a jagged rock, but a *scrupulus* or *scripulum* is a tiny unit
of measure, or a small source of worry like our "scruple."

PART III.   RHETORICAL TREATMENT

A.   The Best Life Is without Emotion (4.34–38)

*All honorable activities arise from virtue, while the turbulent impulses which are the
emotions arise from the contrary state. Every emotion makes us wretched; the wise person, by
contrast, is not only admirable but also happy.*

Cicero now proceeds to the "sailing," the rhetorical treatment promised
in 4.9. Assuming his most eloquent and forceful style, he presents anew the
case against the thesis, which is to stand against the counterarguments of
the Peripatetics in the section following.

Despite the difference in the manner of presentation, the claim made
here largely reiterates that of 4.10–12. Cicero again distinguishes the normatively rational state of the virtuous from the flawed state of ordinary experience, arguing that since the emotions are defined as movements of the
flawed state, it is impossible in principle for the virtuous person to experi-

ence them. But whereas the earlier passage was concerned primarily to explain the theory, the present passage seeks also to motivate the reader to self-improvement by bringing out the disadvantages of fault and the corresponding attractions of virtue.

That virtue is a desirable condition might not seem to require much argument. It is far from obvious, however, that one who possesses virtue will necessarily recognize his own condition as a happy one, or that to be without virtue is necessarily to be miserable. Cicero will strive to make this stronger position plausible by developing a pair of contrasting psychological portraits. On one side we see a person racked by strong emotions; on the other, a fine description of what virtue is like for its possessor. Powerful feelings are disagreeable for us in part because the sensations involved are themselves unpleasant: not only are distress and fear "bitter," "crushing," and so forth, but even the "more cheerful" emotions of desire and delight involve a variety of deplenished, burning, and dissolving sensations. More fundamentally, though, emotions are uncomfortable for us because their cognitive basis is unstable. Assent to what is false necessarily sets us at variance with our deepest intuitions about the world, and the resulting state—one of "witlessness" or "anarchy in the mind"—is one the rational being cannot find fully satisfactory. If this is what emotions are, then to say that the wise or virtuous person lacks them is not to rob him of enjoyment. We need not think that such a person suppresses or denies emotions; rather, he is so constituted as to lack any inclination toward them. Aware of the magnitude of the universe, he will not think any event in a human life great or serious; mindful of all possible events, he cannot be taken by surprise; resourceful in his responses, he will always be able to find strategies for avoiding upset. Meanwhile, he finds contentment "in himself."

A precondition for this understanding of virtue is that the normatively rational person does not need emotion in order to act. This claim is integral to the Stoic position on virtue which Cicero states, closely following his sources, in the first half of 4.34. After giving a formal definition, the same as we find in other Stoic texts, he goes on to list activities which "proceed from virtue," namely honorable "volitions," "sayings," "actions," and "all right reasoning." That is, virtue, being a condition of mind, can be put into action by various kinds of impulses, either well-reasoned affects (of which "volition" is an example, as in 4.12), or right actions. (Compare Stobaeus, *Ecl.* 2.7.11e (96.18–22 W), where the activities of virtue include not only actions such as "prudent walking" and "temperate conversation" but also feelings of joy and cheerfulness.) Though made here without any special emphasis, the point is important, since it asserts that human nature has everything it needs for active engagement with the world even without the motivations supplied by desire and fear. This is the claim which in 4.48–56 undergirds the Stoics' argument that emotions lack real utility.

For the literature on well-reasoned affect see comm. 4, IIA (on 4.10–14). The musical analogy in "harmonious" (4.34) is treated in detail in Long 1991.

4.34   **a consistent and harmonious condition of mind:** The definition is given in this form also by Stob., *Ecl.* 2.7.5b1 (60.7–8 W), and by Seneca, *Ep.* 31.8. "Harmonious" *(conveniens)* translates *sumphōnēs*, the musical metaphor emphasizing the importance of agreement with oneself. Compare also *On Ends* 3.21, Seneca, *Ep.* 74.30.
   makes its possessors worthy of praise: As at D.L. 7.100.
   without considering its utility: Virtue is a final, not an instrumental, good, yet it does not lack utility; in fact, it is the only thing that is genuinely useful in Stoic theory (Stob., *Ecl.* 2.7.11h (100.25–27 W)).
   vitiositas **or "faultiness":** The explanation for Cicero's choice of translation is repeated from *On Ends* 3.40; see Powell 1995, 298–99. But *On Ends* uses just "fault" *(vitium):* the more abstract *vitiositas* is coined for the present work.
   turbulent and agitated movements ... tranquillity of life and thought: The imagery suggests bodies of water; see on 4.10 tranquillity.
4.35   **extreme delight of mind:** The source, according to *On Ends* 2.13, is the comic poet Trabea; see Ribbeck 2.36. As the thought expressed is very close to that of 4.67, we may suspect that the quotation here belongs to the same context as the lines quoted there. See also *Fam.* 2.9.2.
   Tantalus in the underworld: The version of Tantalus's punishment which depicts him cowering beneath an overhanging boulder is known from Pindar (*Olympian* 1.54–64) and from Euripides's *Orestes* (see on 4.63); it is used also by Lucretius (3.980–81). In contrast to the *Odyssey* account (11.582–92), which assigns unsatisfied desire as punishment for his baiting of the gods, this version assigns fear as punishment for his pride of place.
   for his crimes and his anarchic mind: The source of the quotation is unknown.
4.36   **frugality:** See comm. 3, IIA (on 3.13–21), section 3.
   grand and paradoxical: The claim that the wise person does every-

thing well (cf. Stob., *Ecl.* 2.7.5b10 (66.14–15 W)) counts as one of the *mirabilia* or paradoxes (*Acad. Pr.* 2.136); see on 3.10, and compare *On Ends* 3.75–76, which similarly expands on the paradoxes in a description of the sage.

4.37   **must be downcast:** Must lower *(demittere)* his spirits, as at 4.14.

what in human life . . . which he does not anticipate: The practice of pre-rehearsing possible misfortunes is again associated with great-ness of spirit, as at 3.28–30, 3.34.

B.   The Position of Our Opponents (4.38–47)

The Peripatetics hold that emotions should not be eliminated altogether but merely kept within certain limits; however, they fail to establish any convincing basis for limitation. They also argue, again unsuccessfully, that each of the emotions serves a valid function. The Aca-demics also treat the subject but do not set forth any definite position.

The Peripatetic position is presented as one which will have some ap-peal for many readers (note the interlocutor's endorsement at 4.46) but which is nonetheless deeply flawed in its conception. It advocates the limi-tation, rather than extirpation, of ordinary emotions. Even emotions which are destructive in extreme versions need not be censured if kept within cer-tain absolute limits. Further, they may serve some useful purpose—anger and desire above all, but also fear and some forms of distress. The claims about utility are a tempting target, and Cicero means to deal with them at some length in the section following. First, however, he will offer some briefer objections to the claims about limitation.

We need not doubt that Cicero believes the Peripatetic position as stated here to be the position of Aristotle himself, for the same set of views is attributed in *Prior Academics* 2.135 (quoted on p. xxv) to Crantor and the early Academics, whose views on such matters are supposed to be identical with those of Aristotle; see Appendix A. Cicero may or may not be famil-iar with the sources which lead Seneca, in his work *On Anger*, to attribute this same position directly to Aristotle and Theophrastus (*On Anger* 1.9.2, 1.12.3, 1.14.1, 1.17.1, 3.3.1). But while the position reported by Cicero and Seneca has clear affinities with Aristotle's actual views, it is not in fact the Aristotelian position. Aristotle argues in the *Nicomachean Ethics* that to be virtuous is, among other things, to be in a middle or "mean" state which is neither ex-cessive nor deficient in disposing us to emotions such as fear or anger (*NE* 2.5–7). But this does not mean, for Aristotle, that the emotion itself, i.e., each particular episode or "movement," should remain at some moderate level, but that the frequency and extent of our emotions, and the occasions on which we experience them, should all be as reason indicates. Aristotle holds, also, that emotions are to be classed with that set of appetitive and perceptive functions which we share with non-human animals, in such a way that any animate being which can perceive its surroundings will also be able to desire and pursue some objects and to fear and avoid others (*NE* 1.13, *On the Soul* 2.2–3). In this he provides the foundation for the Peripatetics' assumption that our capacity for various kinds of praiseworthy action is inseparable from our capacity for emotions. But the Peripatetics go beyond Aristotle insofar as they insist that to fight bravely, for instance, one must not only possess the capacity for anger and other emotions but must actually be angry. Traces of their position can also be found in later Platonist texts; see esp. Alcinous, *Handbook of Platonism* 32.4.

Cicero's attack on the claims about moderation and limit is on two fronts. On the one hand, he argues that no response which *needs* to be limited can be treated as natural and good. Thus in conceding that emotions can be carried to undesirable extremes, the opponents have already given up any basis for including them in the human norm. Compare the standard Stoic observation that while justice, for instance, is always a good thing, wealth, good reputation, and the like are not always good for us and thus not inherently good at all (D.L. 7.103). Seneca, too, asserts in this connection that if a thing is a genuine good, then to have it in greater degree is always better for us, and in lesser degree worse. Since this is not the case with anger, then anger cannot be good or useful "by nature." To recommend moderate emotion, then, is to recommend a moderate evil (*On Anger* 1.10.4, 1.13.1–2).

The second line of attack is to question whether it is even possible for us to limit our responses in the way the Peripatetics recommend. Cicero gives us two reasons to think that limitation is not practicable. First, he points out that since we have no control over the circumstances which, on the Peripatetic view, necessitate emotional response, we cannot expect to set any firm limit on the extent of that response. For new causes can always be added which will necessarily heighten the response. (Compare Seneca, *On Anger* 2.6.3–4.) Note that this argument does not work unless by "moderate emotion" the opponents mean one which does not exceed some absolute limit (*modus*) relative to the capacity of humans to generate emotions. If the Peripatetics' moderate response were simply a response coming from Aristotle's "mean state," it might go to any extent, so long as that extent was appropriate to the circumstances presented.

A further reason to deny that limitation is practicable concerns the nature of the mind itself. Once the mind has initiated an emotional movement, Cicero argues, it does not have within itself any mechanism for stopping its own movement, just as a person who has jumped from a cliff cannot subsequently reverse the downward movement he has himself begun. This looks like an application of Chrysippus's analysis of "excessiveness" (above, comm. 4, IIB (on 4.14–22), section 2). For Chrysippus's analogy of the runner seeks to show that while the mind does indeed lose control of itself during an emotional movement, that loss of control should be described not as an inability of the reasoning mind to overpower some other part of the self, but as its inability to countermand its own previous impulse. Again, Cicero's use of the Stoic argument is elucidated by comparison with similar material in Seneca. See especially *On Anger* 1.7–8, 2.35, *Ep.* 116.6, and compare *On Anger* 1.8 with the Plutarch passage quoted on p. 141.

On limitation and "moderate amounts" see Dillon 1993, 188–89, and 1983; Annas 1993, 59–66; Classen 1989. On excessiveness, see the works cited under 4 IIB (on 4.14–22).

4.38   **the position:** Cicero's phrase *oratio et ratio* is difficult to translate; it is both "philosophical view" and (with a note of disparagement) "talk."
          what they call a "limit": The Greek term appears to have been *horos* (Plutarch, *On Moral Virtue* 443c; cf. the related verb at 444b, c).
4.39   **Will you set a limit:** I.e., *merely* set a limit, and not eliminate it altogether.
          which even the foolish find less potent over time: Cicero is thinking primarily of distress, as the remainder of the sentence indicates; see 3.53–54, 3.74–75. The point could in theory be applied also to delight, which likewise depends on a fresh belief (4.14), but not to fear or desire.
4.40   **in the writings of Fannius:** Gaius Fannius wrote a history of his own times; he is perhaps to be identified with the Fannius who was consul in 122 (*Att.* 12.5b). As son-in-law to Laelius, he will have been favorable to the Scipiones (*Brutus* 101). Publius Rupilius and his unfortunate brother were proteges of P. Cornelius Scipio Aemilianus (*On Friendship* 73).
4.41   **hurls himself off the cliff at Cape Leucatas:** The promontory on the island of Leucas was romanticized as a lover's leap. Sappho was said to have committed suicide there for love of Phaon (*Leucadia* fr. 1 Kassel-Austin; see Nagy 1990 227–34).
4.42   **takes the part of fault:** Cicero's expression "takes the part of" (*partem suscipit*) may be understood either literally or figuratively ("be-

comes an advocate for"). Seneca, in a similar context, favors the advocacy metaphor (*On Anger* 1.10.2, 2.13.1).

4.43   **"the whetstone of courage":** The phrase is Crantor's; see *Acad. Pr.* 2.135, quoted on p. xxv. Seneca attributes to Aristotle several similar phrases: "kindles the spirit," "the arms of courage," and "the spur of courage" (*On Anger* 1.9.2, 1.17.1, 3.3.1). Compare also "the flame of the spirit" in 4.48.

    they disapprove of the orator who speaks … without the stimulus of anger: Seneca gives them the same position (*On Anger* 2.17).

    That trait which we call "gentleness": Stoics use the positive term "gentleness" (*praotēs*) for the condition of one who never becomes angry at all (Stob., *Ecl.* 2.7.11s (115.10-12 W)). Aristotle, by contrast, reserves *praotēs* for the mean state which experiences anger as only reason directs, admitting however that gentleness "inclines toward the deficiency." For the deficiency itself he coins the term *aorgēsia*, "angerlessness" (*NE* 4.5; see also *Rhet.* 2.3).

    lenitas … lentitudo: Who is responsible for the play on words? Were there Peripatetics writing in Latin?

4.44   **the trophies of Miltiades:** Miltiades received much acclaim for his generalship after the Athenian victory at Marathon in 490. Themistocles' most noted military achievements came some ten years later, when he commanded the Athenian forces at Artemisium and Salamis. The anecdote given here is told also by Plutarch, *Themistocles* 3.3–4.

    Demosthenes: His work habits were proverbial; see for instance Plutarch, *Demosthenes* 7.3–8.4.

    Pythagoras, Democritus, and Plato: The three are listed together as great travelers also in *On Ends* 5.50; see also *Tusc.* 5.115; D.L. 8.3, 9.35.

4.45   **Even distress … has … a useful purpose:** Later Platonists list uses for hatred, indignation, pity, and shame, as well as anger and desire; see Plutarch, *On Moral Virtue* 451e; Alcinous, *Handbook of Platonism* 32.4.

    the bite of conscience: The metaphor was standard for all forms of distress: see comm. 4, IIb (on 4.14–22), section 1, and on 3.83.

    the familiar line of Afranius: L. Afranius (late 2d century) was a composer of *fabulae togatae*, comedies in Italian rather than Greek settings. The title of the play mentioned here is not known.

4.46   **Even rivalry … and jealousy:** Cicero does not say what uses the Peripatetics assign to these emotions. Aristotle notes in *Rhet.* 2.11 that

rivalry motivates us to try to secure the goods others have, while envy
(for Aristotle a bad emotion) motivates us to try to keep others from
getting them. See comm. 4, IIB (on 4.14–22), section 3.

   fear: Note that fear is listed here as a species of distress; see on 4.64.

4.47   **how reserved the Academics are:** These must be the skeptical Academics, whose stance, with its emphasis on the discovery of the probable ("what has the clearest semblance of the truth"), Cicero claims as
   his own. See above, comm. 3, Ic (on 3.12–13).

C.   The Stoic Position Defended (4.47–57)

*The Stoic position is based on a carefully formulated definition and has more of substance
to it than the Peripatetic position. It is not true that one needs anger in order to act courageously,
for courage is inherently reasonable, while anger is closely connected with insanity. In fact, neither anger nor any other emotion is required for humans to act energetically, rightly, and effectively. Once the best life is properly understood, it is clear that emotion can be no part of it.*

Cicero now responds at greater length to the Peripatetics' claims about
usefulness. His response concentrates disproportionately on anger, in keeping with the the importance of that emotion in the philosophical and literary tradition. Cicero may not be aware that the Epicurean Philodemus,
whom he knew by sight, had written a treatise *On Anger,* but he undoubtedly
knows other sustained treatments of the subject. A work by the second-
century Stoic Antipater of Tarsus is mentioned in Athenaeus (14.643f), and
Philodemus mentions a separate treatise by Bion (c. 335–c. 245) as well as
Chrysippus's fourth book *On Emotions* (Philodemus, *On Anger* col. 1.15–20;
for the Chrysippan material see Appendix C, passage [1]). Anger was also
of great importance in the rhetorical tradition: Cicero's *On the Orator,* like
Aristotle's *Rhetoric,* devotes more space to it than to any other emotion.
Especially important for the present discussion, though, is the treatment of
thumos as the middle part of the mind or soul in book 4 of Plato's *Republic.*
For there anger serves as the chief representative of a broad array of emotions (so that *thumos* is sometimes better rendered by the more general
"spiritedness"), and there also it is essential to Plato's argument to maintain that anger plays an important role in the defense of the state. But
Cicero is not inclined to grant this: the Stoic definitions of courage and of
wisdom do not require anger, and his own experience has shown him that
anger is not necessary for effective public speaking.

   Although the presentation is diffuse and rhetorical rather than closely reasoned, the underlying argument is clear enough. While emotions often do move us to act, this does not make them useful, since humans can also generate other, less dangerous forms of impulse which would appropriately serve the purposes in question. A soldier who strikes his enemy simply because he believes it appropriate that he should do so (4.43) enacts an impulse belonging to that broad class which Stoics call "selection" (*eklogē*, Stob., *Ecl.* 2.7.7g (84.24–85.11 W), *On Ends* 3.20). To "select" an object, one need not believe that it is genuinely good for oneself, but only that it is in accordance with nature. On this basis non-sages, as well as sages, may engage in appropriate actions (*officia, kathēkonta*), the difference being that because sages act on the basis of knowledge and not merely correct opinion, their actions can also be termed *katorthōmata* or right actions. Sages also have volition and caution (4.12–14) as possible bases for pursuit and avoidance. The availability of these other, more suitable forms of motivation drains the force from any claim on behalf of emotions as stimuli for action. Anger might still be usable in war, but such suppositious utility will hardly defend its existence. Seneca remarks in a similar vein that even shipwrecks are useful at times (*On Anger* 1.12.6).

The Peripatetic claim about the use of anger in public speaking touches closely on Cicero's own area of expertise. The ability to manipulate the emotions of the juror was essential to the success of the forensic orator, and Cicero's *Orator*, circulated in 46, finds no difficulty in boasting of its author's achievements in that area (*Orator* 128–32). In *On the Orator*, some ten years earlier, Cicero had allowed his principal speaker, the elder M. Antonius, to argue that orators, like actors and even playwrights, are able to arouse emotions in their audiences only insofar as they feel those same emotions even more strongly themselves (2.189–96). Against this view, which is clearly that of the Peripatetics, Cicero will now argue the Stoic position: neither the orator nor the actor needs to experience anger himself in order to create it in others, for feigned anger will serve the purpose just as well (compare Seneca, *On Anger* 2.17). This is perhaps a reversal of views; if so, Cicero is at some pains to mark the new position as his own, for he refers emphatically to his own practice as a speaker and author of circulated speeches and uses for his example of acting technique a personal friend, Aesopus, who, according to Plutarch, had coached him in his own delivery (*Cicero* 5.3–4).

Readers may be surprised at Cicero's use of a Stoic definition to prove his point about courage: why should non-Stoics be expected to accept conclusions drawn from Stoic definitions? The answer is that Stoic definitions are meant to articulate or "unfold" concepts *(notiones, ennoiai)* which are shared by all speakers of the language (Augustine, *City of God* 8.7, D.L. 7.42). All parties to the discussion are expected to agree that the definition spells out what they themselves mean when using the term in question. If they do not, then further argumentation will be needed.

On Philodemus's *On Anger,* see Procopé 1993, Annas 1989; text in Indelli 1988. On selection, Irwin 1998a, 227–34, and 1998b; Brennan 1998, 35–36; Inwood 1985, 194–215. On anger and other emotions in public speaking, see Wisse 1989, 282–96, Solmsen 1938; on the apparent conflict with *On the Orator,* Wisse 1989, 257–68. On Stoic definitions and shared conceptions, Scott 1995, 179–86; Long and Sedley 1987, 1.193–94.

4.48 **an even temper:** The same word *constantia* often refers to the wise person's consistency *(homologia)* of belief and action. But Cicero does not mean that gladiators are often wise.

    meet and converse: The line is metrical (see the note in Dougan and Henry 1934), but its source is not known.

    Yes, I'll kill him: Lucilius book 4, lines 176–81, Warmington 3.58–59. A related fragment from the same book (lines 172–75, Warmington 3.56–57), tells of a match between one Aeserninus, "a filthy fellow, deserving of that life and low degree," and Pacideianus, who is called "the best by far of gladiators since the human race began." Pacideianus, then, is as admirable as a gladiator can be, yet his prowess in hand-to-hand combat is still grounded in rage and hatred.

4.49 **Homer's Ajax:** Cicero adheres closely to the Homeric account of Ajax's fight with Hector in *Iliad* 7; see esp. 7.189–92 and 211–17.

4.49–50 **Torquatus … Marcellus … Scipio Africanus:** Three war heroes from the upper classes. T. Manlius Torquatus was supposed to have earned his cognomen in 361 by removing a golden chain from his opponent in single combat. An excerpt in Aulus Gellius 9.13 from the *Annals* of the historian Q. Claudius Quadrigarius gives a sense of how such incidents were handled in the literature of Cicero's youth. M. Claudius Marcellus when he was consul in 222 killed the opposing general in single combat at Clastidium in Cisalpine Gaul (Plutarch, *Marcellus* 7.1–3). The incident involving P. Cornelius Scipio Aemilianus Africanus is not otherwise recorded.

4.50 **Lucius Brutus:** L. Junius Brutus is the famous ancestor of Cicero's addressee. According to Livy 2.6.6–9, he was killed in a cavalry engagement with Arruns Tarquinius.

4.51   **Scipio, the great Pontifex Maximus:** P. Cornelius Scipio Nasica Ser-
apio (consul 138), during civil unrest of 133, led the Senate in an assault
on Tiberius Gracchus which cost the latter his life. The cry "let those
who wish to save the Republic follow me" amounts to a declaration of
martial law. As a private citizen, Nasica could not legally utter it, but
Cicero implies that his action was justified by the needs of the moment.

4.52   **Whether I myself have performed any brave action:** False modesty: Cicero alludes to his own actions in thwarting the conspiracy of
Catiline in 63. This implies that the anger displayed in the orations
against Catiline was feigned as suggested in 4.55.

    their quarrel in Homer: *Iliad* 1.122–305.

    bravest of all in his frenzy: The madness of Ajax has already been
mentioned in 3.11 as an example of *furor* or insanity as commonly conceived; see comm. 3, I_B (on 3.8–11). Cicero attributes his state to the
effects of extreme anger, as does Sophocles (*Ajax* 40–41). But while
Sophocles and others make Ajax's anger a response to the awarding of
Achilles' arms to Odysseus, Cicero here speaks as if Ajax were already
insane much earlier, when he drove the Trojans from the ships (*Iliad*
15.674–746).

    A great deed he performed: The lines belong to the old Latin
drama on grounds of meter but cannot otherwise be identified.

4.53   **the definitions of courage:** Parts of all four definitions are attested
elsewhere; see esp. Stob., *Ecl.* 2.7.5b1, 5b5 (59.10–11, 63.20–22 W); Sextus, *AM* 9.158 (*SVF* 3.263); Philo of Alexandria, *Allegorical Laws* 1.68 (*SVF*
3.263). Since Cicero's case rests on what is *not* said in the definitions, he
is unusually exact in his report.

    Sphaerus: Sphaerus of Borysthenes (mid-3d century) studied
with Zeno and Cleanthes, later settling in Alexandria (D.L. 7.177).
His works included a treatise *On Definitions* as well as one *On Emotions.*

4.54   **it is cases like this:** Cases like those of Ajax and Achilles, otherwise
good persons who are spoiled by anger. The paragraph is connected in
thought with 4.52 and comes in here as an afterthought.

    "all fools are insane": See on 3.10.

    morose: *Morosus* regularly means "peevish" (Seneca, *On Anger* 1.4.2).
A derivation from the stem in *mores* (which Cicero takes for granted)
would suggest a more general meaning (e.g., "immoral").

4.55   **Does no one punish:** For Accius see on 3.20; the line is from his *Atreus*
(Warmington 2.390).

    Do you think that Accius was angry: *On the Orator* 2.193–94 makes
exactly the opposite claim, using Pacuvius for the example and claim-

ing for its authority the remarks of Plato and Democritus on the madness *(mania)* of poets.

the centurion ... the standard-bearer: Either might have occasion to exhort soldiers to fight; neither would have received the education in oratory and philosophy which Cicero regards as indispensable if one is to make use of reasoned argument in public speaking.

lest I reveal the secrets of orators: To go further in this direction would be to write a work on rhetorical theory rather than on ethics.

4.56   **rivalry ... and jealousy, and pity:** The claims are made at 4.46.

4.57   **full of longing, irascible, anxious, and timid:** All are listed as "proclivities" in 4.27–28.

the knowledge of things divine and human: The same definition is found in Sextus, *AM* 9.13 (*SVF* 2.36).

like a sea exposed to the winds: See on 4.10 **tranquillity.**

the roots of error: For the imagery, see on 3.83.

PART IV: CURES FOR THE EMOTIONS

A.   Introduction to Therapeutic Approaches (4.58–62)

Perhaps what you really want is to be free of emotions yourself. Philosophy does offer remedies, which are worth pursuing, although they require concentrated effort. More than one therapeutic strategy is possible. One principal sort of therapeutic discourse is directed at beliefs about what kinds of things count as good or evil; a second is directed at the emotion itself. While either can be effective, at least in theory, the latter is more generally useful and is available to all schools of philosophy.

Just as the end of book 3 made practical recommendations for the consolation of distress, so the end of book 4 will discuss philosophical remedies for the emotions in general. Distress is still named as the paradigm emotion, especially in 4.59–61, but others, in particular erotic love and anger, will soon claim the spotlight. Again as in book 3, Cicero begins with general principles for the therapeutic endeavor. As before, he professes a willingness to be flexible as to the strategies to be employed; in fact, however, he gives serious attention to two methods only, both of Stoic origin, and unqualified approval to only one of these. This, he says, can and should be adopted by all philosophers regardless of their position on value.

The difference between the two approaches in question is made clearer by comparison with 3.76–79. The method which tries to convince the hearer that the object at which the emotion is directed has no genuine value or disvalue is clearly a more general form of Cleanthes' consolation, which "teaches the sufferer that what happened is not an evil" (3.76). About the other method, the "specific and more reliable cure," Cicero says only that it "addresses the emotion itself" or "teaches that the emotions are wrong in and of themselves." This is not very helpful, but a repetition of the "Alcibiades" case from 3.77 makes it clear that the recommended method is the one there attributed to Chrysippus. One is now to show for every emotion, and not only for grief, that the belief about appropriateness (the second component identified at 3.25) is false. For although the emotion is indeed dependent on a belief that the object at hand or in prospect is a genuine good or evil, it is best to leave this belief unchallenged for the time being, since it is the one the hearer is least likely to relinquish. Emotions will be eradicated just as effectively by eliminating the necessary belief that emotional feelings and behaviors are appropriate in some circumstances. Moreover, this strategy has the advantage of flexibility in addressing those who cannot accept the Stoic position on value. For even if one adheres to the Aristotelian position on the "three classes of goods" (see on 4.62, p. 174) or thinks, like the hedonists, that pleasure is the good, it should still be possible to argue that emotional responses to those goods (or to the corresponding evils) are inappropriate. So says Chrysippus himself, on behalf of his own method, in Appendix C, passage [m].

All this seems considerably too easy. Two objections present themselves immediately. First, a practical objection: Convincing one's hearers that no emotion is ever appropriate seems hardly easier than convincing them that the objects of their present emotions have no real value. Second, a theoretical objection: It was implied in the discussion of well-reasoned affect (4.12–13) that our belief in the appropriateness of elevation, reaching, and withdrawing may in some circumstances be perfectly correct. It is not the movements themselves that are problematic, but movements generated in the wrong way, wrong usually through false ascriptions of value. Only full-scale contraction can never be right, and then only because the wise person can never be in the presence of a genuine evil. Cicero here seems oblivious to both these objections, despite the reservations he has himself expressed at 3.79. We may surmise that Chrysippus was less incautious, though we can only speculate as to how his suggestion might have been refined. For instance, the second objection might be forestalled by particularizing the belief to be removed (viz., "it is never appropriate to be elated over winning an election," cf. 4.66).

This would make the proposed therapy more time-consuming, since each object-type would require its own arguments, but would surely improve its prospects of success.

On the three classes of goods see Dillon 1996, 9, 74–75.

4.58 **so many means of cure for our bodies, and none for our minds:** The thought is Chrysippan; compare Appendix C, passage [j], and 3.4.

4.59 **several different kinds:** Cicero lists three different ways therapeutic approaches may vary: (1) they may be addressed to different species within a broad genus such as distress (cf. 3.83); (2) they may be addressed either to emotions in general or to a single genus or species; (3) they may be addressed either to evaluations of objects or to beliefs about what responses are appropriate. Only the third sort of variation will be considered here.

4.60 **The other method . . . is indeed more useful:** The approach which concentrates on the value of the object can be considered "more useful" in that if it succeeds, it will eliminate all future emotions concerned with the same or similar objects. At the same time it "cannot be applied to the uneducated" (the *vulgus*, as in Lucretius 1.945), i.e., to those who are not currently even studying philosophy. For these will be so unfamiliar with philosophic discussions about value that they will not be willing to listen to this sort of advice at all.

4.61 **upset about his own lack of virtue:** In addition to its practical limitations, the Cleanthean approach is not even of theoretical utility against emotions directed at moral goods or evils. See further comm. 3, VA (on 3.75–79).

responsibility or integrity: "Responsibility" is *officium*, a sense of what actions are appropriate for oneself. "Integrity" is *honestas*, a sense of what actions are honorable or morally excellent. The same words are also used more technically, to render *to kathēkon* and *to kalon*.

all of them ought to agree: This looks like special pleading, since other philosophers may not concede that emotions are inherently unreasonable. But Cicero will appeal to ordinary moral intuitions which regard calmness and largeness of view as especially praiseworthy.

it is a fault: As a movement, an emotion is not, strictly speaking, a fault (4.30), but it is still *vitiosus*, still "faulty" or "a matter of fault," since it can only occur in those who are in a state of fault.

great-spirited or a brave man: The language is gendered: *virtus* is not only virtue but also courage and manliness; see *Tusc.* 2.43. For great-spiritedness see on 3.15.

4.62   **three classes of goods:** Goods of the body (health, strength), of the mind (good memory, learning, the virtues), and "of life," i.e., external goods (wealth, reputation). The classification is regularly identified as Peripatetic or early Academic (*Tusc.* 5.24, 5.85; *On Ends* 3.43; *Acad.* 1.19–22) but is called "ancient" already in Aristotle, *NE* 1.8. Compare Plato, *Laws* 3.697b.

B.   Arguments to Be Used against Individual Emotions (4.62–79)

I have already mentioned how distress is best treated by setting the present sufferings in the context of the common lot of humanity. Fear is closely related to distress and can be treated similarly. Gladness and desire, too, need therapeutic treatment. Rather than arguing that the objects of gladness are not good things, we should show that it is not proper to become excessively elated over them. Erotic love is a shameful thing, even though it is condoned by poets and indeed philosophers. Of several cures for love, the best is to show the lover what a disturbed state of mind love is. Anger is a particularly dangerous emotion, akin to insanity. Yet both love and anger are dependent on belief and thus voluntary.

Pursuing the program laid out in 4.59, Cicero now takes up each of five important emotions and offers a sample of the remarks that might be made against each. The series is organized in accordance with the now-familiar fourfold classification, but the four genera are not treated equally. Distress and fear receive only a cursory treatment, since the former has already been treated at length in book 3, and the latter is concerned especially with death and pain, the subjects of books 1 and 2. The emotions directed at the apparent good are presented at greater length: there is a brief review of method and then, in a heightened tone and with numerous illustrations from the poets, full-scale attacks on gladness, erotic love, and anger.

By far the most interesting of these is the long section which argues the disadvantages and inherent impropriety of erotic love. Love has not previously been mentioned, and the silence is significant. For the mainstream tradition represented by Plato and the Stoics offers some enthusiastically positive accounts of this emotion and its role in the philosophical education. Only the Epicureans strictly exclude *erōs* from the wise person's experience (see on 4.70, and compare the powerful attack in Lucretius at 4.1058–1191). If Cicero is to include love in his sequence of negative treatments here—and it is hard to see how he could avoid the topic altogether—he will be in the odd position of arguing against his own favorite philosophers and in favor of a view identified with his chief opponents. In the context of a serious exposition of ethical fundamentals, this would hardly have been possible; here, the relaxed liveliness of the therapeutic section makes it somewhat easier. Aristocratic Roman prejudices against the cultural institutions of Greek cities are on his side here also, and he does not hesitate to exploit them.

Given Cicero's usual hostility to Epicurean ethics, his apparent endorsement of Epicurus's position on erotic love has surprised some commentators. But the appeal to Epicurus is sheer hyperbole, meant to point up the extreme unfitness of the Platonic and Stoic stance. The singling out of male—male *erōs* in 4.71 is likewise a rhetorical move rather than a substantive objection to homosexual behavior. Cicero is quite willing to jeer at Ganymede in order to make his point against Plato and the Stoics, both closely associated with the Athenian norms elevating pederasty to a cultural ideal. But there is no corresponding endorsement of heterosexual love: the examples from *Medea*, especially, make it clear that the condemnation is meant to apply equally to relations between the sexes. Had he wished to use an illustration from Roman poetry involving love between males, he could easily have done so, since he knew well the works of Afranius, which are known to have included more than one homosexual intrigue (Quintilian, *Instruction of the Orator* 10.1.100).

In complaining against Plato, Cicero is undoubtedly thinking of those passages in the *Symposium* and *Phaedrus* which make the experience of erotic love a necessary part of the philosopher's intellectual development. These were far more damaging to his own case than were the biographical claims of Dicaearchus mentioned in 4.71, since Plato might have been in love himself without recommending love to others. The Stoics, too, no doubt taking their clue from Plato, elevated erotic love to an ethical ideal. The doxographic accounts note that according to Zeno and other Stoic writers "the wise person will fall in love with young persons who through their form give an impression of a good natural endowment for virtue" (D.L. 7.129). To reconcile this claim with their general condemnation of the *pathē*, they take the startling position that genuine erotic love is not an emotion at all. Cicero's failure to include love in his list of species-emotions at 4.16—21 might be due to other causes, but there can be no accident about the definition that he reports in 4.72. For this canonical definition, which we have from many sources, does not allow that love is a species of desire. Rather it is "an effort to form a friendship, due to an impression of beauty." What is meant by an "effort" *(conatus, epibolē)* is not at all clear. We know, however, that effort is a species of impulse, apparently one concerned in some way with the future ("an impulse before an impulse," Stob, *Ecl.* 2.7.9a (87.18 W)). This confirms that it is replacing desire (also an impulse) in the definition, no doubt to make the point that love is a movement which does not commit the agent to any false evaluation. Probably, then, love is a "consistency," presumably as a species of "volition." See comm. 4, IIA (on 4.10–14), section 2.

But it would hardly make sense to deny that ordinary persons, as well as sages, can fall in love. In answer to this obvious objection, the Stoics appear to have identified also a second form of erotic love which is indeed a species of desire. Evidence for the second definition can be gleaned from D.L. 7.113: "Love is [a species of] desire, but not among the virtuous, for [among the latter] it is an effort [viz.,] to form a friendship, due to an impression of beauty." Compare also Stob, *Ecl.* 2.7.5b9 (65.17–20 W):

> There are two senses in which one may speak of the "erotic person"; one in reference to virtue, as one quality of the righteous person, and one in reference to vice, as if blaming someone for "love-madness."

If the second definition was known to Cicero, he might easily have chosen to direct his remarks against it only, reserving judgment on the wise version of love as Panaetius is supposed to have done (in an anecdote reported by Seneca, *Ep.* 116.5). He would then be arguing on behalf of the Stoics against a form of love which they, too, consider to be unnatural and destructive. But the sarcastic tone of 4.70–72 reads as a condemnation of the Stoic position in general. Either Cicero is unaware of any negative treatment of *erōs* within the Stoa, or he has specific reasons for wishing to raise questions about their positive account. He may wish to eliminate recourse to the Stoic definition on the part of ordinary persons using it to defend their less high-minded affections.

In his remarks on the means of cure for both love and anger, Cicero comes near to the observations of Chrysippus on excessiveness in passage [1] of Appendix C. The "frenzy" mentioned here is not, of course, the frenzy of mental derangement as in 3.11, but it is akin to it and may lead to it: see comm. 3, IB (on 3.8–11). In attacking gladness, too, he has some token support from Chrysippus (Appendix C, passage [e]). But his speech on gladness is poorly developed and awkward. Symmetry demanded that such an attack be included, but the theme is not very promising, and it is not likely that even Chrysippus expanded upon it at any length.

For Platonic *erōs* see esp. Halperin 1990, 113–52; Price 1989. For the Stoics, and for the relation between the Platonic and Stoic views, Nussbaum 1995; Inwood 1997; Schofield 1991, 26–56. On Epicurus's position, Nussbaum 1994, 149–54. For the relation of 4.68–76 to Lucretius, Brown 1987, 138–39.

4.62 **to set in view what it is to be a human:** The method recommended in 3.30 and 3.34.

4.63 **No tale is so terrible:** The opening lines of Euripides' *Orestes*, followed immediately by the Tantalus story as given in 4.35. By quoting the lines out of context, Cicero changes their meaning somewhat. For Euripides, the tendency of humans to take on divinely inflicted misfortunes will be illustrated by the audacious crimes of Tantalus and Atreus.

    applied a remedy to the mind's swelling while it was still fresh: The thought is a commonplace of consolation literature, given a philosophical interpretation by Chrysippus; see comm. 3, Vᴀ (on 3.75–79).

    the force of nature: The "force of nature" is the persuasive force of the argument from the human condition, which reminds the sufferer of the regular restrictions on human nature (3.34, 3.57).

4.64 **some have called it a species of distress, and others have named it "foregrief":** Both remarks seem to belong to the Peripatetic/Platonist tradition. A classification scheme which treats (mental) pain and pleasure as the primary genera of emotion is explicitly attested by Alcinous (*Handbook of Platonism* 32.2–3) and forms the basis of Aristotle's definitions in *Rhet.* 2.1–11. "Foregrief" (*praemolestia*) looks like a translation of a Greek term, perhaps *prolupēsis* (Plato, *Republic* 9.584c).

    to speak contemptuously about the ... objects of fear: To argue that the objects of fear are not evils.

4.66 **cannot ever feel gladness:** As the wise person is never in the presence of an actual evil, so the non-wise is never in the presence of an actual good. The cases differ, however, in that the non-wise person will often have erroneous beliefs about what is good and may experience gladness on that basis. Thus the argument Cicero calls "easy" could not succeed even on Stoic terms.

    the most plausible position: Cicero here gives the palm to the Stoic position on value. Yet he is still speaking as an Academic, in that the view he endorses is not said to be true, but only "what is most plausible" (*quae maxime probatur*).

    Pouring out the mind in gladness: "Outpouring" (*ecfusio*) is equivalent to "elevation"; see on 4.14–15. The emphasis rests on the word "gladness," since elevation itself need not be contrary to right reason (4.13, 4.67).

confidence: This word is something of a surprise: we might have expected "caution" (*cavere*) to complete the parallel with 4.13, and some editors emend the text accordingly. But the reading *confidere* has impressive support in a quotation by Nonius in the fourth century, and 4.80 similarly offers *fidentia* as a paradigm of well-reasoned affect. The occurrence of *tharros*, again "confidence," in two lists of *eupatheiai* in Stobaeus would seem to confirm the reading (*Ecl.* 2.7.5b, 5g (58.8, 72.2 W)). See Lundström 1964, 159 and Giusta 1984 ad loc. "Confidence" is similarly prominent in Aristotle's discussions of emotion, where it is merely the opposite of fear (*Rhet.* 2.5, *NE* 3.6–9). In a Stoic discussion, however, confidence must be a response in the sage to the prospect of a moral evil in the self, e.g., of committing an injustice. The substitution of confidence for caution is perhaps in response to an epistemological worry: will the sage not be aware that no genuine evil can even be in prospect for him? He will certainly "withdraw" from such evils, but he will also feel confident of his ability to avoid them, and the impulse should be specified accordingly.

for the purposes of teaching: The distinction is serious enough. Cicero means that *gaudium* and *laetitia* are not so carefully distinguished in ordinary usage, whatever may have been the case with Gr. *chara* and *hēdonē*. Seneca similarly distinguishes *gaudium* from *voluptas* in *Ep.* 59.1–2.

4.67   **Glad am I, father:** From Naevius's tragedy *Hector's Departure* (Warmington 2.118).

   The madam's greased with silver: From an unidentified comedy (Ribbeck 2.36); see also on 4.35 **extreme delight of mind.**

4.68   **Not only is it shameful:** The transition from gladness to erotic love is rapid, without the usual introductory statement. The heightened tone corresponds to the inflammatory subject matter.

   Love is the greatest god: From an unidentified comedy (Warmington 1.548–49). Compare Euripides, fr. 269 Nauck.

4.69   **What a fine moral guide:** The disparagement of poetry echoes Cicero's own words in the first part of *Tusc.* 2.27–28, just as the disparagement of philosophy that follows echoes the second part.

   You saved me for the sake of love: From Ennius's *Medea in Exile* (fr. 107 Jocelyn). See on 3.63.

   I had him for my husband: From another play on the Medea legend, perhaps Pacuvius's *Medus* (Warmington 2.262).

4.70 **even Jupiter:** The philosophers' treatment of Jupiter was very different; see especially Cleanthes' *Hymn to Zeus* (*SVF* 1.537).

Epicurus ... was not far from speaking the truth: Epicurus denies that erotic love, which he defines as "an intense desire for intercourse" (Hermias, *On Plato's Phaedrus* 76, fr. 483 Usener) is compatible with happiness: D.L. 10.118 reports that "they [the Epicureans] do not think that the wise person will fall in love ... nor that love is a thing sent by the gods. ... Intercourse, they say, has never benefited anyone; one is lucky if it has not even done harm." Compare *Tusc.* 5.94. But Epicurus does not condemn sexual activity per se; compare 3.41.

a love whose object is friendship: *amor amicitiae*; cf. the Stoic definition in 4.72.

Disgrace begins with nudity: Fr. 176 Jocelyn, from an unidentified tragedy.

4.71 **Euripides' Laius:** The story of Laius's abduction of Chrysippus, the son of Pelops, was recounted in Euripides' lost *Chrysippus*. Pacuvius wrote a play based on the same legend.

Alcaeus ... Anacreon ... Ibycus: Greek lyric poets, all three of whom included some homoerotic material in their output. Alcaeus saw combat both in his native Mytilene and abroad.

We philosophers: Sarcasm for rhetorical effect, as at *Tusc.* 2.28. In neither passage is Cicero rejecting philosophy itself; he merely expresses dissatisfaction with certain philosophical views.

the charges of Dicaearchus: Dicaearchus (late 4th century) was a pupil of Aristotle. Two works of his on the nature of the soul are named as sources in *Tusc.* 1.21, 1.77. The "charges," which must be charges of sexual misconduct, were probably in his work *On Lives*.

4.72 **an effort to form a friendship, due to an impression of beauty:** The same definition appears in a number of sources, e.g. Stob., *Ecl.* 2.7.11s (115.1–4 W), D.L. 7.130. The mention of beauty is puzzling: Why should wise persons restrict their affections to those who are physically attractive? Would the sage fall in love with a fifteen-year-old Socrates? But there is no guarantee that the beauty noticed by the sage will conform to conventional standards. A person's character is "graspable from his form" (D.L. 7.173), but the characteristics of form that mark one as being "of good endowment for virtue" are chiefly to be seen in bearing and deportment (Clement, *Pedagogue* 3.11.74 (*SVF* 1.246)). Compare Plutarch, *On Common Notions* 1073b, and see on 4.32 **natural endowments.**

If such a love exists ... then so be it: Let it be true that the wise person will fall in love (*amaturum ... sit*), provided it can be shown that a feeling recognizable as erotic love could be completely free of desire. The point of the if-clause is not that wise love happens not to be instanced anywhere in the world—that objection could be raised against any of the consistencies. Rather, it is that love as specified in the definition is not even a conceivable form of affect: it is a thing impossible in the universe, like a square circle.

this talk is about desire: Ultimately the Stoic definition reduces to a definition of desire. *Oratio* "talk" is used contemptuously of an opponent's words, as often, e.g. 4.23, 4.38.

But if there is any love . . . : The sentence is left grammatically incomplete, giving the impression that the need for careful argumentation is now swept away by the force of the examples. As *sin*, "but if," regularly introduces the second part of a biconditional, we are apparently meant to assume the following train of thought: "But if the kind of love described by the Stoic definition does *not* exist in nature, then all love is of the kind instanced in *Leucadia*—which certainly does exist—and that kind is little short of insanity."

the lover in *Leucadia*: The quotations are from the comedy adapted from Menander by Sextus Turpilius (2d century), Ribbeck 2.116. The story involved the love of Sappho for Phaon and, according to Ribbeck, at least one other pair of lovers. Sappho's suicide would illustrate Cicero's point well enough; see on 4.41. But the speaker here is male.

4.73   **Neptune omnipotent:** The best manuscripts have an *a-* before *omnipotens,* and for this reason some editors print *amnipotens,* "river-powerful," a possible though otherwise unattested epithet for Neptune. But "omnipotent" is better suited to a plea for divine assistance. See further Lundström 1986, 71–72.

4.74   **the cure that should be applied:** Two of the suggestions made here resemble remedies offered in Lucretius 4.1069–72: that the lover should be distracted with other pursuits, and that he should satisfy the sexual urge "somewhere else or in some other way," i.e. by the use of prostitutes or slaves. Compare also Epicurus, *Vatican Sayings* 18: "Take away the sight of beloved, and the association and daily contact, and the experience *(pathos)* of love is dissolved." But the thought is commonplace enough.

4.75   **one nail is knocked from its hole by another:** Proverbial, as in Aristotle, *Politics* 8.1314a.

4.76   **The wrongs, the suspicions:** Terence, *Eunuch* 59–63.

if love were natural: Individual variation in the way we experience love is sufficient to show that love is dependent on character, and this is enough to make it voluntary in the weak sense explained in 3.64–71.

4.77   **Is there anyone in all the world:** Perhaps from Ennius's *Iphigeneia*, a favorite play of Cicero's; see Jocelyn, 321.

A greater weight, a greater ill: This and the following quotation are from Accius's tragedy *Atreus* (Warmington 2.382, 390). The passage is quoted at greater length in *ND* 3.68.

out of control: The point is as in 4.22; see comm. 4, IIв (on 4.14–22), section 2, and compare Chrysippus's remarks in Appendix C, passage [l].

4.78   **the scattered parts of the mind:** "Parts" can hardly refer to the quasi-Platonic division of soul from 4.10. Probably we should interpret in terms of the "limbs" or "parts" mentioned by Chrysippus in Appendix C, passage [j], these being the "things of which reason is composed," i.e., the judgments. During an emotional movement the mind is at variance with itself to an exceptional degree, since the assent involved in the emotion overrides, through its excessiveness, any subsequent impulse to the contrary. Dougan and Henry 1934 suggest an interpretation in material terms, as a diffusion of the vital heat away from the center; compare next note. The two explanations are not mutually exclusive.

ceases to boil: In Aristotle (*On the Soul* 1.1.403a29–31) the "boiling of the blood around the heart" provides a material account of the movement of anger, and this formulation was used in the later tradition as well; see Galen, *On Preserving Health* 2.9 (*SVF* 2.878); Nemesius, *Nature of the Human* 21 (*SVF* 3.416). See also on 4.21 *thumōsis*.

After **ceases to boil** there follows in the received text a short sentence offering a definition of *defervescere* ("*defervescere* means, surely, a burning of the mind aroused against the will of reason"). This must, I think, be a scribal gloss: not only does it suggest the wrong interpretation for the verb ("boil up" rather than "cease to boil" or "boil away"), but its inclusion leaves *ex quo* "for this reason" too far separated from the clause to which it refers (*ut differant in tempus aliud* "to put it off").

Archytas: So also *On the Republic* 1.59. Archytas of Tarentum, the Pythagorean philosopher and mathematician, was a contemporary of Plato. The same anecdote was told both of Socrates (Seneca, *On Anger* 1.15.3) and of Plato (Seneca, *On Anger* 3.12.5, D.L. 3.78).

4.79   **those who claim that anger ... is natural:** Primarily the Peripatetics, as at 4.43.

Alexander ... after he had killed his comrade Clitus: The anecdote is recounted in more detail in Seneca, *On Anger* 3.17.

C.   Conclusion to Book Four (4.79–84)

Indeed, every emotion arises from false belief, whereas the "consistencies" arise from knowledge. While we do have proclivities, even innate proclivities, to one emotion or another, these need not determine our actual behavior. Hence the great value of our discussions here: it is by such intellectual activity that philosophy provides healing.

The conclusion to the practical discourse, which also concludes the book, gives a brief review of two points covered early in book 4, then in a somewhat grander style looks back at what has been achieved in all the work to this point. It is only because emotions are belief-dependent that philosophic discourse, which deals in belief, can claim to have any influence in this area; if Cicero has become repetitive on the point, it is because he recognizes its importance for his enterprise. Efforts at practical therapy must also meet objections based on the theoretical discussion of "sicknesses" and "proclivities" (4.23–28). Cicero now indicates that inborn proclivities do not disappear completely even in those whose training has been completely successful; compare Lucretius 3.307–22. The sicknesses, by contrast, are entirely culpable and should be removed altogether. But the process of therapy will be long and difficult, for these are not short-lived episodes but conditions ingrained by habit.

Because of textual corruption, we cannot be certain what the first part of 4.80 is supposed to add to the discussion. The reading adopted here attempts to rescue what I take to be a gesture toward the epistemological basis of the distinction between emotions and consistencies *(eupatheiai)*. Considered from an epistemological standpoint, a "consistency" is an instance of what Stoics call "grasping" *(katalēpsis)*, while an emotion is an instance of ordinary "weak" or ill-grounded assent. The contrast between confidence and fear serves as an example of this, confidence *(fidentia, tharros)* being a consistency as in Stob., *Ecl.* 2.7.5b (58.8 W). (In view of 4.13, we might have expected to see caution, rather than confidence, as the consistency opposed to fear, but the substitution is not made here alone; see on 4.66.) But Cicero confuses the issue slightly by also identifying confidence as a form of knowledge: as a movement, a consistency ought not to be knowledge but rather an activity of knowledge. However, we do have record in Stobaeus also of a virtue called *tharraleotēs;* a species of courage (*Ecl.* 2.7.5b2 (60.21–22 W)). This would presumably be that particular form of knowledge which disposes the sage to *tharros.* Cicero, or his source, may have confused the movement with the similarly named condition.

A brief reprise of the theory on proclivities and faults is augmented by a curious anecdote involving the ancient practice of physiognomics or the reading of character from external appearance. The point made is similar to that at *On Fate* 7–10, which recounts the Zopyrus anecdote in more detail (see on 4.80). Neither passage makes it clear, however, whether the physiognomical addendum comes through Stoic sources or is put forward by their Academic opponents. The early Stoa did maintain the validity of that peculiar science, asserting—not altogether strangely, for thoroughgoing materialists—that a person's character is "graspable from his form" (D.L. 7.173, and see on 4.72). But physiognomic material was popular with more than one school, and various conclusions could be drawn from it. Thus while the Zopyrus anecdote might well be taken to imply that tendencies to particular emotions may be innate, we should be cautious about attributing any such claim to the Stoics. See comm. 4, IIc (on 4.23–33), section 2.

On physiognomics in the ancient world see Tsouna 1998a; Evans 1969; Sharples 1983, 130; in Stoicism, Schofield 1991, 115–18, conceptual background in Sedley 1993. On Phaedo's *Zopyrus*, Giannantoni 1990, vol. 1, I-C.49, III-A.11.

4.79   **greed and desire for glory:** See on 4.25.

4.80   **confidence, or a firm assurance of mind:** Cicero's expression *firma animi confisio* corresponds well with the definition of confidence cited as Stoic by the scholiast to *Iliad* 5.2 (*SVF* 3.287), "an unerring trust in oneself, that one will not encounter anything terrible." On the word *fidentia* see also 3.14.

    a serious opinion on the part of one who does not assent rashly: Error in the non-wise is the result of assenting "rashly" to impressions which are unclear or not graspable; see esp. Stob., *Ecl.* 2.7.11m (112.5–8 W), and *Acad.* 1.42. *Opinio* is used of the beliefs of the wise also at 4.31.

    so also is fear an opinion: The translation is based on Heine's conjecture restoring *opinio* in place of *diffidentia*. Fear is not an opinion in the same sense as confidence, since the latter is a "serious opinion" or *katalēpsis* rather than an ordinary opinion *(doxa)*. But the two are comparable in that both take the form of assent to some proposition, and this is the point here.

    hope is an expectation of good: The present passage seems to present hope as an *eupatheia*, and this may also be the view of Philo of Alexandria at *The Worse Defeats the Better* 140. But hope is not usually treated as an affective response in Stoic theory, but merely as a belief about the future.

After **so also with the other emotions,** the manuscripts add the words *sunt in malo,* "they are in bad. . . ." Not much can be gotten out of these, and as the text yields reasonably good sense without them, they are omitted from the translation. For a history of efforts to restore the paragraph see Lundström 1964, 213–24, with Giusta 1984 ad loc.

Zopyrus: His interactions with Socrates were the subject of a dialogue by Phaedo of Elis, a contemporary of Plato. In *On Fate* 10, Zopyrus deduces from the absence of certain hollows about the throat that Socrates is dull-witted and also overfond of women. Alcibiades bursts out laughing—but Zopyrus turns out to be correct.

he had cast them out by reason: That is, by philosophy *(ratio).* Alexander of Aphrodisias, reporting the same anecdote for the Peripatetics, has "through the practice *(askēsis)* that comes from philosophy" (Alexander, *On Fate* 171.11–17).

4.83   **because we think it appropriate:** Cicero opts yet again for the Chrysippan therapy of 3.76.

4.84   **philosophy consists in comparing:** The day's discussion ends as it began (4.7), with a reminder that judgments are free.

APPENDIXES:
SOURCES FOR CICERO'S ACCOUNT

A P P E N D I X A

CRANTOR AND THE

CONSOLATORY TRADITION

Cicero's immediate response to bereavement was to read. He read not only his friends' letters of sympathy and consolation (see pp. xiii–xv) but, more ambitiously, in the writings of the philosophers. "At your house I read everything that anyone has ever written on the alleviation of sorrow," he wrote to Atticus on March 8, some three weeks after Tullia died, "but my grief defeats every consolation" (*Att.* 12.14.3). These readings must have included, among other things, the letter of Panaetius mentioned in 4.4 and an epistle or short treatise by Crantor of Soli, titled *On Grief*. It was also at this time that he composed a consolatory work addressed to himself, "a consolation like no other" (*Att.* 12.14.3). This was more than an exercise in personal writing: it was meant for circulation, required research (*Att.* 12.20.2, 12.22.1), and is listed in *On Divination* 2.3 as a philosophical work in its own right. The *Consolation* is lost to us, but we know from later sources that Cicero claimed to have "followed" Crantor in it (Pliny, *Natural History pref.* 22; Jerome *Letter* 60.5); this means, probably, that he imitated the format of Crantor's work and at least some of its language and content. The present work adopts a more critical stance in relation to Crantor (3.12, 3.71); nonetheless, it too may owe a considerable debt both to his work and to other works in the consolatory tradition.

Surviving fragments of Crantor's treatise are not sufficient to tell us whether it pursued a clear philosophical agenda; nonetheless, it is clear that Cicero both in the *Tusculans* and in the slightly earlier *Academics* considers it a fair representative of the "Old Academic" position on emotion in general.

Prior Academics 2.135 (quoted on p. xxv) associates the work with three broad claims: that emotions should be kept within certain naturally ordained limits, that within these limits emotions are natural (and thus acceptable and ineliminable), and that such "moderate" emotions serve useful purposes in human life. These are of course the same views as are attributed in the present work to the Peripatetics (3.71–74; 4.38–47).

The identification of Old Academic and Peripatetic views is not surprising, since Cicero regards all Academics before Arcesilaus as holding substantially the same views as Aristotle (*On the Orator* 3.67, *Acad.* 1.22, *On Ends* 5.7), and since the reported claims have clear Aristotelian antecedents (see comm. 4, IIIB (on 4.38–47)). It is noteworthy, though, that a work of consolation should be named in evidence of a position which concerns not grief alone but emotions in general, and which is, moreover, of very broad ethical significance. Cicero is taking Crantor's work seriously as philosophy, pressing the implications of points made in the context of consolation and setting them against general Stoic (and, in *Prior Academics,* Antiochan) claims about impassivity *(apatheia).* At least as concerns the central issues of nature, functionality, and limit, Crantor can figure as a representative opponent for the view which he, taking the Stoic line, means to attack. This does not mean, however, that he has to reject everything in the consolatory tradition, since many standard consolatory remarks could be made to support the Stoic side as easily as the Peripatetic.

In tracing the influence of Crantor in particular, it is helpful to compare the *Tusculan Disputations* with a later consolatory epistle, the *Consolation to Apollonius* preserved in the corpus of Plutarch. Written in Greek, this relatively late work (probably second century C.E.) shares Cicero's fondness for Crantor's treatise. Indeed, a close comparison of the pseudo-Plutarchan work with Cicero's helps to confirm the influence of Crantor on both works, for the verbal and thematic correspondences between them are extensive, involving some ten passages from *Tusculans* 3–4 and a number of others from the treatment of death in book 1. Of these, five are linked to Crantor by explicit citations in one or the other of the two works. Moreover, the nature of the correspondences makes it clear that neither author is at all concerned to document every one of his borrowings from this source. Thus in passage [b], ps.-Plutarch represents as his own the first part of the paragraph which Cicero quotes as Crantor's in 3.12. Likewise in a long passage from *Cons. Ap.* 108f–116c there is a string of eight examples and quotations which correspond closely to material in *Tusculans* 1 and 3; of these, three are attributed by ps.-Plutarch to Crantor but offered by Cicero as if his own, while a fourth has the attribution in Cicero only. It is a fair guess, then, that at least some of the corresponding passages not labeled Crantoran by either author were also in fact taken from his work, especially since several of these involve quotations from Euripides, whom Crantor is known to have quoted frequently (D.L. 4.26). Others may have been taken by both authors from other works of a similar nature. It would hardly be reasonable, for instance, to posit any single point of origin for the Anaxagoras anecdote in [j] and 3.30, which is given in near-identical words by Panaetius (fr. 115 van Straaten), Posidonius ([g] in Appendix D), and many later authors.

The value of the *Consolation to Apollonius* is all the greater when we consider the possibility that its versions of the consolatory commonplaces may have been derived directly from Crantor, without the mediation of Chrysippus or other Stoic authors. For while the consolations of Seneca likewise exhibit many points of similarity with *Tusculans* 3–4, these resemblances cannot tell us anything about what was contained in Crantor's work, since both Seneca and Cicero are known to have read extensively in Stoic works on grief and consolation. With the author to Apollonius, the case for dependence on Stoic sources is much less clear. To be sure, he does share with Chrysippus and Posidonius some anecdotal material and literary quotations, as noted later in this Appendix. But no theme endemic to Stoic ethics is sounded in his work (for impassivity, mentioned in [b], does not belong exclusively to Stoicism), and no Stoic author is ever mentioned by name. It may be, then, that the points of resemblance between his work and various Stoic texts should be explained in another way: the Stoic authors have themselves read and reflected on the very work of Crantor which the author to Apollonius takes as his model, along with (probably) other works from the early consolatory tradition. In that case, the pseudo-Plutarchan work actually provides us with a point of reference in studying Stoic interpretations of various standard consolatory themes. As Cicero himself had studied some Stoic works, at least those by Chrysippus (Appendix C) and Panaetius (see on 4.4), the mingled approbation and criticism with which he responds to Crantor and the consolatory tradition in the *Tusculans* may represent either his own view or that of his Stoic sources.

Themes shared between Cicero and the pseudo-Plutarchan *Consolation* include all of the following:

(1)   In offering consolation, as in applying medical treatment, it is important not to attempt a cure while the wound or illness is still "inflamed" ([a]) or "swollen" (*Tusc.* 4.63). The author to Apollonius uses this as an explanation of why his work arrives some time after the actual

bereavement, while Cicero notes it as a peculiarity of his own *Consolation* that it was written very soon after the event. As in [a], Cicero at 3.76 makes this same point with a quotation of *Prometheus Bound* 380–81.

(2)   While grief is a natural human response and cannot, indeed should not, be eliminated, it should only go so far. As noted above, two portions of [b], only the second of which is there attributed to Crantor, are near-identical with the passage cited as Crantoran by Cicero at 3.12. The first sentence of [b] also resembles the remark that "grief comes by nature," attributed at 3.71 to Cicero's Peripatetic opponents but also associated in that context with Crantor. The reference to "moderate emotion" in [b] resembles the thought in [h] and in 4.38 as well as in *Acad. Pr.* 2.135.

(3)   Bereavements and other supposed misfortunes are much less distressing if one has prepared oneself for them in advance, just as a town is less likely to be captured when it has warning before the attack ([g]). Compare 3.39 and 3.52. In support of the point, ps.-Plutarch quotes Euripides fr. 964 Nauck. Cicero quotes the same passage at 3.29 along with the much-repeated Anaxagoras anecdote [j], which ps.-Plutarch uses to support (4).

(4)   What has happened to the mourner is one of the regular occurrences of human life and so does not merit any extreme reaction. In itself something of a platitude (*Fam.* 5.16.2, *Att.* 12.11.1), the commonplace as used in [c], [d], [g], [h], [i], and in *Tusc.* 3.30, 3.34, 4.62–63, bears some distinctive features. The repetitions in [i] ("a share . . . things shared; the human lot . . . humans should") are strikingly phrased in Greek; see the notes on 3.30 and 3.34, where Cicero gives Latin equivalents. Both Cicero (3.59) and ps.-Plutarch ([f]) support the point by quoting Euripides fr. 757 Nauck; the excerpt in [f] is fuller by two lines. Both also connect it with the importance of citing many examples of persons who have borne such events calmly; such examples are helpful, it is said, because they lessen our sense of the importance of the loss ([e]; compare 3.58). The consolatory use of the meditation on the human condition can be seen also in [d], which Mette accepts as Crantoran.

(5)   Grief is of no use: it will not bring the dead person back and does him or her no service. The observation is as old as the *Iliad* (24.524, quoted in *Cons. Ap.* 105c) and recurs a number of times in the *Consolation to Apollonius;* in the passages quoted here it can be found in [a], [h], and [i]. The Demosthenes anecdote [k] supports this point: Demosthenes' suppression of grief is commended as patriotic, since it enables him to perform a service for the community. Cicero in 3.63 presents the same

anecdote but interprets it differently: Aeschines' attack serves as evidence that he and his audience are committed to a belief that grief is appropriate in certain circumstances.

It should be noted that while both (2) and (4) involve some material associated with Crantor, Cicero's criticism of the Old Academic/Peripatetic position is restricted to (2). None of the shared claims in (1)–(5) requires any commitment to characteristically Stoic positions; however, we do have some evidence, discussed in Appendix C and Appendix D below, that Chrysippus mentioned elements of (1), (2), (3), and (5), and that (3) and the last part of (2) were treated in some detail by Posidonius. If we are correct in assuming that ps.-Plutarch did not draw these elements from the Stoic tradition itself, then these will be points at which the Stoic authors take over existing consolatory themes and offer their own explanations for their efficacy. In that case, Cicero's own treatment of the consolatory material is likely to have been influenced by the treatment he finds in Chrysippus or other Stoic authors.

The fragments of Crantor are collected in Mette 1984. Hani 1972 provides an edition with commentary of the *Cons. Ap.* and a helpful review of scholarship, and makes as strong a case as can be made for Chrysippan influence. For the consolatory commonplaces see Kassel 1958, 49–98, together with the works cited under 3 IVA (on 3.52–61).

[a] *Cons. Ap.* 102a–b
At that time, so close to the moment of death, it would have been improper for me to accost you and encourage you to endure as a human should the thing that has happened, since you were laid low in body and soul by the unthought-of misfortune.... For when infections are acute, even the best doctors do not bring in medicinal remedies right away; rather, they let the worst of the inflammation subside on its own, without applying any salve from the outside. But now that time ... has passed since your misfortune ... I feel that it is well to share with you some words of comfort, to ease your grief and put an end to your pointless cries of mourning. For

words may be doctors to the mind's disease,
at least if one soothes the heart at the right time.

[b] *Cons. Ap.* 102cd = Crantor fr. 3a Mette
The painful bite of grief which one feels at the death of a son has its origin in nature and is not in our power. For I myself cannot agree with

those who extol that uncouth and hard impassivity. For that is neither possible nor beneficial, since it will remove the good will which comes from
mutual affection, and that is more to be preserved than anything else. But
when one is carried away beyond the measure, and increases one's griefs,
that, I say, is contrary to nature and happens through bad belief. So let that
go, since it is harmful and bad and not proper to men who are morally serious, but one need not get rid of moderate emotion (*metriopatheia*). For let
us not be ill, says Crantor the Academic, but if we are, let us feel it, even if
some part of our body should be cut open or amputated. For this absence
of pain comes to a person at a high price: such a one will no doubt become
like a wild beast both in body and in mind.

[c] *Cons. Ap.* 103f

The best medicine to free us from distress is reason and preparation
through reason for all the changes of life. For we should know not only that
we are mortal by nature, but also that we have a share in mortal life and in
circumstances which easily reverse themselves.

[d] *Cons. Ap.* 104c = Crantor fr. 4 Mette

Crantor, too, when he comforts Hippocles on the death of his children,
says, "All this old philosophy tells you these things and exhorts you. . . .
And this uncertain fortune has attended us all along from the beginning . . .
and a portion of evil is mingled with our nature at birth. For indeed, the
seed was already mortal and shares in this cause through which there creep
upon us defects of mind and the 'sicknesses and myriad cares of mortals.'"

[e] *Cons. Ap.* 106b–c

The poet Antimachus, when his wife died whom he dearly loved, composed as a consolation for himself an elegiac poem, the *Lyde*, in which he
enumerated the misfortunes of the heroes, making his own grief less
through the ills of others. It is obvious, then, that one who consoles another
in time of grief by demonstrating that what has happened is shared by many
others, and is in fact less than theirs, changes the mourner's belief and con-
vinces him, in a way, that what has happened is less serious than previously
thought.

[f] *Cons. Ap.* 110f

There is some value, it would seem, in the comfort which Amphiaraus
in the poet [Euripides] offers to the mother of Archemorus, who was upset
over the death of her son in infancy, so long before his time. He says,

No mortal lives who does not suffer pain,
who does not bury children and bear new ones,
and die himself. And mortals grieve at this,
returning earth to earth. Necessity
insists that life be mowed, like wheat at harvest,
one to exist, another not. Why weep, then,
at natural transitions? There is nothing
to fear in what must come to everyone.

[g] *Cons. Ap.* 112d

"But I did not expect to experience this," he says, "and did not think ahead for it." But you ought to have been thinking ahead and making an advance judgment about human affairs, how they are both uncertain and of no importance. If you had done so, you would not now be unprepared, like one taken over by the sudden attack of enemies. For it is a fine thing how Theseus, in Euripides, is seen to have prepared for things like this. For he says,

I learned this from a wise man: setting my mind
on worries and disasters, I imagined
exiles from my homeland, deaths untimely,
and other kinds of evil that might happen.
Thus, if at any time I should encounter
such things as these, they would not be new to me
and bite me more.

[h] *Cons. Ap.* 114c–e, *in part* = Crantor fr. 6a Mette

Crantor says that not being responsible for one's own misfortune makes it much easier to bear. . . . But love and affection for the departed lie not in distressing ourselves, but in benefiting the one we loved. And it is a benefit to those taken from us when we honor them by a good memorial. For no good person deserves dirges, but hymns and paeans . . . since he has departed to a more godlike life, in exchange for one full of the cares and calamities which mortals necessarily undergo. . . . For this reason, right-minded persons should not devote themselves to grief beyond the natural measure of mental pain, for grieving is barbaric and achieves nothing.

[i] *Cons. Ap.* 118b–c

Taking these things to heart, we will find release from the pointless and empty heaviness of grief. . . . It is also well to recall the words which we have perhaps used on some occasion with relatives or friends who have undergone similar misfortunes, comforting them and persuading them to endure these experiences, of which all have a share, as things shared, and to bear the human lot as humans should *(pherein . . . ta anthrōpina anthrōpinōs)*. For it is not well to be able to free others from distress but derive no benefit ourselves from remembering the "healing medicines of reason" through which we ought to cure the mind's pain. For if there is one thing we should not delay, it is freedom from distress.

[j]   *Cons. Ap.* 118d

According to tradition, Anaxagoras was speaking with his acquaintances about natural science when someone told him of his son's death. He paused for only a moment, then said to those who were present, "I knew my child was mortal."

[k]   *Cons. Ap.* 119bc

Demosthenes, the orator, . . . [continued his activities] when he lost his only and much-beloved daughter. About her Aeschines, thinking to accuse him, speaks as follows: "On the seventh day after his daughter's death, not yet having mourned or done what is customary, he put on a garland, clothed himself in white, and performed a state sacrifice, against convention. . . ." He said this with the intention of accusing him, as orators do, not knowing that by these words he was praising him for setting aside his grief and showing patriotism rather than his feelings for his own kin.

$\mathscr{A}$ PPENDIX $\mathscr{B}$

EPICURUS AND THE CYRENAICS

For most of the philosophical material he uses, Cicero makes no very consistent effort to document his dependence on Greek authors, assuming, no
doubt, that those of his contemporaries who are likely to care which author
he is following in any given passage will also have no difficulty recognizing
the source for themselves. For Epicurean material, however, he is considerably more careful, often citing specific texts, sometimes even by title, and
frequently quoting word for word. Reasons for this more studious presentation are not far to seek. For while Cicero's own allegiance lay elsewhere,
there were many among the prospective readers of his circulated works who
were likely to scrutinize Epicurean material with the zeal of confirmed adherents. Epicureans among Cicero's own circle of acquaintances included
not only avowed enemies like L. Calpurnius Piso Caesoninus, but others
whom he could still hope to influence, men like Vibius Pansa and the young
Trebatius Testa (*Fam.* 15.19.3, 7.12). Atticus, too, considered himself an
Epicurean (see comm. 3, IIID (on 3.47–51)). In attacking Epicurus's views,
then, Cicero cannot risk any appearance of unfairness: he must be able to
demonstrate that he has not attributed to Epicurus any view not contained
in his writings. This means that where he singles out specific Epicurean
teachings for criticism, we should in general assume that he has some textual basis for attributing those views to his opponent, though of course we
need not agree with the construction he puts on them. Moreover, where his
reports of Epicurus's positions touch on that philosopher's controversies
with the Cyrenaics, we should at least give serious consideration to the

possibility that the report was derived from Epicurus's own writings and thus has the authority of contemporary witness.

In both the *Tusculans* and *On Ends*, Cicero makes use of Epicurus's non-extant *On the End (Peri Telous)*, which he quotes at 3.41–42. He also quotes some material known to us from Epicurus's *Principal Doctrines* and *Epistle to Menoikeus*. For the most part, this is corroborated testimony, since Cicero's chief interests are in Epicurus's description of the highest good, in the relation between pleasures of state ("katastematic" pleasures) and pleasures in movement ("kinetic" pleasures), and in the dependence of mental pleasures on the body—all points on which we have abundant evidence elsewhere. But the present work also takes up a set of Epicurean claims concerning the causation and management of mental pain—necessarily mental, since pain of body has already been treated in book 2. This is an area of Epicurus's philosophy of mind on which we are much less well informed. It will be of some use, then, to bring together here those bits of outside evidence which have a bearing on the points mentioned. We will then be in a better position to assess the validity of Cicero's testimony.

The claims attributed to Epicurus in 3.28 and 3.32–35 are as follows:

(1)   Mental pain comes about "naturally" and "necessarily" when one directs one's attention toward ("gazes upon," *intueri*) comparatively serious present evils.

(2)   We have available two means for easing mental pain: we can distract or "call away" (*avocare*) the mind from the distressing circumstance, and we can also redirect or "recall" it (*revocare*) toward pleasures.

(3)   The Cyrenaics are wrong to recommend the pre-rehearsal of future evils. This practice actually increases our experience of evil.

(4)   Distress does not diminish over time.

The first of these claims should probably be connected with the epistemological role of pleasure and pain (the "feelings," *pathē*) as criteria of truth. Agreeable or disagreeable sensations, whether of body or of mind, are important to the philosopher as one basis on which we can make valid assertions about the world ([a]). "Necessary" in *Tusc.* 3.32 and also in [b] may therefore have some epistemological significance. If there is not *some* reliable connection between our inner experience and the way the world is, including what it is best for us to pursue and avoid, then there is no way for us to plan our activities at all. Thinking in this way, it is not unreasonable to say that the wise person will have to have a capacity for "feelings," not only for pleasure and for pain of body (as in [c]) but for mental pain as well.

But the "ways one attends in thought" are also named as a criterion of truth, in [a] and also by Epicurus himself in *Epistle to Herodotus* 38 and *Principal Doctrine* 24. The significance of these "attendings" or "focusings" *(epibolai)* has been much disputed. From what Lucretius says in [d], it appears that they explain our ability to *do* something: to pick out from the endlessly varied stream of thought-images those we choose to think about. Likewise in [e] it is probably the same "attendings" which enable us to summon up images of dead friends. But the way we attend or fail to attend can also provide a suitable explanation for our ability *not* to do certain things: not to observe objects which are before our eyes, not to think all the thoughts available to us at any given moment. It may be the negative ability which gives the "attendings" their epistemic role. Since what we see clearly is only that to which we are attending, failure to see a thing to which we are not attending does *not* prove that that thing is not present. To know what is and is not present, then, we must consider both our sense-perceptions and where our attention is directed. Similarly, the superiority of the wise person to pain of body and distress of mind does not show that those feelings are not grounded in reality. The sage may simply not be attending to those evils.

The second reported claim links this epistemological point to the management of present distress. Cicero's paired terms *avocatio* and *revocatio* must refer to the same control of attention as is described by Lucretius. But Cicero, like Plutarch in [g] (who uses the verb *epiballein*), attributes to Epicurus a practical application of this ability, based on our ability to derive (mental) pleasure from circumstances in the past or future ([h] and [i]). Just because we do not experience, or do not experience keenly, what we disregard, it is sometimes to our advantage *not* to attend closely to our present circumstances, when those circumstances are such as would necessarily cause us pain.

It is through the power of attention that Epicurus, in [f], is able to deploy the remembrance of past pleasures against present pain of body with such success that he remains, on balance, happy. This often-repeated anecdote illustrates not only the wise person's ability to remain happy in the midst of bodily pain (compare [c]), but also the means by which he remains happy: through the remembrance of goods, or, as [g] has it, through "memory, reasoning *(epilogisis)*, and gratitude that such-and-such has happened to oneself." See also Plutarch, *That a Follower of Epicurus Cannot Live Pleasantly* 1099d, fr. 436 Usener; Seneca, *On Benefits* 3.4. Note the association in [g] between memory and *epibolē*, cashed out in [e] as the power to pick out thought-images surviving from the past (cf. Lucretius 4.33–45). But while [e], [f], and [g] all lay special emphasis on memory, there does not seem to be any reason in the theory why a secure expectation of *future* goods should not be used in the same way, as Cicero indicates in *Tusc.* 5.96 and in *On Ends* 1.57, quoted on p. 100. What is important is that the remembered or anticipated goods should be of sufficient magnitude to outweigh the cause of distress.

Points (3) and (4) should be taken together, since both concern Epicurus's controversy with the Cyrenaics. Here, too, Cicero may well be drawing on Epicurus's *On the End.* The matter is best approached through [i]. Because the Cyrenaics treat pleasure only as a movement, they insist that it has a limited lifespan and conclude from this that we cannot increase our experience of pleasure by borrowing from the past or future. They reason, perhaps, that it is not *possible* for us to derive further enjoyment from past goods, the movement being already exhausted; while with future goods it is not *expedient* to exhaust the movement prematurely. Thus "only the present is ours" ([j]). If this point is allowed to hold, then Epicurus's method for reducing present pain is not viable. Epicurus needs to insist that past pleasures do in some cases remain available for our use in the present, and that the anticipation of future pleasures does not lessen our enjoyment of those same objects later on. It may be for this reason that he asserts, in [k], that the future is "not completely *not* ours."

So the Cyrenaic point about diminishment implies that where pleasure is concerned, we should concentrate exclusively on the present, not anticipating our goods but allowing each pleasure to burst upon us at its freshest and most forcible. When it comes to pain, however, the implication is just the reverse. If anticipating an event brings it about that we experience less powerful feelings in relation to that event when it occurs, then it may well be to our advantage to anticipate as many as possible of our future misfortunes. To be sure, the anticipation may itself be painful in some degree. The Cyrenaics perhaps reason that because distress in relation to future events always views those events as uncertain, it can never be so intense as to ruin one's enjoyment of life in the present; but that even these mild pains, if experienced every day, will suffice to blunt the force of the movement. This sort of concern for one's lifelong surplus of pleasure over pain is not, I think, ruled out by any authoritative report on Cyrenaic ethics; indeed, considerable support can be found for it in D.L. 2.87–88.

Epicurus responds in *Tusc.* 3.32 that if we anticipate what is uncertain, we must experience distress over some events which will never happen at all. Moreover, there is no reason why anticipatory distress must be limited in intensity, since for Epicurus mental experience dominates over bodily ([h]). Just as the remembrance or expectation of goods may overbalance present pain of body, so pre-rehearsal could be so distressing as to cancel out any present pleasure we might be experiencing. Where circumstances are potentially painful, then, it is better to concede that the future is not ours and should not be anticipated (again, [k]).

If passage [l] makes a specifically Epicurean point at all, it must be related to the first claim above, that mental pain is in some circumstances a necessary feeling. But [l] is probably better understood as evidence that even Epicurus sometimes made use of conventional expressions of condolence, sounding for the moment like Crantor in passage [b] of Appendix A.

For Epicureans at Rome, see the works cited under 3 IIId (on 3.47–51). On directing the attention ("focusing"), see esp. Asmis 1984, 85–94 and 118–26; Long and Sedley 1987, 1.90; Annas 1992, 165–66; on the Epicurean criterion more generally, Long and Sedley 1987, 1.87–90; Asmis 1984; Striker 1974. Kassel 1958, 29–32, gathers further evidence on Epicurean consolation. Accounts of Cyrenaic thought and of the history of the school vary widely; for a fuller version of the interpretation given here see Graver n.d. for other views, Tsouna 1998, esp. 15–18; Laks 1993; Annas 1993, 227–36; Irwin 1991; Döring 1988. The surviving evidence is collected in Giannantoni 1990, and see his suggestive remarks on Cicero's report in vol. 4, 183. For Lucretius's argument in [d] see Asmis 1981.

[a] D.L. 10.31

So Epicurus says in the *Standard (Kanōn)* that the means of judgment *(kriteria tes aletheias)* are sense-perceptions, preconceptions, and feelings *(pathē)*. But the followers of Epicurus say that the ways one attends in thought to impressions are also [a means of judgment]. And Epicurus says this also, in the *Epistle to Herodotus* and in the *Principal Doctrines.*

[b] *KD* 29 (D.L. 10.149)

Some desires are natural and <necessary, some natural but> not necessary, and some are neither natural nor necessary but arise through empty opinion.

[c] D.L. 10.117, 118, 119

The person who has once become wise . . . will be more subject to the feelings *(pathē)*; this would not be any impediment to his being wise. . . . Even if the wise person is tortured, he will be happy. . . . but he will still cry out and groan. . . . And the wise person will experience pain (or "distress," *lupē*), according to Diogenes in book 5 of the *Excerpts.*

[d] Lucretius 4.802–4, 807, 809–15

Because the images are slight, the mind,
unless it strains at them *(contendit)*, cannot discern

them sharply. All the others perish, save
the ones for which it has prepared itself. . . .
Do you not see the eyes as well, how, when
they start to see some tiny thing, they strain,
readying themselves, and how, without this, we
cannot discern things sharply? And besides,
even when things are obvious, if you fail
to pay attention *(advertere animum)*, it may be as if
your object were set off by all of time
and far away. Why, then, is it surprising
that the mind should lose all things except the ones
to which it has devoted its attention *(quibus est deditus ipse)*?

[e] Plutarch, *That a Follower of Epicurus Cannot Live Pleasantly* 1105e, fr. 213 Usener
    "Sweet on every side is the remembrance of a dear one who is dead,"
says Epicurus . . . and they think that they can receive and view appearances
and images of friends who have died . . .

[f] Epicurus, *Letter to Idomeneus*, fr. 138 Usener (D.L. 10.22)
    I write to you on a day of happiness which is also my last, saying this: I
am assailed by feelings of urinary blockage and abdominal cramp such as
could not be surpassed in magnitude, yet against all of these is deployed the
joy that is in my mind through the memory of conversations I have had.

[g] Plutarch, *That a Follower of Epicurus Cannot Live Pleasantly* 1091b, fr. 423 Usener
    Epicurus says, likewise, that the nature of the good comes into being
from the very escape of evil, and from memory, reasoning, and gratitude
that such-and-such has happened to oneself. "What produces unsurpassed
gladness," he says, "is the comparison [? text uncertain] with the great evil
one has escaped. And this is the nature of the good, if a person directs his
attention *(epibalēi)* rightly, then stands still and does not walk about prattling
vainly about the good."

[h] D.L. 10.136–37
    He differs from the Cyrenaics concerning pleasure. For they do not rec-
ognize the pleasure of state, but only that which is in movement, while he
recognizes both. . . . Also in regard to the Cyrenaics: their view is that bodily torments are worse than those of the mind, seeing that wrongdoers are
punished in body, but he holds that torments of mind are worse, seeing
that the flesh experiences only the storms of the present, while the mind

experiences those of the present, the past, and the future. In the same way, he says that the pleasures of the mind are greater [than those of the body].

[i] D.L. 2.89
    The Cyrenaics deny that pleasure is gained from the memory or expectation of goods, which is the Epicurean claim, for they say that the movement of the mind diminishes with time.

[j] Aelian, *Miscellaneous History* 14.6, Giannantoni IVA.174
    Aristippus . . . told people not to exert themselves over things past nor to exert prospective effort *(prokamnein)* over things to come. . . . And he instructed them to have thought for today, and again, to have thought for that part of the day within which one is acting or thinking. For he said that neither what is gone nor what is expected is ours, but only the present. For the one is lost already, and the other, even if it is to be, is uncertain.

[k] Epicurus, *Epistle to Menoikeus* 127 (D.L. 10.127)
    One should remember that the future is neither ours nor completely not ours. Thus we should neither anticipate it *(prosmenein)* nor give up hope of it as a thing which will absolutely not be.

[l] Plutarch, *That a Follower of Epicurus Cannot Live Pleasantly* 1101ab, fr. 120 Usener
    They contend against those who exclude grief *(lupē)* and tears and lamentations over the deaths of dear ones, and they say that the kind of freedom from pain which amounts to impassivity comes of another and greater evil, which is savagery, that is, an unmixed and crazed urge for fame. For this reason it is better to have some feeling and some grief, and by Zeus even to wear out one's eyes with weeping, and whatever else they say in their writings, making a display of their feelings so as to seem tender and affectionate. For Epicurus said this especially in *On the death of Hegesianax,* which is addressed to Sositheos and Pyrson, the father and brother of the deceased.

APPENDIX C

THE EARLY STOICS AND CHRYSIPPUS

We know that treatises *On Emotions* or *On the Absence of Emotion* were written by many different Stoic authors. In addition to the fundamental work by Zeno of Citium, treatises were written during the third century B.C.E. by Herillus, Dionysius of Heraclea, Chrysippus, and Sphaerus, and the topic was later taken up by Hecaton and Posidonius. But our knowledge of the contents of these works is mostly derived from later summaries and critiques: apart from Cicero, we are chiefly dependent on various works of Seneca (particularly his treatise *On Anger*), on some passages in Epictetus, on Plutarch's treatise *On Moral Virtue*, on Galen's *Precepts of Hippocrates and Plato*, and on doxographic accounts 0by Diogenes Laertius, *Lives and Opinions of Eminent Philosophers* 7.84–131, and Stobaeus, *Ecl.* 2.7.5–12, the last probably derived from a summary written by Arius Didymus, a generation after Cicero. Most of these authors tend to speak of the position of "the Stoics" generally, as if the views of all Stoics who wrote on this topic were essentially the same. Only Galen makes any consistent effort to attach the names of specific authors and treatises to the views he reports. For this reason, the *Precepts of Hippocrates and Plato* is of primary importance to the study of Cicero's sources on the issues that are of interest to Galen, namely the genesis of emotion and the relation between emotion and reason. At the same time, Galen's evidence must be handled with caution, for his own strong preference for an opposing position may lead him to misrepresent the intentions of the Stoic authors he has read.

Parallels cited throughout the commentary reveal the depth of Cicero's familiarity with the general Stoic position as that position is known to us. In 4.11–32, especially, he appears to have made an abridgement of the same text as is summarized in Stobaeus, and he seems to have followed Stoic material closely in many other passages as well, including some which he does not identify as being of Stoic origin. But only occasionally does he mention specific Stoic authors by name, and even when he does so, it is not in such a way as to give us clear information about what books he has read. For instance, he says in 4.47 that the definition of emotion "was given correctly . . . by Zeno," but he need not have encountered Zeno's definition in Zeno's own writings, since the definition is an obvious candidate for repetition in any Stoic work. Much the same might be said about Sphaerus's definition of courage in 4.53, and perhaps also about the remark on "swelling" attributed to Dionysius of Heraclea in 3.19. The recommendation of Cleanthes on consolation, which Cicero presents as inadequate (3.76–77), might have been similarly criticized in a source which favors the approach of Chrysippus. Chrysippus himself is mentioned with some regularity, at 3.52, 3.59, 3.61, 3.76, 3.79, 4.9, 4.23, 4.53, and 4.63. The frequency of mention may be significant but does not in itself show that Cicero has read Chrysippus's treatise.

When we consider the passages from Chrysippus's *On Emotions* preserved in Galen, however, it is hard to escape the conclusion that Cicero did rely on that work, or something very similar to it, for a number of important points in his theory. For Cicero does not resemble Chrysippus only on those terms and doctrines which our sources attribute to the Stoics generally: he also shares with him a number of themes which Galen and others associate specifically with this author. The following seem to me especially significant:

(1)   Chrysippus emphasizes the role of belief in emotion ([a] is one of many examples), as does Cicero throughout his account (see esp. 3.24). Although he does not eliminate discussion of the psychophysical "effects" ([b] tells against Galen's own assertion in *PHP* 5.1–3 and elsewhere), Chrysippus is most interested in analyzing emotions as judgments, i.e., not only as impulses but as assents to certain kinds of propositions.

(2)   Chrysippus insists, in keeping with the point just mentioned, that the mind functions as a unity in emotional experience and explains carefully how what is in the most important sense a judgment can nonetheless carry us away as emotions do ([c], [d], [l]). Cicero does not repeat the full explanation, but he echoes language highly characteristic of it in *Tusc.* 4.22 and 4.42.

(3)   Chrysippus identifies two important components in the complex beliefs specified in the definitions of the genus-emotions, a misevaluation
and a belief about obligation ([b]). According to Cicero's own report
in *Tusc.* 3.76–79, he points out that grief could be combatted by refut-
ing either the first or the second component, whereas Cleanthes based
his entire strategy on the misevaluation. The advantages of a consolation based on the obligation-belief are explained in the Origen passage,
[m]. Not only does it defer direct confrontation with the belief which
"preoccupies" the mind of the emotional person, but it is usable even
with those who are deeply committed to other philosophic positions
on value. Cicero's therapeutic sections similarly favor attacking the second, rather than the first, belief-component; see especially 4.60–63, together with his direct endorsement of Chrysippus at 3.79.

(4)   Chrysippus borrows and develops several points from consolation literature. The consolatory commonplace about the pointlessness of grief
seems to have been mentioned in some way in his discussion of
"excessiveness" ([e]), and the diminishment of grief over time is
treated as a phenomenon to be explained in his account of causes ([g]).
He may also have spoken about "dwelling in advance," i.e., pre-
rehearsal; see Appendix D. Other commonplaces about anxiety, about
"inflammation," and about timing come into his discussion of arguments against the emotions ([f], [l], [m]). See Appendix A, and compare Cicero's treatment of the same points in 3.67, 3.76, 4.63. The remark about Euripides fr. 757 Nauck which Cicero mentions (without
context) at 3.59–60 attests to the same kinds of interests in Chrysippus;
compare [f] in Appendix A.

(5)   Chrysippus makes extensive use of a comparison between conditions
of mind and conditions of body, and in particular between emotions
(or states predisposing to emotion) and bodily illness ([h]–[k]).
Cicero complains that the analogy with the body is overused by "the
Stoics, especially Chrysippus" (4.23); nonetheless, 4.30–31 compares
health, strength, quickness, and beauty of body to qualities of mind
bearing the same names, in language strongly reminiscent of [j] and [k].
In contexts where the medical analogy is prominent, Chrysippus sometimes borrows a medical usage and makes *pathos* mean "sickness," equat-
ing it with what is elsewhere in the theory called *nosos* or *nosēma*; so [j]
and apparently also [h], and compare the use of *apathēs* in Appendix D,
passage [d]. Cicero is clearly familiar with this usage; see *Tusc.* 3.7.

(6)   In the same vein, Chrysippus describes philosophy as a medical science
for the mind. The comparison was widely used, notably in Epicurus

(Porphyry, *To Marcella* 31, fr. 221 Usener) and in the consolatory tradition (see passage [a] in Appendix A), but Chrysippus may have been the first to give it a Stoic application. He expresses it emphatically in [j] and also in [m], and it is he who labels the final section of his treatise the "therapeutic" book. Cicero echoes the beginning of [j] in 3.1, 3.5–6, and 4.58.

(7)   Chrysippus's account of the origins of error is twofold ([n], and perhaps also [o]), in contrast to the single explanation offered in Cleanthes' *Hymn to Zeus.* That *Tusc.* 3.2–5 gives the same twofold account is argued in pref. to 3 above. If the language in [n] about praise and glory reflects language in Chrysippus (i.e., if it does not originate with Posidonius; compare Appendix D, passage [e]), then *Tusc.* 3.3–4 will have a particularly Chrysippan ring.

Some of these themes may also have figured large in other authors: the subject matter of (3), for instance, was a particular interest of Posidonius as well. But the match between Chrysippus's attested views and emphases and the themes Cicero sounds in the *Tusculans* is close enough to suggest that Chrysippus was the direct source for much of Cicero's Stoic material, unless indeed there were other works, unknown to us, which shared these same features.

Not specifically identified as Chrysippan, but possibly originating with him, is a more detailed discussion of the twofold cause of error preserved for us in Calcidius's commentary on Plato's *Timaeus*, [o]. Similarities between that Stoic account and the preface to Cicero's third book are striking: as in Cicero, the child falls into error even through the ordinary and proper attentions of nursemaids, parents, and teachers; through the natural appeal of money and pleasure; and through the impressive productions of the poets: but a particularly important inducement is the inherent resemblance between popular acclaim and (true) glory, which is "the testimony to virtue" and worthy of pursuit by the wise. Calcidius does not derive his account from Cicero himself, since he would not have found there the phrase "twofold corruption," and since he adopts different Latin equivalents for standard Greek terms. The easiest explanation for the resemblance between the two texts is that the shared material is derived ultimately from some work earlier than Cicero (perhaps at several removes in the case of Calcidius). Related material in Cicero's *On Laws* (1.31–32, 1.47) and in Seneca (*Ep.* 94.52–55, 115.11–12) supports the same conclusion. If, however, the source Cicero used resembled what we have in Calcidius, then his adaptation was brilliant: he has obscured the characteristically Stoic terminology without losing the force of its explanation, has restructured the account for conciseness and emphasis, and has added imagery borrowed from Plato's Cave allegory.

The discussion of sources in Dougan and Henry 1934, xxx–xlvii, comes to similar conclusions and also provides a helpful resume of earlier scholarship on the problem. Among the older studies, note especially that of Pohlenz 1906.

[a] Galen, *PHP* 4.1.14,17 = *SVF* 3.461

In the entirety of *On Emotions*, the three books in which he investigates rational questions about them and also the "therapeutic" book, which some call the "ethical" book, he tries to show that it would be better to suppose that the emotions are judgments, and not things which follow upon judgments, forgetting what he wrote in the first of his two books *On the Soul*, that erotic love belongs to the desiderative power and resentment to the spirited.

[b] Galen, *PHP* 4.2.1–5 = *SVF* 3.463

In the definitions for the genus-emotions which he gives first . . . he defines distress as a fresh belief that an evil is present, fear as an expectation of evil, pleasure as a fresh belief that a good is present . . . In the definition of desire . . . he says that it is an irrational reaching . . . And reaching . . . he defines as a rational impulse toward something which pleases to the extent that it should. . . . In some of the definitions that follow . . . he defines distress as a lowering at what is thought to be a thing to avoid, delight as an elevation at what is thought to be a thing to pursue. And . . . he also mentions contractions and outpourings.

[c] Galen, *PHP* 4.2.8–12 = *SVF* 3.462, from Chrysippus, *On Emotions*, book 1

Writing about the definition of emotion, he keeps saying that it is "an irrational movement of the mind, contrary to nature," and "an excessive impulse." Then, explaining the word "irrational," he says that it means "apart from reason and judgment.". . ."First, one must realize that the rational animal is by nature such as to follow reason and act in accordance with reason as with a guide. But often, also, it goes after or withdraws from things in another way, a way disobedient to reason, when pushed 'in excess' (*epi pleion*). Both definitions include a reference to this push, when [the first says that] the movement contrary to nature happens 'irrationally,' and when [the second says that] the impulses are 'excessive.' For 'irrational' should be understood here to mean 'disobedient to reason' and 'turned away from reason.' We speak of this push even in ordinary talk, when we say that some people are 'carried away' and proceed 'irrationally' or 'without reasoned judgment.' For we do not use these expressions to signify that the person is proceeding in error, perceiving something wrongly through reason, but rather to refer to the push that he [Zeno] subjoins [to the definition]. For to be moved in this way is not in the nature of a rational animal; rather, its nature is to be moved through reason."

[d] Galen, *PHP* 4.2.14–18 = *SVF* 3.462, from Chrysippus, *On Emotions*, book 1
   "It is also in reference to this [push] that we speak of the 'excessiveness' of the impulse. [We say the impulse is excessive] because it oversteps that measure in impulses which is natural and is through oneself. What I mean would be more comprehensible through the following. When one walks through impulse, the movement of the legs is not excessive, but is to some extent fitted to the impulse, so that if the person wishes to stop or make a change, he can do so. But when people run through impulse, this is no longer the case: the movement of the legs is excessive and contrary to the impulse, so that they are carried away and [the legs] do not obediently make a change right when one initiates it, as in the previous case. I think that something very similar happens also in the impulses [involved in emotion], because of overstepping the measure that is in accordance with reason, so that when one has an impulse [of this kind] one is not being obedient to reason. In the case of running, the excessiveness is called 'contrary to impulse,' but in the case of the impulse [in question], it is called 'contrary to reason.' For the due measure of a natural impulse is a measure which is in accordance with reason and which is to the extent that reason thinks right. Therefore when there is an overstepping in this connection and happening in this way, it is said to be an 'excessive' impulse and 'contrary to nature' and an 'irrational' movement of the mind."

[e] Galen, *PHP* 4.6.35, 38, 40–41, 43–46 = *SVF* 3.478, from Chrysippus, *On Emotions*
   "It is quite suitable, also, that those who are angry in this way are said to be 'carried away.' They are like those persons at the races who are carried forward through what is excessive [in their impulse]: in the one case [the impulse is] contrary to one's impulse in running; in the other, contrary to one's own reason. For of these, at any rate, one would not say that they are moved through themselves, controlling their own movement, but that they

are moved through some other force external to themselves.".... And he cites the conversation between Heracles and Admetus, as written by Euripides. It goes like this: Heracles says,

what would you gain by choosing to grieve always?

and Admetus replies,

I know, and yet some passion (*erōs*) still compels me.

And he also cites what Achilles says to Priam [*Iliad* 24.549–51]:

Refrain; let not your spirit grieve unceasing.
Nothing is gained by mourning for your son.
You will not bring him back to life; rather, you suffer more.

He says that when Achilles says this, he is speaking "in his right mind" (*par' hautōi*)—these are his very words—but that "in the midst of events he is often outside of these same judgments and cannot control himself, being conquered by emotion."

And he says, "For that in us which is agitated and in an altered state (*parēllachos*) and disobedient to reason comes about just the same in the case of delight."

And again, "For in disappointment we are 'outside of' or 'beside' ourselves and, in a word, blinded, so that sometimes, if we have a sponge or a bit of wool in our hands, we pick it up and throw it, as if that would achieve something. And if we happened to be holding a dagger or some other weapon, we would do the same with that. ... And often, through the same blindness, we bite keys, and beat at doors when they do not open quickly, and if we stumble over a stone we take revenge on it by breaking it or throwing it somewhere, and we say very odd things on all such occasions. ... From such things we may realize both how irrational the emotions are and how we are blinded in such moments, as if we had become different people from those who were previously conversing."

[f] Galen, *PHP* 4.7.26–27 = *SVF* 3.467, from Chrysippus, *On Emotions,* book 2
   "As concerns distress, also, some people seem to depart from it as if sated. Thus the poet speaks as follows about Achilles, when he was grieving for Patroclus, saying that

> when he was sated with weeping and rolling on the ground
> and the desire had gone from his thoughts and his limbs,

he then began to comfort Priam, demonstrating to him the irrationality of his grief. From this account one retains a hope that with the passage of time, as the emotional inflammation subsides, reason will sneak in and, as it were, take a stand and demonstrate the irrationality of the emotion."

[g] Galen, *PHP* 4.7.12–17 = *SVF* 3.466, from Chrysippus, *On Emotions*, book 2
"One might inquire into how it happens that distress diminishes, whether it happens when some belief changes or while all the beliefs remain the same, and why this happens. I think that the belief remains the same—namely that the thing which is now present is an evil—but that it is by the passage of time that the contraction yields and also, in my view, the impulse toward contraction. Perhaps, also, the belief remains but the consequences do not follow because in this situation some other condition *(diathesis)* is also present, one difficult to reason out. For that is why people stop crying, or cry without meaning to, when they get different impressions from their circumstances, and when something does or does not interfere. For it is reasonable that the same kind of thing should happen in the case of those others [whose grief diminishes] as happens when people stop mourning and lamenting, since things move us more when just beginning. It is like what I said happens when one is moved to laughter, and cases like that."

[h] D.L. 7.111
They think that the sicknesses *(pathē)* are judgments, as Chrysippus says in his work *On Emotions*. For [he says that] fondness for money is a supposition that money is a fine thing, and similarly with drunkenness, stubbornness, and so forth."

[i] Galen, *PHP* 4.5.21–22 = *SVF* 3.480, from Chrysippus, *On Emotions*, book 4
"For these are not called 'infirmities' only because one judges each of these objects to be a good, but also because one [in these states] falls into them [i.e., into the corresponding movements] 'in excess' of what accords with nature. Thus it is not unreasonable that some people are said to be 'mad about women' or 'mad about birds.'"

[j] Galen, *PHP* 5.2.22–24, 26–27, 31–33, 47, 49 = *SVF* 3.471, 471a, from Chrysippus, *On Emotions*, book 4
"It is not the case that there is a method, which we call 'medical,' concerned

with the diseased body, but no method for the diseased mind. Nor does the latter method fall short of the former, either in item-by-item theory or in treatment. Therefore, just as it is appropriate for the doctor concerned with bodies to be, as they say, 'inside' the sicknesses (*pathē*) which befall them and the proper cure for each, so also it falls to the doctor of the mind to be 'inside' both these things [i.e., the mental sicknesses and their cure] in the best way he can. And one can learn that this is so even from the analogy with these things that I set forth at the beginning. For the fitness of the analogy will suggest, I think, that there is also a similarity of therapies, that is, an analogy between the methods of cure for each.

"For just as one can observe in the body both strength and weakness, good tension and lack of tension, and also health and sickness, good condition and bad condition, so also there are certain states in the rational mind which are analogous to all of these in composition and in name. It is, I think, the similarity and analogy between them which is responsible for their having the same name. For we do also say in reference to the mind that some people are strong or weak or have good tension or lack tension, and also that they are sick or healthy, and it is also in the same way that we speak of sickness (*pathos*) and infirmity and things like that in the mind.

..."Therefore Zeno's account continues suitably. The sickness (*nosos*) of mind is very similar to an unsettled condition (*akatastasia*) of body. It is said that the sickness of the body is a lack of proportion among its constituents, the warm and the cool, the dry and the wet ... and health of body is a good mixture and proportion among the things mentioned. A 'good state' of body is, I think, the optimal mixture of the things named.

..."Therefore the mind, too, will be called beautiful or ugly by analogy, in reference to the proportion or lack of proportion among some such parts. For the mind does have parts, of which its reason and its condition in reason are composed. And the mind is beautiful or ugly insofar as its directive part is in one condition or the other as concerns its own 'limbs.'"

[k] Galen, *PHP* 4.6.5–7, 11 = *SVF* 3.473, from Chrysippus, *On Emotions*, book 4
"Furthermore, in the case of the body we likewise speak of tensions which are either 'lacking in tension' or 'good tensions,' referring to the way our tendons are when we are or are not able to perform tasks, and in the same way, perhaps, the tension of the mind is called a 'good tension' or a 'lack of tension.' For just as in things which one does by means of tendons, like running, grasping an object, and so forth, there is a constitution which is such as to perform the task and one which is such as to give way because the tendons are slack and yielding, even so, by analogy, there is some such

way for the tendons to be in the case of the mind. It is in this connection that we say, metaphorically, that some people are 'without tendon' and others 'have tendons.' One person retreats in the presence of what is frightening, another slackens and gives way when rewards or penalties are offered, and there are many similar cases. ... Therefore, since all the base act this way, retreating and giving way for many reasons, one might say that they perform every action 'weakly' and 'badly.'"

[l] Galen, *PHP* 4.6.24–25, 27, 31–32, 34–35 = *SVF* 3.475, from Chrysippus, *On Emotions*, book 4

"For this reason we also treat those stirred by emotion in the same way we treat those who are out of their minds, and make speech to them as to those who are in an altered state *(tous parēllachotas)* or who are beside themselves or are not themselves. This altered state or this departure from self comes about through that very 'turning away from reason' which I mentioned earlier.

"This is also why when people are in love or have some other strong desire, or are angry, one can hear people say things like 'they want to indulge their feelings' and 'let them be, whether it is better or not,' and 'say nothing to them' and 'they have to do it, no matter what, even if it is a mistake and not to their advantage.' ... They reject the [therapeutic] speech as one whose chastisement is ill-timed and who is no arbiter of the affairs of love, as a human who sees fit to give ill-timed advice at a time when even the gods see fit to let them swear false oaths. 'Let us follow our desire,' they say, 'and do whatever occurs to us.'"

When he explains the expression "being beside oneself," or "not oneself," he says, "Those who are angered in this way are properly said to be 'carried away,' similarly to those who are carried forward in running: in the one case there is an excess contrary to one's impulse in running, in the other case an excess contrary to one's own reason. For one would not say that they move through themselves in the same way as those who are in control of their movement, but that they move through some other force external to themselves."

[m] Origen, *Against Celsus* 8.51 = *SVF* 3.474, from Chrysippus, *On Emotions*, book 4

"For even if it should be that there are three classes of goods, even so one should work to cure the emotions. But during the critical period *(kairos)* of the inflammation one should not waste one's efforts over the belief that preoccupies the person stirred by emotion, lest we ruin the cure which is

opportune by lingering at the wrong moment over the refutation of the beliefs which preoccupy the mind. And even if pleasure is the good and this
is the view of the person who is overcome by the emotion, one should
nonetheless assist him and demonstrate that every emotion is inconsistent
[i.e., with their doctrine] even for those who assume that pleasure is the
good and is the goal."

[n] Galen, *PHP* 5.5.13–14, 17, 19–20 = *SVF* 3.229a, from Chrysippus, *On Emotions*

He admitted that even if children were brought up only by a philosopher
and never saw or heard any example of fault, they would still not necessarily
become philosophers. For the cause of corruption is twofold: one comes
about through the verbal influence (*katēchēsis*) of the many, the other through
the nature of things themselves. ... But [in reference to the second cause,]
what necessity is there that they should go toward praise and glory and rejoice in them, and should dislike and avoid blame and dishonor? ... We
must ask him, What is the reason why pleasure gives us the persuasive impression that it is a good, and pain the persuasive impression that it is an evil?
And likewise, Why is it that we are readily persuaded when we hear the many
praise and congratulate people for having statues put up of them, as if that
were a good thing, and speak of defeat and dishonor as if they were bad?

[o] Calcidius, *On the Timaeus of Plato* 165–66 = *SVF* 3.229

They say that misdeeds do not come about without cause, since every
animate being, in that it partakes of the divine, does indeed pursue the good
but errs sometimes in its judgment of what things are good and what are
evil. ... There is more than one cause for error. First is that which the Stoics call the "twofold corruption." This arises both from circumstances
themselves and from the transmission of rumor. For the very experience of
being born involves some pain, because one is moving from a warm and
moist place into the chill and dryness of the surrounding air, and as a remedy for this the midwife provides a warm bath and swaddling to recall the
womb, to ease the young body with pleasant sensation and quiet it. Thus
... there arises a kind of natural belief that everything sweet and pleasurable is good, and that what brings pain is bad and to be avoided. Older children learn the same thing from the experience of hunger and satiety, and
from caresses and punishments.

As they mature, they retain this belief that everything nice is good, even
if not useful, and that everything troublesome, even if it brings some advantage, is bad. Consequently they love riches, which are the foremost

means of obtaining pleasure, and they embrace fame (*gloria*) rather than honor. For humans are by nature inclined to pursue praise and honor, since honor is the testimony to virtue. But those who are wise and engaged in the study of wisdom know what sort of virtue they ought to cultivate, while people do not know about things and so cultivate fame, that is, popular esteem, in place of honor. And in place of virtue they pursue a life steeped in pleasures, believing that the power to do what one wants is the superiority of a king. For humans are by nature kingly, and since power always accompanies kingship, they suppose that kingship likewise accompanies power. . . . Similarly, since the happy person necessarily enjoys life, they think that those who live pleasurably will be happy. Such, I think, is the error which arises "from circumstances" to possess the human mind.

But the one which arises "from transmission" is a whispering added to the aforementioned error through the prayers of our mothers and nurses for wealth and fame and other things falsely supposed to be good, and a disturbance from the bogeys which frighten young people very much, and from comfortings and everything like that. Yes, and think of poetry, which shapes the minds of older children, and of the impressive productions of other authors! How great an influence concerning pleasure and suffering do they convey to the novice mind! What about painters and sculptors? Do they not deliberately lead the mind toward sweetness?

. . . So those who are to become wise have need of a liberal education and of precepts directing them to what is fine, and also of training in seclusion from people in general, and they should see and study things conducive to wisdom.

A P P E N D I X *D*

P O S I D O N I U S

Among those with whom Cicero studied on his eastern tour of 79–77 was the Stoic philosopher, historian, and scientist Posidonius of Apameia and Rhodes (c. 135–c. 51). In later years, Cicero would make the most of what must have been a very limited personal acquaintance: even in the writings of 45 the older man is still "my teacher" (*On Fate* 5, *ND* 1.6), "my dear friend" (*noster familiaris, On Ends* 1.6, *ND* 2.88), and, in *Tusc.* 2.61, "my friend (*noster*) Posidonius, whom I have seen many times in person . . . a very distinguished philosopher." He also read from among Posidonius's many treatises, which he cites enthusiastically, though not always with approval, when relevant to his topic (see esp. *On Fate* 5–7, *ND* 1.123, *On Divination* 2.35, *Off.* 3.7–10). We might have expected, then, that Posidonius would be mentioned by name also in *Tusculans* 3 and 4. For Posidonius, too, wrote a treatise *On Emotions,* and surviving fragments of that work indicate that it contained extensive discussions of several of the same issues as are treated by Cicero. We cannot say for certain, however, whether Cicero had read the Posidonian treatise. The question needs to be considered carefully, for it has important implications both for Cicero, whose work takes on quite a different character if it is intended as an answer to Posidonius, and for Posidonius himself, whose relationship to the rest of the Stoic tradition on this topic is still a matter of dispute.

Almost everything we know of Posidonius's *On Emotions* is preserved in the same treatise of Galen to which we are indebted for fragments of

Chrysippus's treatise on the same subject. But where Galen objects strongly to Chrysippus's views on the relation between emotion and belief, he claims Posidonius as an authority for the (roughly) Platonic view which he himself favors. He insists that the reason Posidonius criticizes his predecessor's causal account and advocates a different method of treatment is that he follows Plato in his own psychology, distinguishing sharply between the mind's emotional and rational powers. The similarity between Galen's own position and that which he attests for Posidonius has led some interpreters to question the reliability of the report. These scholars argue that while the verbatim quotations in Galen's work do seem to indicate that Posidonius's views diverge to some extent from those of Chrysippus, Galen's interpretation may take Posidonius to have said considerably more than was intended. Others have defended Galen as a responsible, though opinionated, reporter. In considering the relation of Cicero to Posidonius, then, we will need to allow for a range of possibilities in the latter's actual views: he may in fact have abandoned the mainline Stoic position on these issues (it was not only Chrysippan), or he may be developing that position in essentially sympathetic ways, or he may be trying to find some middle ground between the Stoa and its opponents.

Similarities between Cicero's work and the Posidonian material quoted and paraphrased by Galen are striking: not only do both authors treat many of the same issues—notably pre-rehearsal, freshness, and the diminishment of grief—but they sometimes give very similar examples and even, on two occasions, quote the same passages from Euripides. But their differences on these same points are equally striking. For where Posidonius is reported to us as expressing objections to Chrysippus point by point, arguing against the validity of his causal analysis and the details of his mind–body analogy, Cicero, on all but one relatively minor point, offers arguments to support the cognitivist analysis.

This means that if Galen is right about Posidonius's relation to the earlier tradition, then Cicero, if he knows Posidonius's work, must be attempting to overturn its central arguments. This does not seem at all likely. Even supposing Cicero were to undertake such a refutation, it would be very unlike him to do so without mentioning his distinguished opponent by name. For while Cicero does not always feel obliged to name the authors from whom he borrows material, an attack *sine nomine* would sit very oddly with his own proud claims regarding Posidonius's tutelage. He could hardly expect such a breach of decorum to go unrecognized by his more educated readers. He might perhaps have remained silent about a predecessor whose views he regarded as essentially similar to his own. But it is difficult to see how he could have thought this about Posidonius if he had read the treatise of which Galen speaks. Even allowing for considerable distortion on· Galen's part, we can hardly suppose that Posidonius took the fully intellectualist line which Cicero reports for the Stoa on the causation of emotions, on pre-rehearsal, and on freshness. And these are the very points in which Cicero is most interested himself.

If, on the other hand, Cicero has not read Posidonius's work, then we need some other explanation for the points of similarity. This is not difficult to supply. We know from Galen and from the evidence cited in Appendix C that both Posidonius and Cicero had made a detailed study of Chrysippus's *On Emotions*. Both authors may well have restated or simply repeated material from that treatise in their own works, either with approbation or for the purposes of criticism. In this case, our comparison of the two later authors provides us with interesting, though limited, information about the contents of Chrysippus's treatise, including some points not otherwise attested for that work.

The apparent points of contact between Cicero and Posidonius can be divided into two groups. First, there are a number of points on which we have, from Galen and others, clear evidence as to what Chrysippus's position was. On all of these we find Posidonius expressing some opposition to Chrysippus, although the nature and significance of the objection is not always fully clear. Cicero, however, expresses the same views as Chrysippus on all points except (4).

(1) Posidonius differs from Chrysippus in some way on how, in general, emotions are related to beliefs and to the mind's reasoning powers ([a]). Unfortunately, Galen never quotes his exact words on this point, and the nature of the difference between the two Stoics remains unclear, especially as Chrysippus too sometimes refers to "spirited" and "desiderative" powers ([a] in Appendix C). Cicero says firmly that the cause of emotions lies "entirely in belief" (3.24).

(2) Posidonius in [b] and [c] expresses dissatisfaction with Chrysippus's position on why grief diminishes over time. The loss of "freshness," he says, is not an adequate explanation: the matter is not at all "difficult to reason out" (cf. [g] in Appendix C), if one assumes that distress is a movement of a mental part or power distinct from the rational. (The discussion continues in the first part of [g].) Cicero recognizes that the phenomenon of diminishment might serve as the basis for an

objection to the account he presents, but he feels that if "freshness" is properly interpreted—that is, not interpreted in terms of time only—it suffices to explain the phenomenon (3.52–54, 58, 74–75).

(3)   In [d], Posidonius objects to Chrysippus's terminology of proclivities to certain emotions. Since all bodies are susceptible to disease, Chrysippus cannot use an analogy with susceptibility to bodily disease as a way to talk about an individual's particular tendency to experience some one emotion. It would make better sense to speak of such tendencies by analogy to actual diseases, since it is this that would be the activation of a capacity which all possess. Cicero uses the proclivities analogy in exactly the manner to which Posidonius objects.

(4)   Also in [d], Posidonius points out a problem with the body–mind analogy: bodies are never immune to disease, but minds, in Stoic theory, can be immune to what the analogy calls "sicknesses." Cicero, too, thinks this is a weakness in the analogy (4.31, and compare also 3.6).

(5)   In [e], Posidonius is dissatisfied with Chrysippus's twofold account of the origins of error, the same account which Cicero uses in his preface to book 3.

(6)   In [f], Posidonius grants spirit (*thumos*, also translatable as "anger") and desire (*epithumia*, i.e., the desiderative power) to animals. Compare 4.31, where Cicero, like Chrysippus, denies emotions to animals.

The fourth of these points is the only one on which Cicero and Posidonius appear to be taking the same side on a point made *against* the Chrysippan theory. Their agreement is worth noting, but is not in itself very significant, as the criticism is a fairly obvious one to make from a close study of the terminology of infirmities (*Tusc.* 4.23–31) and could well have occurred to both writers independently. Neither is the criticism particularly troublesome for the Stoic theory; indeed, the point could have been conceded by Chrysippus himself without damage to his own case, which uses the analogy only for illustrative purposes.

But there are also two other matters on which Cicero's remarks resemble those of Posidonius. On these we have little or no direct evidence as to what Chrysippus's position was, if indeed he took a position. We can see, however, that Cicero's expressed views differ from those of Posidonius in much the same way as they differ in (1)–(6).

(7)   In [g], Posidonius discusses the same recommendation about pre-rehearsal as Cicero puts forward in 3.28–31, connecting it, as Cicero does also (3.52, 3.58), with the issue of diminishment and freshness.

Like Cicero, Posidonius mentions a specific term for the exercise
(*proendēmein*, "dwell in advance") and cites in connection with it the
Anaxagoras anecdote and the two Euripides fragments, 964 and 821
Nauck (as at 3.29–30, 3.67). But while Cicero accepts an explanation for
the efficacy of pre-rehearsal in terms of alterations in belief, Posidonius stresses what seem to be non-rational processes of habituation
and visualization ("model or stamp out an image"). (Note that Galen's
report does not always indicate clearly which remarks belong to Posidonius and which to Chrysippus. It looks, however, as though the term
proendēmein was already in Chrysippus, since what is attributed to Posidonius is a new interpretation of its meaning. Also, the observation
that "everything which is unrehearsed" is more upsetting than what is
foreseen strongly resembles a remark which Cicero, in the same context,
attributes to Chrysippus (3.52).)

(8) In [h], Posidonius makes a pair of objections to Chrysippus's definition of emotion in terms of evaluative beliefs. If evaluative beliefs are a
sufficient cause, he says, then sages should rejoice over their own virtue,
and progressors should be terribly upset that they have not yet man-
aged to rid themselves of faults. He seems to claim that a sufficiently
strong evaluative belief will in itself produce the belief that a certain
emotional response is appropriate. Cicero, by contrast, feels that it is
entirely possible to hold the strong evaluative belief without being
committed to the belief about appropriateness: he depends on this
possibility both to explain the lack of distress in imperfect philosophers and to provide a means of cure for progressors who are indeed
distressed over their faults (3.68–70, 3.77, 4.61).

The differences between Cicero and Posidonius on these two points are easiest to explain if we assume that Chrysippus, too, discussed both (7) and
(8) in his work. Chrysippus may perhaps have raised these issues as apparent points of difficulty which his theory had the explanatory resources to
surmount. (Compare his interest in Medea's wavering and in Odysseus's
self-admonishment; Galen, *PHP* 3.3.2–3, 13–24.) Cicero will then have taken
from him both the problems themselves and the solutions, which he, unlike
Posidonius, regards as adequate.

Again, conclusions drawn here are similar to those of Henry; see bibliographical note to Appendix C. The translation given here follows the text established in Edelstein and Kidd 1989; see also
the valuable commentary by Kidd 1988. For various interpretations of Posidonius's position see
Sorabji 1998; Cooper 1998; Gill 1998; Price 1995, 175–78.

[a] Galen, *PHP* 4.3.2–4, fr. 157 Edelstein and Kidd, lines 1–8

He [Chrysippus] is in conflict both with Zeno and with himself and with many others of the Stoics, who do not think that the emotions are the mind's judgments themselves but that they are the irrational contractions, lowerings, and bitings, and its elevations and outpourings. But Posidonius departed completely from both views. For he holds that the emotions are not judgments, nor do they follow upon judgments, but that they come about through the spirited and the desiderative power. . . . And several times in his work *On Emotions* he asks Chrysippus's supporters what is the cause of the excessive impulse. For reason could not exceed its own deeds and measures.

[b] Galen, *PHP* 4.7.24–25, 32–33, fr. 165 Edelstein and Kidd, lines 99–103, 134–43

And he [Posidonius] himself shows how the emotions are from spirit (or anger, *thumos*) and from desire, and why they subside over time, even if the beliefs and judgments still persist that a bad thing exists or is coming into existence for oneself. And he calls to witness even Chrysippus himself [in Appendix C, passage [f]].

. . . It is quite easy to collect from the poets not only these but many other such examples of how people become sated with grief, tears, crying, anger, victory, honor, and everything like that. In these cases it is by no means "difficult to reason out" why the emotions cease in time and reason gains control of the impulses. For just as the emotional [part or power] strives after certain objects of pursuit proper to it, so also, when it obtains them, it becomes sated and at that point halts its movement which was controlling the animal's impulse and was of its own accord driving [the animal] wrongly toward its object.

[c] Galen, *PHP* 5.6.29–31, fr. 166 Edelstein and Kidd, lines 1–4, 7–14

Next he [Posidonius] tells why it is that emotions become quieter and weaker over time, [a point] about which Chrysippus in the second book of *On Emotions* admitted he was puzzled. . . . For one thing, this emotional [part or power] of the mind becomes satiated over time with its own objects of desire, and for another, it grows weary of movements lasting a long time. For both these reasons, then, it grows quiet and makes only moderate movements, whereupon the reasoning [part or power] can take control. It is like when a runaway horse carries off its rider by force and then, when it becomes tired with running and also sated with what it wanted, the rider can again use the reins to gain control and stop it.

[d] Galen, *PHP* 5.2.2–7, fr. 163 Edelstein and Kidd, lines 1–30

Both of them [Chrysippus and Posidonius] are in agreement that this movement does not arise in the minds of the refined [i.e., sages]. But they do not give the same explanation concerning what kind of mind inferior persons have during emotions and prior to emotions. For Chrysippus says that it is analogous to bodies which have a tendency to incur fevers or diarrhea or things like that upon a slight and chance pretext. Posidonius criticizes this comparison: he says that the mind of the inferior person should not be compared to such bodies but simply to healthy bodies, since with regard to their experiencing the emotions and incurring them at all it makes no difference whether they become feverish for great or small causes: the point of difference is that some incur them easily, others only with difficulty.

So, he says, Chrysippus is wrong to compare health of mind to bodily health and [mental] sickness to the state of body which falls easily into disease. For there is a soul which becomes free of emotion (*apathēs*)—that of the wise person, of course—but no body is free of sickness (*apathēs*). But it would have been more just to compare the minds of inferior persons either to bodily health, which includes a proneness to sickness (for that is the term Posidonius uses), or to sickness itself, since it is a condition which can only be either disease-ridden or actually diseased.

Yet even he is in agreement with Chrysippus in that he says that all inferior persons are sick in mind and that their sickness resembles the above-mentioned states of body. In fact, this is what he says: "For this reason, also, sickness of mind does not, as Chrysippus thinks, resemble a disease-ridden condition of body through which it is subject to incur irregular non-periodic fevers; rather, mental sickness resembles either bodily health, which includes a proclivity to sickness, or the sickness itself. For bodily illness is a condition already diseased, but the sickness Chrysippus is talking about is more like a proclivity to fevers."

[e] Galen, *PHP* 5.5.9–11, 21, fr. 169 Edelstein and Kidd, lines 38–44, 77–84

Posidonius, reasonably I think, criticizes and refutes Chrysippus on all these points [in his account of the origins of error]. For if children had from the start an orientation toward what is honorable, then fault would have to come about not from within or from themselves, but only from without. Yet one sees, surely, that even if they are brought up in excellent habits and suitably, they always go wrong in some way. Even Chrysippus admits this . . . [Then follows [n] in Appendix C.]

Posidonius criticizes these things, too, and tries to show that the causes of all the false suppositions come about in the theoretical [part or power] through lack of learning, but in the emotional [part or power] through the emotional "pull."

[f] Galen, *PHP* 5.6.37, fr. 33 Edelstein and Kidd, lines 2–4

Chrysippus ... takes emotions away from irrational animals, even though [such animals are] obviously governed by desire and by spirit, as Posidonius, too, explains at length about them ...

[g] Galen, *PHP* 4.7.1–5, 7–11, fr. 165 Edelstein and Kidd, lines 1–17, 22–50

I now turn to some of Posidonius's responses to Chrysippus. "This definition of distress," he says, "clearly refutes his own view, as do many of the other definitions stated by Zeno and recorded by Chrysippus. For he says that distress is a fresh belief that something is present which is bad for oneself."... He [Posidonius] says that what is "fresh" is what is recent in time, and he demands to be told the reason why the belief about evil contracts the mind when it is fresh, but when time passes it either does not contract it at all, or no longer does so in the same way. But if what Chrysippus says is true, the word "fresh" ought not even to have been included in the definition. For by his view it would have been better to say that distress is a belief about a great or unendurable or unconquerable evil, as he himself often says, rather than about a fresh [evil]. . . .

He [Posidonius] asks the reason why it is not the belief that an evil is present, but only the fresh belief [to that effect], which produces [distress]. And he [Posidonius?] says it is because "everything which is unrehearsed (*ameléton*) and strange, if it comes upon a person all of a sudden, upsets him and takes him out of his previous judgments; but if one has practiced and habituated oneself to it over time, it either does not affect him in this way and thus occasion an emotional movement, or does so only to a very small extent."

It is for this reason that he [Chrysippus or Posidonius] also says that one ought to "dwell in advance" on things which are not yet present as if they were present. To Posidonius, the term "dwell in advance" means to model or stamp out an image, as it were, within oneself of what is going to happen, and to habituate oneself to it little by little as to something that has already happened. It is for this reason that he [Chrysippus or Posidonius] also took up the anecdote about Anaxagoras, how when someone told him his son had died, he said very calmly, "I knew my child was mortal"; and how Euripides, taking this thought, portrayed Theseus saying

I learned this from a wise man: setting my mind
on worries and disasters, I imagined
exiles from my homeland, deaths untimely,
and other kinds of evil that might happen.
Thus, if at any time I should encounter
such things as these, they would not be new to me
and would not bite me.

And he says that the following words are spoken in the same way:

If this had been the first sad dawn for me,
if I had never sailed far into troubles,
no doubt I would have shied from this, as does
the newly bridled colt, when tightly reined.
But now I am stolid, broken by misfortunes.

[h]   Galen, *PHP* 4.5.26–28, fr. 164 Edelstein and Kidd, lines 12–25
"When Chrysippus says this kind of thing, one might be puzzled first
as to how it is that the wise, who regard all things honorable as great and
unsurpassable goods, are not stirred with emotion by them, desiring the
things they reach out after and becoming extremely joyful about those same
things when they obtain them. For if it is the magnitude of the things
thought to be good or evil that moves one to suppose that it is appropriate
and worthwhile to be moved emotionally when they are present or in
prospect, and not to admit any speech about how one ought to be moved
differently by them, then those who think what is around them is unsurpassable [in goodness] should experience the same thing. But we do not observe this happening. Similarly [one might be puzzled] concerning progressors, who suppose that great harm is present to them because of their
faults. They should be overcome with fear and with immoderate distress,
but this does not happen either."

BIBLIOGRAPHY

Abel, K. 1983. Das Propatheia-Theorem: Ein Beitrag zur stoischen Affektenlehre. *Hermes* III, 78–97.

Algra, K., J. Barnes, J. Mansfield, and M. Schofield, eds. 1999. *Cambridge History of Hellenistic Philosophy.* Cambridge.

Angeli, A., and M. Colaizzo. 1979. I frammenti di Zenone Sidonio. *Cronache Ercolanesi* 9, 47–113.

Annas, J. 1999. *Platonic Ethics, Old and New.* Ithaca and London.

———. 1993. *Morality of Happiness.* Oxford.

——— 1992. *Hellenistic Philosophy of Mind.* Berkeley.

———. 1989. Epicurean emotions. *Greek, Roman, and Byzantine Studies* 30, 195–213.

———. 1980. Truth and knowledge. In Schofield, Burnyeat, and Barnes 1980, 84–104.

Asmis, E. 1984. *Epicurus' Scientific Method.* Ithaca, N.Y.

———. 1981. Lucretius' explanation of moving dream figures at IV.768–76. *American Journal of Philology* 102, 138–45.

Bailey, D. R. Shackleton. 1971. *Cicero.* London.

Bailey, D. R. Shackleton, ed. 1980. *Cicero: Epistulae ad Quintum fratrem et M. Brutum.* Cambridge.

———. 1977. *Cicero: Epistulae ad familiares.* 2 vols. Cambridge.

———. 1966. *Cicero's Letters to Atticus,* vol. 5. Cambridge.

Barnes, J. 1997a. *Logic in the Imperial Stoa.* Leiden.

———. 1997b. Roman Aristotle. In Barnes and Griffin 1997, 1–69.

———. 1989. Antiochus of Ascalon. In Griffin and Barnes 1989, 51–96.

Barnes, J., and M. Griffin, eds. 1997. *Philosophia togata II: Plato and Aristotle at Rome.* Oxford.

Bobzien, S. 1998. *Determinism and Freedom in Stoic Philosophy.* Oxford.

Braund, S., and C. Gill, eds. 1997. *The Passions in Roman Thought and Literature.* Cambridge.

Brennan, T. 1998. The old Stoic theory of emotions. In Sihvola and Engberg-Pedersen 1998, 21–70.

Brown, R. D. 1987. *Lucretius on Love and Sex.* Leiden and New York.

Brunschwig, J. 1986. The cradle argument in Epicureanism and Stoicism. In Schofield and Striker 1986, 113–44.

Brunschwig, J., and M. Nussbaum, eds. 1993. *Passions and Perceptions: Studies in Hellenistic Philosophy of Mind.* Cambridge.

Castner, C. J. 1988. *Prosopography of Roman Epicureans from the Second Century B.C. to the Second Century A.D.* Frankfurt.

Classen, C. 1989. Die Peripatetiker in Cicero's Tuskulanen. In Fortenbaugh and Steinmetz 1989, 186–200.

Cooper, J. 1999. *Reason and Emotion.* Princeton, N.J.

————. 1998. Posidonius on emotions. In Sihvola and Engberg-Pedersen 1998, 71–112. Also in Cooper 1999, 449–84.

————. 1988. Some remarks on Aristotle's moral psychology. *Southern Journal of Philosophy* 27 Supplement, 25–42. Also in Cooper 1999, 237–52.

De Lacy, P., ed. 1978. *Galen: On the Doctrines of Hippocrates and Plato. Corpus medicorum Graecorum,* vol. 5, no. 4.1.2. Berlin.

Diels, H., ed. 1879. *Doxographi Graeci.* Berlin. Repr. Berlin and Leipzig, 1929.

Dihle, A. 1982. *The Theory of the Will in Classical Antiquity.* Berkeley.

Dillon, J. 1997. Medea among the philosophers. In *Medea: Essays on Medea in Myth, Literature, Philosophy, and Art,* ed. J. Clauss and S. Johnston, 211–18. Princeton, N.J.

————. 1996. *The Middle Platonists.* Ithaca, N.Y.

————. 1983. *Metriopatheia* and *apatheia:* Some reflections on a controversy in later Greek ethics. In *Essays in Ancient Greek Philosophy,* vol. 2, ed. J. Anton and A. Preus. Albany, N.Y., 508–17.

Dillon, J., ed. 1993. *Alcinous: The Handbook of Platonism.* Oxford.

Donini, P. 1995. Struttura delle passioni e del vizio e loro cura in Crisippo. *Elenchos* 16, 305–29.

Döring, K. 1988. *Der Sokratesschüler Aristipp und die Kyrenaiker.* Stuttgart.

Dougan, T., ed. 1905. *M. Tulli Ciceronis Tusculanarum disputationum libri quinque,* vol. 1. Cambridge.

Dougan, T., and R. Henry, eds. 1934. *M. Tulli Ciceronis Tusculanarum disputationum libri quinque.* 2 vols. Cambridge. Repr. 1988, with Dougan 1905. Salem, New Hampshire.

Douglas, A. E. 1995. Form and content in the *Tusculan Disputations.* In Powell 1995, 119–26.

Dyck, A. 1996. *A Commentary on Cicero, De Officiis.* Ann Arbor.

Edelstein, L., and I. G. Kidd, eds. 1989. *Posidonius: The Fragments.* Cambridge.

Engberg-Pedersen, T. 1990. *The Stoic Theory of Oikeiosis.* Aarhus.

Erskine, A. 1997. Cicero and the expression of grief. In Braund and Gill 1997, 36–47.

Evans, E. C. 1969. Physiognomics in the ancient world. *Transactions of the American Philosophical Society* 59.5. Philadelphia.

Everson, S., ed. 1998. *Ethics.* Cambridge.

Fortenbaugh, W. 1989. Cicero's knowledge of the rhetorical treatises of Aristotle and Theophrastus. In Fortenbaugh and Steinmetz 1989, 139–60.

Fortenbaugh, W., and P. Steinmetz, eds. 1989. *Cicero's Knowledge of the Peripatos.* New Brunswick, N.J.

Frede, M. 1986. The Stoic doctrine of the affections of the soul. In Schofield and Striker 1986, 93–110.

Garbarino, J., ed. 1984. *M. Tulli Ciceronis fragmenta.* Turin.

Gersh, S. 1986. *Middle Platonism and Neoplatonism: The Latin Tradition.* Notre Dame, Ind.

Giannantoni, G., ed. 1990. *Socratis et Socraticorum reliquiae.* 4 vols. Naples.

Gill, C. 1998. Did Galen understand Platonic and Stoic thinking on emotions? In Sihvola and Engberg-Pedersen 1998, 113–48.

———. 1997. The emotions in Greco-Roman philosophy. In Braund and Gill 1997, 5–15.

———. 1983. Did Chrysippus understand Medea? *Phronesis* 28, 136–49.

Giusta, M. 1991. *Il testo delle Tusculane.* Turin.

Giusta, M., ed. 1984. *M. Tulli Ciceronis Tusculanae Disputationes.* Turin.

Glibert-Thirry, A., ed. 1977. *Pseudo-Andronicus de Rhodes* ΠΕΡΙ ΠΑΘΩΝ. Leiden.

Glucker, J. 1978. *Antiochus and the Late Academy. Hypomnemata* 56. Göttingen.

Görler, W. 1977. ᾺΣΘΕΝΗΣ ΣΥΓΚΑΤΑΘΕΣΙΣ: Zur Stoischen Erkenntnistheorie. *Würzburger Jahrbücher* N.F. 3, 83–92.

———. 1989. Cicero und die 'Schule des Aristoteles.' In Fortenbaugh and Steinmetz, ed., 1989, 246–64.

Gosling, J. C. B.; Taylor, C. C. W. 1982. *The Greeks on Pleasure.* Oxford.

Gottschalk, H. B. 1987. Aristotelian philosophy in the Roman world. *Aufstieg und Niedergang des römischen Welt* 2.36.2, 1079–174.

Graver, M. n.d. Managing mental pain: Epicurus vs. Aristippus on the pre-rehearsal of future ills. *Proceedings of the Boston Area Colloquium in Ancient Philosophy* 17. Forthcoming.

———. 1999. Philo of Alexandria and the origins of the Stoic προπάθεια. *Phronesis* 44, 300–25.

Gregg, R. C. 1975. *Consolation Philosophy: Greek and Christian Paideia in Basil and the Two Gregories.* Cambridge, Mass.

Griffin, M. 1997. The composition of the Academica: Motives and versions. In *Assent and Argument: Studies in Cicero's Academic Books,* ed. B. Inwood and J. Mansfield, 1–35. Leiden.

———. 1995. Philosophical badinage in Cicero's letters to his friends. In Powell 1995, 325–46.

———. 1989. Philosophy, politics, and politicians at Rome. In Griffin and Barnes 1989, 1–37.

Griffin, M., and J. Barnes, eds. 1989. *Philosophia togata: Essays on Philosophy and Roman Society.* Oxford.

Grilli, A., ed. 1962. *M. Tulli Ciceronis Hortensius.* Milan.

Hadot, I. 1969. *Seneca und die griechisch-römische Tradition der Seelenleitung.* Berlin.

Halperin, D. 1990. *One Hundred Years of Homosexuality.* New York.

Hani, J., ed. 1972. *Consolation à Apollonios [de] Plutarque.* Paris.

Heine, O., ed. 1892–96. *M. Tulli Ciceronis Tusculanorum disputationum libri V.* Leipzig.

Heylbut, G., ed. 1889. *Aspasii In Ethica Nicomachea quae supersunt commentaria* (= *Commentaria in Aristotelem Graeca,* vol. 19). Berlin.

Hubert, C., et al., eds. 1925–38. *Plutarchi Moralia.* Leipzig.

Hutchinson, G. O. 1998. *Cicero's Correspondence.* Oxford.

Indelli, G., ed. 1988. *Philodemus, De ira.* Naples.

Inwood, B. 1997. Why do fools fall in love? In Sorabji, ed. 1997, 57–70.

———. 1993. Seneca and psychological dualism. In Brunschwig and Nussbaum 1993, 150–83.

———. 1985. *Ethics and Human Action in Early Stoicism.* Oxford.

Inwood, B., and L. Gerson. 1997. *Hellenistic Philosophy.* Indianapolis.

Ioppolo, A. M. 1980. Carneade e il terzo libro delle Tusculani. *Elenchos* 1, 76–91.

Irwin, T. H. 1998a. Stoic inhumanity. In Sihvola and Engberg-Pedersen 1998, 219–42.

———. 1998b. Socratic paradox and Stoic theory. In Everson 1998, 151–93.

———. 1991. Aristippus against happiness. *Monist* 74, 55–82.

Jocelyn, H. D., ed. 1967. *The Tragedies of Ennius.* Cambridge.

Johann, H. 1968. *Trauer und Trost, Eine quellen- und strukturanalytische Untersuchung der philosophischen Trostschriften.* Munich.

Kalbfleisch, K., ed. 1907. *Simplicii In Aristotelis Categoriis commentarium* (= *Commentaria in Aristotelem Graeca,* vol. 8). Berlin.

Kassel, R. 1958. *Untersuchungen zur griechischen und lateinischen Konsolationsliteratur.* Munich.

Kassel, R., and C. Austin, eds. 1983–95. *Poetae comici Graeci.* 8 vols. Berlin.

Kidd, I. G. 1988. *Posidonius: The Commentary.* Cambridge.

Kühn, D. 182135. *Claudii Galeni opera omnia.* 20 vols. Leipzig.

Laks, A. 1993. Annicéris et les plaisirs psychiques: Quelques préalables doxographiques. In Brunschwig and Nussbaum 1993, 18–49.

Lee, A. G., ed. 1953. *M. Tulli Ciceronis Paradoxa Stoicorum.* London.

L'Hoir, F. Santoro. 1992. *The Rhetoric of Gender Terms.* Leiden.

Long, A. A. 1996. *Stoic Studies.* Cambridge.

———. 1995. Cicero's Plato and Aristotle. In Powell 1995, 37–62.

———. 1992. Stoic readings of Homer. In R. Lamberton and J. J. Keaney, ed., *Homer's Ancient Readers,* 41–66. Princeton. Repr. in Long 1996, 58–84.

———. 1991. The harmonics of Stoic virtue. *Oxford Studies in Ancient Philosophy* supplement, 97–116. Repr. in Long 1996, 202–23.

———. 1986. *Hellenistic Philosophy: Stoics, Epicureans, Sceptics.* Berkeley.

———. 1983. Arius Didymus and the exposition of Stoic ethics. In Fortenbaugh, W., ed., 1983, *On Stoic and Peripatetic ethics: The work of Arius Didymus,* 41–66. Repr. in Long 1996, 107–33.

———. 1978. Dialectic and the Stoic sage. In *The Stoics,* ed. J. Rist, 101–24. Berkeley. Repr. in Long 1996, 85–106.

————. 1971. The logical basis of Stoic ethics. *Proceedings of the Aristotelian Society* 71, 85–104. Repr. in Long 1996, 134–52.

Long, A. A., and D. Sedley, eds. 1987. *The Hellenistic Philosophers*. 2 vols. Cambridge.

Long, H. S., ed. 1964. *Diogenes Laertii Vitae philosophorum*. 2 vols. Oxford.

Lundström, S. 1986. *Zur Textkritik der Tusculanen*. Stockholm.

————. 1964. *Vermeintliche Glossema in den Tusculanen*. Uppsala.

MacKendrick, P. 1989. *The Philosophical Books of Cicero*. New York.

Marcus, R., ed. 1953. *Philo, Questions and Answers on Genesis*. London and Cambridge, Mass.

Meineke, A., ed. 1855. *Joannis Stobaei Florilegium*. 4 vols. Leipzig.

Mette, H. J. 1984. Zwei Akademiker heute: Krantor von Soli und Arkesilaos von Pitane. *Lustrum* 26, 7–93.

Mitsis, P. 1988. *Epicurus' Ethical Theory*. Ithaca and London.

Moraux, P. 1973. *Der Aristotelismus bei den Griechen: Von Andronikos bis Alexander von Aphrodisias*, vol. 1. Berlin.

Murphy, T. 1998. Cicero's first readers: Epistolary evidence for the dissemination of his works. *Classical Quarterly* 48, 492–505.

Nagy, Gregory. 1990. *Greek Mythology and Poetics*. Ithaca, N.Y.

Nauck, A. 1964, ed. *Tragicorum Graecorum fragmenta*. Hildesheim.

Nussbaum, M. 2001. *Upheavals of Thought: The Intelligence of Emotions*. Cambridge.

————. 1995. Eros and the wise. *Oxford Studies in Ancient Philosophy* 13, 231–67. Repr. in Sihvola and Engberg-Pedersen 1998, 271–304.

————. 1994. *The Therapy of Desire: Theory and Practice in Hellenistic Ethics*. Princeton, N.J.

————. 1993. Poetry and the passions: Two Stoic views. In Brunschwig and Nussbaum 1993, 97–149.

Petit, F., ed. 1978. *Philon D'Alexandrie: Quaestiones in Genesim et in Exodum, fragmenta Graeca*. Paris.

Plasberg, O. 1922. *M. Tulli Ciceronis Academicorum reliquiae cum Lucullo*. Repr. 1980. Stuttgart.

Pohlenz, M., ed. 1918. *M. Tulli Ciceronis Tusculanae Disputationes*. Repr. 1982. Stuttgart.

————. 1906. Die dritte und vierte Bücher der Tusculanen. *Hermes* 41, 321–55.

————. 1911. Die Personenbezeichnungen in Ciceros Tusculanen. *Hermes* 46, 627–29.

Pohlenz, M., and O. Heine, eds. 1957. *Ciceronis Tusculanarum Disputationum libri V*. Stuttgart.

Pomeroy, A. J., ed. 1999. *Arius Didymus, Epitome of Stoic Ethics*. Atlanta, Ga.

Powell, J. G. F. 1995. Cicero's translations from Greek. In Powell, ed., 1995, 273–300.

Powell, J. G. F., ed. 1995. *Cicero the Philosopher: Twelve Papers*. Oxford.

Price, A. W. 1995. *Mental Conflict*. London and New York.

————. 1989. *Love and Friendship in Plato and Aristotle*. Oxford.

Procopé, J. 1993. Epicureans on anger. In *Philanthropia kai Eusebeia. Festschrift für Albert*

Dible zum 70. Geburtstag, ed. G. Most, H. Petersmann, and A. M. Ritter, 363–86. Göttingen. Repr. in Sihvola and Engberg-Pedersen 1998, 171–96.

Rabel, R. 1981. Diseases of soul in Stoic psychology. *Greek, Roman, and Byzantine Studies* 22, 385–93.

Rawson, E. 1985. *Intellectual Life in the Late Roman Republic*. Baltimore.

Reid, J., ed. 1885. *M. Tulli Ciceronis Academica*. London.

Reynolds, L. O. 1998. *M. Tulli Ciceronis De finibus bonorum et malorum libri quinque*. Oxford.

Ribbeck, O., ed. 1898. *Comicorum Romanorum fragmenta*. Leipzig.

Richlin, A. 1996. Producing manhood in the schools. In *Roman Eloquence: Rhetoric in Society and Literature*, ed. W. Dominik, 90–110. London.

Rist, J. 1969. *Stoic Philosophy*. Cambridge.

Ronnick, M. 1991. *Cicero's "Paradoxa Stoicorum": A Commentary, an Interpretation, and a Study of Its Influence*. Frankfurt am Main.

Rorty, A., ed. 1996. *Essays on Aristotle's Rhetoric*. Berkeley.

Ruch, M. 1958. *Le Préambule dans les oeuvres philosophiques de Cicéron*. Paris.

Runia, D. 1989. Aristotle and Theophrastus conjoined in the writings of Cicero. In Fortenbaugh and Steinmetz 1989, 23–38.

Schofield, M. 1991. *The Stoic Idea of the City*. Cambridge.

Schofield, M., M. Burnyeat, and J. Barnes, eds. 1980. *Doubt and Dogmatism: Studies in Hellenistic Epistemology*. Oxford.

Schofield, M., and G. Striker, eds. 1986. *The Norms of Nature: Studies in Hellenistic Ethics*. Cambridge.

Scott, D. 1995. *Recollection and Experience: Plato's Theory of Learning and Its Successors*. Cambridge.

Scourfield, J. 1993. *Consoling Heliodorus: A Commentary on Jerome, Letter 60*. Oxford.

Sedley, D. 1993. Chrysippus on psychophysical causality. In Brunschwig and Nussbaum 1993, 313–31.

———. 1989. Philosophical allegiance in the Greco-Roman world. In Griffin and Barnes 1989, 97–119.

———. 1980. The protagonists. In Schofield, Burnyeat, and Barnes 1980, 1–19.

Sharples, R. W. 1983. *Alexander of Aphrodisias: On Fate*. London.

Sihvola, J., and T. Engberg-Pedersen, eds. 1998. *The Emotions in Hellenistic Philosophy*. Dordrecht.

Solmsen, F. 1938. Aristotle and Cicero on the orator's playing upon the feelings. *Classical Philology* 33, 391–404. Repr. in Solmsen, F., 1982, *Kleine Schriften*, 216–30. Hildesheim.

Sorabji, R., 2000. *Emotion and Peace of Mind: From Stoic Agitation to Christian Temptation*. Oxford.

———. 1998. Chrysippus—Posidonius—Seneca: A high-level debate on emotion. In Sihvola and Engberg-Pedersen 1998, 149–70.

———. 1997. Is Stoic philosophy helpful as psychotherapy? In Sorabji, R., ed., 1997, 197–210.

————. 1993. *Animal Minds and Human Morals.* Cornell.

Sorabji, R., ed. 1997. *Aristotle and After. Bulletin of the Institute of Classical Studies,* Supplement 68. London.

Stokes, M. C. 1995. Cicero on Epicurean pleasures. In Powell 1995, 145–70.

Striker, G. 1996a. *Essays on Hellenistic Epistemology and Ethics.* Cambridge.

————. 1996b. Emotions in context: Aristotle's treatment of the passions in the *Rhetoric* and his moral psychology. In Rorty 1996, 286–302.

————. 1993. Epicurean hedonism. In Brunschwig and Nussbaum 1993, 3–17. Repr. in Striker 1996a, 196–208.

————. 1991. Following nature: A study in Stoic ethics. *Oxford Studies in Ancient Philosophy* 9, 1–73. Repr. in Striker 1996a, 221–80.

————. 1974. Κριτήριον τῆς ἀληθείας. *Nachrichten der Akademie der Wissenschaften zu Göttingen,* 1. Phil.-hist. Klasse, 2, 4–110. Repr. (in English) in Striker 1996a, 22–76.

Tsouna, V. 1998a. Doubts about other minds and the science of physiognomics. *Classical Quarterly* 48, 175–86.

————. 1998b. *The Epistemology of the Cyrenaic School.* Cambridge.

Usener, H. 1887. *Epicurea.* Leipzig.

van Straaten, M. 1962. *Panaetii Rhodii fragmenta.* Leiden.

Vander Waerdt, P. A. 1985. Peripatetic soul-division, Posidonius, and Middle Platonic moral psychology. *Greek, Roman, and Byzantine Studies* 26, 373–94.

von Arnim, J., ed. 1921. *Stoicorum veterum fragmenta.* 4 vols. Leipzig.

Wachsmuth, C., and O. Hense, eds. 1884–1912. *Ioannis Stobaei Anthologium.* 4 vols. Berlin.

Warmington, E., ed. 1956–1982. *Remains of Old Latin,* vols. 1–3. Cambridge, Mass.

Waszink, J. H. 1962. *Timaeus a Calcidio translatus commentarioque instructus.* London.

White, S. 1995. Cicero and the therapists. In Powell 1995, 219–46.

Wilson, M. 1997. The subjugation of grief in Seneca's 'Epistles.' In Braund and Gill 1997, 48–67.

Wisse, J. 1989. *Ethos and Pathos from Aristotle to Cicero.* Amsterdam.

INDEX LOCORUM

Locators in **boldface** refer to quoted passages.

General Index

A and M, 79
Academics, xiv, xxxii n.13, 86
Academy (walkway at Tusculan house), 5, 42, 79
Academy
    Old, xvii, xxxiv n.37, 83–84, 120, 187, 188 (*see also* Crantor)
    skeptical, xxiv, xxxii n.17, 41, 55, 83, 84, 107, 167 (*see also* Carneades)
Accius, 11, 28, 58, 90
Achilles, 10, 57
action
    appropriate, xxiii, 32, 83, 110, 111, 154, 168 173
    (not) requiring emotion, xvii–xviii, xxii–xxiii, 161–62, 168
    right or virtuous, xi, 51, 161–62, 168
    Stoic theory, xx–xxi, 86–87, 88, 91–92, 110–11
    See also assent; impressions; moral responsibility; voluntary action
Aeetes, 14, 19, 95
aegritudo, xxxviii, 12–13, 94
Aemilius Paullus, 31, 116
Aeschines, 28, 112
Aeschylus, 34
Aesopus, 58, 168
Afranius, 55, 59, 166, 175
Agamemnon, 28, 46, 57, 67
Ajax, 7, 31, 56, 57, 81, 98, 103, 170
Alcaeus, 65, 179
Alcibiades, 34–35, 122–23, 124, 172, 184

Alcinous, xxxiii n.25, 138. *See also* Platonists
Alcmaeon, 7, 82, 146
Alexander the Great, 12, 67, 90, 181
Amafinius, 41, 129, 130, 131–32
Anacreon, 65, 179
Anaxagoras, 15, 26, 98, 189, 190, 219
Andromache, 103–4
Andronicus of Rhodes, 133–34. *See also* pseudo-Andronicus
anger, 11, 67–68, 144, 166
    defined, 46, 144, 147
    and oratory, 54, 167
    as species of desire, 7, 11, 45, 46, 54
    species, 46, 142, 147
    treatises on, 167
    uses for, 54, 56–58, 167–68
    and vital heat, 147, 181
    See also irascibility; *lentitudo; thumos*
animals, xvii–xviii, xxxiii n.23, 50, 159–60, 218
Antiochus of Ascalon, xxiv–xxv, xxxiii n.22, xxxiv n.39, 27, 109, 130
Antipater of Tarsus, 167
antiquarianism, 82, 130, 130
anxiety, 48, 144, 151; defined, 45
apatheia. See impassivity
aphormai, 3, 74, 77
Appius Claudius Caecus, 40, 131
Appuleius, xiii
Arcesilaus, xxiv, xxxii n.17, 83, 84
Archytas, 67, 181
Aristippus. See Cyrenaics
Ariston of Chios, 156